Sounding Funny

Genre, Music and Sound

Series editor: Mark Evans, Macquarie University, Sydney

Over the last decade screen soundtrack studies has emerged as a lively area of research and analysis mediating between the fields of cinema studies, musicology and cultural studies. It has deployed a variety of cross-disciplinary approaches to illuminate an area of film's audio-visual operation that was neglected for much of the mid–late 1900s. Equinox's *Genre, Music and Sound* series extends the emergent field by addressing a series of popular international film genres as they have developed in the post-war era (1945–present), analysing the variety and shared patterns of music and sound use that characterize each genre.

Published

Terror Tracks: Music, Sound and Horror Cinema
Edited by Philip Hayward

Drawn to Sound: Animation Film Music and Sonicity
Edited by Rebecca Coyle

Earogenous Zones: Sound, Sexuality and Cinema
Edited by Bruce Johnson

The Music of Fantasy Cinema
Edited by Janet K. Halfyard

Forthcoming

Movies, Moves and Music: The Sonic World of Dance Films
Edited by Mark Evans and Mary Fogarty

The Singing Voice in Contemporary Cinema
Edited by Diane Hughes and Mark Evans

Ludomusicology: Approaches to Video Game Music
Edited by Michiel Kamp, Tim Summers and Mark Sweeney

Sounding Funny

Sound and Comedy Cinema

Edited by
Mark Evans and Philip Hayward

Equinox Publishing Ltd

Sheffield, UK Bristol, CT

Published by Equinox Publishing Ltd

UK: Office 415, The Workstation, 15 Paternoster Row, Sheffield, South Yorkshire S1 2BX
USA: ISD, 70 Enterprise Drive, Bristol, CT 06010

www.equinoxpub.com

First published 2016

© Mark Evans, Philip Hayward and contributors 2016

All rights reserved. No part of this publication may be reproduced or transmitted in any form or by any means, electronic or mechanical, including photocopying, recording or any information storage or retrieval system, without prior permission in writing from the publishers.

ISBN-13 978 1 78179 099 1 (hardback)
978 1 84553 674 9 (paperback)

British Library Cataloguing-in-Publication Data
A catalogue record for this book is available from the British Library.

Library of Congress Cataloging-in-Publication Data
Sounding funny: sound and comedy cinema/edited by Mark Evans and Philip Hayward.
    pages cm.—(Genre, music and sound)
Includes bibliographical references and index.
    ISBN 978-1-78179-099-1 (hb) – ISBN 978-1-84553-674-9 (pb)
    1. Motion picture music—History and criticism. 2. Film soundtracks—Production and direction—History. 3. Comedy films—History and criticism. I. Evans, Mark, 1973- II. Hayward, Philip.
  ML2075.S676 2015
  791.4502'4--dc23
2014044378

Typeset by Atheus
Printed and bound in Great Britain by Lightning Source UK Ltd., Milton Keynes
and in the USA by Lightning Source Inc., La Vergne, TN

Contents

1. Sounding Funny: The Importance of Hearing the Joke — 1
   Liz Giuffre and Mark Evans

2. The Soundtrack as Appropriate Incongruity — 14
   Marshall Heiser

3. The Sound of Satire; or, *Trading Places* with Mozart — 29
   Ben Winters

4. Parody, Self-Parody and Genre-Parody: Music in *The Magnificent Seven* and *¡Three Amigos!* — 51
   Erik Heine

5. Austin Powers: Intentional Music Man — 74
   Liz Giuffre and Mark Evans

6. Paranormal Product: The Music and Promotion of *Ghostbusters* — 92
   Jon Fitzgerald and Philip Hayward

7. Red in Tooth and Lipstick: Music and Sound Design in *Lesbian Vampire Killers* — 110
   Clarice Butkus and Jon Fitzgerald

8. 'Be a Clown' and 'Make 'Em Laugh': Comic Timing, Rhythm, and Donald O'Connor's Face — 122
   Jonas Westover

9. Sound, Comedy and Cinematic Modernism: *Kaasua, komisario Palmu!* — 148
   Kimmo Laine and Anu Juva

10. Spanish Film Music in the 1940s: Comedy, Subversion, and Dissident Rhythms in the Films of Manuel Parada — 171
    Laura Miranda

11. An Okinawan Romance: Lyrical Dialogue, Comedy and
    Music in *Nabbie's Love*   189
    Philip Hayward

12. A Special Flavour: Comic Song Scenes in the Hindi Cinema   205
    Gregory D. Booth

13. Humour Between the Keys: A Detailed Analysis of *The Cat Concerto*   224
    Peter Morris

Index   257

1 Sounding Funny
The Importance of Hearing the Joke

Liz Giuffre and Mark Evans

Dying is hard. (Defining) comedy is harder

Academics have a problem when engaging with comedy. Developing a definition is necessary for our work but it can also be seen as threatening the experience we wish to explore. It could be contended that comedy that needs to be explained is not very good comedy. Equally, once a joke is explained, it ceases to be funny. Or, as an aphorism attributed to American author E.B. White characterizes it, "Explaining a joke is like dissecting a frog. You understand it better but the frog dies in the process." Academic engagement with comedy is not the same as reception by a more general audience. We explain the effects of cultural practices and works so as to acknowledge their potential and spark further debate. We work towards building definitions to provide boundaries and build foundations for further discussion. We may kill the frog, but in doing so we hopefully explain the meaning of its life.

Defining comedy is a problem that has long been acknowledged, and most often commentators take the challenge by playing with form with a knowing irony. For example, King argues that comedy can be "a mode, genre, adjective or noun" (2002: 3), with the only real consistency being that "comedy, by its definition, is not usually taken entirely seriously" (2003: 2). As Leacock argued in a 1930s textbook, "with honourable exceptions books on humour are written by people who haven't any" (Leacock in Mera, 2002: 94); while in the same piece Mera acknowledges that "humor has many beautiful yet intangible elements that defy analytical description" (*ibid*). Stott observed a similar problem, suggesting that comedy "is a term that can refer equally to a genre, a tone, a series of effects that manifest themselves in diverse environments" (2005: 3), whilst exploring the history of the word 'comedy' via its Greek linguistic origins and relationship to the god Dionysus, as well as various employments of the concept by Dante and Aristotle (2005: 4).

Seeking to formalize the otherwise frivolous, Stott argues that as "a dramatic form, the historical development of comedy appears to conform to the idea of a relatively permeable form adapting to suit the demands of the day" (2005: 3). Inevitably questions of value arise in key discourses around comedy, and Stott concludes that, "even though comedy has been shown to be an object worthy of significant study, it is simultaneously shown to be closer to nature than art, and closer, therefore, to the body than the soul" (2005: 28). He attributes this to "modern critical interest [which] is guilty of retaining the elitist generic divisions that once denigrated comedy, keeping it as the working-class cousin of aristocratic tragedy" (2005: 39).

Connections between comedy, class and value appear to be inescapable. Famously Aristotle defined comedy in terms of value, as "an imitation of inferior people" (1996: 9), something that is related to tragedy but without its apparent motivations. Notably, he argued that "a comic mask is ugly and distorted, but does not involve pain" (*ibid*), a point that has come to be a marker of the apparent lack of skill and gravitas of the comedic performer and writer (as opposed to those performing and writing tragedy). Aristotle notes that despite comedy and tragedy having similar origins in terms of their structures, performance types and various transformations, "because it was not taken seriously, little attention was paid to comedy" (*ibid*). His equation of comedy with a relative blankness of emotion (the absence of pain) is one that is problematic but also political and perhaps unfair – as translator Heath notes, "the loss of the extended analysis of comedy which the original *Poetics* probably contained makes it difficult to be sure what Aristotle's views on comedy would have been" (Heath in Aristotle, 1996: lxii).

Institutions and artists *do* question what, if any, boundaries there are between comedy and other forms, but this questioning can be met with resistance. When the nominations for the annual Golden Globe awards were announced in late 2013, *The Hollywood Reporter* suggested that "The Hollywood Foreign Press Association, which votes for the Globes, adopted a very elastic definition of comedy," with a variety of different types of films nominated for "best comedy or musical" including the *American Hustle* (David Russell), *Her* (Spike Jonze) and *The Wolf of Wall Street* (Martin Scorsese) (Kilday, 2013; online). Reporter Kilday argued this was problematic because "divid[ing] the top acting categories between drama and comedy performers … [will make it harder] securing Academy Award nominations" (*ibid*), an insight that focused on competition strategy rather than broader problems of valuing comedic performance in relation to other genre performances. Other commentators agreed, with Tim Gray of *Variety* arguing that in contemporary filmmaking "it's hard to draw the line between comedy and drama" in terms of institutional categorization, with "Several studios [having] submitted films as comedies to the Hollywood Foreign Press Assn. on the supposition that the race is less competitive than the jam-packed drama race" (Gray, 2013). Gray argues that films need not be exclusively considered either comedy or drama, or at least, that this consideration can be played with. He makes this point by contextualizing genre distinctions in terms of an earlier filmmaking model, where in the early 1940s and into the 50s "Studios programmed movies by genres, which helped theater owners vary the fare for audiences among dramas, comedies, westerns, musicals, and so on" (ibid).

Noting the problems of the Academy Awards' apparent bias against comedy ("laffers get short-changed in Oscar voting"), Gray begins to mount an argument against exclusive categorization of contemporary film by genre. Starting with examples of great performances and films that have been overlooked for awards because they were considered exclusively comedic (Whoopi Goldberg's Sister Mary Clarence in the *Sister Act* films (Emile Ardolino) and Peter Sellers as Inspector Clouseau in Blake Edwards' *Pink Panther* series), he offers for consideration the comedic value in films like *Forrest Gump* (Robert Zemeckis, 1994) and *The Graduate* (Mike Nichols, 1967) that were categorized as drama (and therefore were nominated for, and won, awards). Ultimately, though Gray's case rests on a simple premise, "both [*The Graduate* and *Forrest Gump*] had a lot of laughs, but the endings were sad. In that sense, Hollywood can follow the Shakespearean standard ... based on whether the final scene resolves things happily or not" (ibid). Notwithstanding the accuracy of Gray's claim about Shakespearean categorization here (see for example Leggatt, 2002), his point about a relatively arbitrary classification system remains.

Comedy films or 'comedic actors' seldom receive Academy Award nominations let alone win awards, and established comedy personnel have been acknowledged when working on other genre pieces. Take for example talented director/writers Joel and Ethan Coen, who drew huge box office and audience affection with comic films like *The Big Lebowski* (1998) and *O Brother, Where Art Thou?* (2000), but only gained an Academy Award recognition for Best Film with their non-comedy offering *No Country for Old Men* (2007). Similarly, actors like Robin Williams have had their skills relatively overlooked when they perform in comedies but praised by the Academy for relatively 'dramatic' roles (notably Williams winning Best Supporting Actor for his appearance in Gus Van Sant's *Good Will Hunting* in 1997). There are notable exceptions, such as Woody Allen's three Academy Awards, including Best Picture for 1977's *Annie Hall*, however even then the relationship between the film and genre has been considered as problematic. Symons argued that *Annie Hall* "complicated Woody Allen's reputation" (2013: 119) because of the type of comedy techniques and contexts it employed. His argument split comedy beyond distinctions from drama and towards high and low culture and art, ultimately suggesting that "the critical reaction suggests that, by making *Annie Hall*, Allen was regarded by some critics to have disregarded the expectations of his fans and made a move away from the perceived fundamentals of the 'comedy' genre" (2013: 126).

Symons concludes by comparing Allen's approach to *Annie Hall* with comedian Bill Murray's 2003 "shifted [approach] to performing comedy in a more subtle way in the film *Lost in Translation*" (2013: 127). Here Symons notes the audience Murray had previously built with "zany characters in *Saturday Night Live* (NBC, 1975–), *Caddyshack* (Harold Ramis, 1980), and *Ghostbusters* (Ivan Reitman, 1984) – all of which could be classed as "low" comedies" (2013: 127), yet with *Lost In Translation* (Sophia Coppola, 2003) Murray's performance was considered more sophisticated. Symons recalls how Murray's role was "treated as a departure" (*ibid*) by critics and by the Academy, and here, like Allen, he was both praised and criticized for exploring comedy beyond his previous experiences and contexts.

The sound of comedy: the sound of laughter

There is a common and reasonably reliable method for defining comedy, or at least, for isolating a comedic presence. That method is sonic – when we hear laughter we know that comedy is there – even if the original context or intention wasn't necessarily 'meant to be funny'. Laughter confirms and underlines comedy – as demonstrated with radio and television broadcasting which frequently included pre-recorded 'live' audience laughter (a practice prefigured by eighteenth- and nineteenth-century 'talking machines', which emitted laughter to demonstrate the capabilities of the emerging technologies as well as to amuse onlookers – Smith, 2008: 17). We can extend the importance of the sound of laughter to the viewing experience of cinema goers as well, applying Smith's concept that the sound of laughter provides "an important index of authentic presence used to bridge the gap between recorded sound and the listener" (2008: 15).

When we watch a film in a room with other people who are laughing, we are also inspired to do so (or at least consider the piece in relatively comedic terms). This process of 'perceived funniness' has also been explored by psychologists (Lawson *et al.*, 1998) and other behavioural specialists including Freud's famous exploration of the relationship between jokes and the unconscious (1960) and works exploring the broader health benefits of laughter, including its relationship to socialization (Wolosin, 1975; Weisfeld, 1993; Bennett, 2008; Szameitat *et al.*, 2009). While the addition of 'canned' laughter in a television sitcom might confirm comedy's presence, it has also come to be criticized as leading the audience too forcefully. As Kalviknes Bore notes, "the laugh track permits or demands a reciprocal response [however it also raises questions of] distinctions between authenticity and artifice" (2011: 24). A similar suspicion of laughter (particularly in terms of volume) was also raised in Symons' examination of *Annie Hall*, where the film is described as "a 'high culture' comedy in that it is designed to evoke a less visceral, more muted response – in short, not a loud, raucous laugh" (2013: 124). Even for audiences where sound cannot be heard, laughter and its inclusive effects are still emulated in performance, as in the case of "deaf jokes and sign language humour" where "extensive embodiment" is used by a signer to allow deaf audiences to visually "identify and empathize with characters in the joke" (Sutton-Spence et al., 2012: 316). Interestingly, the study also notes that the misuse of these signs can also entertain a deaf audience, as "poor signing by hearing people who are not part of Deaf Culture is a great source of belly laughs for Deaf people" (Sutton-Spence et al., 2012: 323). In each example laughter (and its equivalent) is something that sounds comedy (and sounds a comedy in progress), but laughter can also be evoked in a variety of (perhaps unreliable) ways.

Laughter's place as a piece of "emotional communication" that is "one of the few vocalizations shared by humans and non-human primates" (Szameitat et al., 2011: 600) also likely contributes to attitudes of laughter (and by association, comedy) with relatively low or primitive cultural capital. To continue with the *Annie Hall* example, Symons argues that for the Academy and other critics, laughter is aligned clearly to cultural status – i.e. "comedy that inspires laughter has a lower cultural status" (2013: 135). At the turn of the twentieth century, English psychologist James Sully published "An Essay On Laughter" (1902), a work aimed at understanding "How did the first [utterances of] laughter, mindless as it may well seem to us, get developed and differentiated into the variety of forms which make up the humorous experience of civilized man?" (Sully, 1902: 22). For Sully it was important to discern types of laughter – the involuntary (perhaps primal) response of the audience to something simplistic and unexpected, from the more sophisticated reaction of audiences to a comic artist who was deliberately trying to illicit a specific reaction. Sully described this as the need to examine "the place of laughter in Art, and the treatment of the sources of merriment by the comedian," questioning "the value which is to be assigned to the laughing propensity, and the proper limits to be set to its indulgence" (1902: 24). This last point about laughter as a possible sonic intrusion is particularly interesting – does any genre other than comedy need to consider how sound is welcome (or not) from the audience? Where else is the sound of the audience in the construction and confirmation of genre considered at all?

If laughter can be 'faked' and simulated in a way that can coerce or confuse the viewer, it can also be used inappropriately as an appraisal of a work of art that may not be considered sophisticated enough for other types of praise.

The sound of laughter may indicate a range of emotions from an audience, including nervousness or uncomfortableness rather than simply amusement (Keltner and Bonanno, 1997; Sideridis, 2006), an expression of desire (Weeks, 2002), a way to deflect attention (O'Connell and Kowal, 2004) and even a way to isolate the fear in individuals suffering from gelotophobia, or the fear of being laughed at (Proyer et al., 2009: 255). However, laughter's connection to comedy (and pleasure broadly) remains the most common and overwhelming interpretation of this distinctive sound. Laughter is used as a metonym for comedy in terms of live venues and productions such as standup comedy venue 'The Last Laugh' in Melbourne, Australia and the 'Just For Laughs' festival in Montreal. More formally, Stott's study of comedy includes an entire chapter dedicated to laugher (2005: 127–145), noting that while laughter has been "variously understood as vice or cowardice, as delight caused by surprise, the product of demamilarization, a means of averting antisocial conflict, or an extra-linguistic bark signalling the limits of understanding" (2005: 127), in each case this relates back to the richness that can be delivered with comedy as a form, mode, genre and method. He concludes that the academic study of comedy should ultimately have "the aim of opening up understanding for the purposes of laughter" (2005: 149).

The connection between comedy and sound, specifically comedy and laughter, has also been acknowledged by practising comedians and narrative comedy writers. For example, in the opening passages of a textbook on writing narrative comedy, Tim Ferguson argues:

> Laughter has several mysterious qualities. Like blushing, adrenalin rushes and erections, laughter is involuntary ... Furthermore, we can't decide to be amused. We might expect to laugh at a standup comedian, but that doesn't mean that we will (2010: 5. Emphasis as original)

Ferguson's point about the 'mystery' of laughter evokes a necessary relationship between the person/thing inspiring laughter and the person actually laughing. In doing so, he also establishes a method by which comedians can systematically provoke laughter, and therefore, confirm their success with creating comedy.

Offering a list of "principles of comedy" (2010: 2–4) for the aspiring comedian to draw on, Ferguson demonstrates how laughter is provoked (as opposed to other involuntary reactions) using a basic example – a parent tickling a baby. In this small action, which he calls "the most reliable stimulus for laughter" (2010: 7), Ferguson also notes the "mock-threatening behaviour" that occurs as the parent reaches for the child (perhaps sneaking up on them to surprise them). He argues that "to be effective, tickling should be an unfolding drama" (*ibid*), explaining how a parent might aim for different 'more ticklish' parts of the child or vary their approach – even, importantly, adding sound effects to heighten the experience. Interestingly, Ferguson highlights the importance of sound here too, asking the tickler: "do you remain silent as you tickle? … of course not" (*ibid*). This rhetorical question confirms that in the most basic comedic interaction a sonic marker is necessary for comedy to work. Without the accompanying sound of the tickler (likely their own laughter to let the toddler know that the interaction is playful rather than malicious), the action could very easily be perceived by the baby as threatening or too dangerous. Citing American comedian Bob Newhart to help support this, Ferguson argues "Laughter gives us distance. It allows us to step back from an event, deal with it, and move on" (Hope in Ferguson, 2010: 6).

Music, comedy and context

Unlike broadcast television or radio, the sound of laughter is rarely (if ever) included nondiegetically in a film. This means the relationship between sound and comedy for film is somewhat different to that of these other forms – laughter can be invited or implied but never directly added, leaving scope for the soundtrack to be manipulated differently. In his volume *Film Comedy*, King defined the relationship between the medium and comedy as "a mode – a manner of presentation" (2002: 2), noting that, "film comedy is so widespread as to be difficult to local as a single or stable generic noun-form" (2002: 3). The music used in film comedies is similarly diverse both in terms of its use as comedy and the uses of music for non-comic effects in comedy films (such as in establishing sequences, 'straight' sequences etc. that might alternate with more overtly comic ones).

In a seminal article on film comedy and music, informed by reference to previous performance traditions (and, most notably, theatre), Mera (2002) argued that music used in comedy is not so much intrinsically comic as rendered comic by context. Some musical traditions, such as the 'ba-dum-bum-ching' drum roll used to signify a comic punchline or the 'wah-wah-wah-wah' descending motif (often played on a trombone) used to signify excessive pathos, have become comic traditions due to their re-iteration in live action and animated films; music is often *rendered* comic by context. Identifying three standard levels of comedy – superiority, incongruity and relief – Mera argues that comic effect is caused by "creating a sense of anticipation that is then subverted or dislocated" (2002: 91). Drawing on Mera, Coyle and Morris identify that film music creates comic effects through deployment of "parody, referentialism, instrumentation, and diegetic/nondiegetic ambiguities" (2010: 202) and, citing screen composer Julian Nott, the authors emphasize music's capacity to cue (rather than *deliver*) laughter.

Drawing on the above and on the critical essays included in this volume, we can identify that musical techniques designed to stimulate and accompany comedy can be classified as follows (with some degrees of overlap between categories):

- familiar comic cues that rely on the audience's knowledge of their comedic traditions
- orchestration, including the use of instruments traditionally perceived as 'funny' (e.g. the tuba) or instruments mismatched to action on-screen
- songs performed within the film's diegesis that are perceived as comic due to aspects of lyrics, performance, instrumentation and/or musical style
- quotation or allusion to other musical excerpts for comedic effect
- nondiegetic music comically juxtaposed with the vision

Of course there are also non-musical sounds that contribute to comedic intent, most notably:

- exaggerated sound effects
- mismatched sound effects
- the removal of all sound to highlight the artifice of film (often found in spoof or parody films)

While the chapters included in this anthology primarily focus on the musical approaches detailed above, elements of sound design are also included with regard to their relation to score and enhancement of musical effects. Individual contributors focus on a variety of comic effects in music and narrative relation as appropriate to either their conceptual overviews, as in the case of Heiser in his analysis of incongruity, or in the case of the other authors, with their studies of particular films and/or composers (and, in the case of Westover, a particular comic dance routine enacted with variation in separate films).

Heiser's chapter complements this introduction to comedy sound by analysing how the combination of incongruent visual and audio events works to produce a truly 'fantastic' comedic moment. As he notes, "the sound and vision components, when experienced separately might be fun, but aren't exactly funny." Yet cinema affords the opportunity to bring the incongruent together in the creation of new comedic moments, moments that are built on playfulness and a knowing wink to the audience. From Jacques Tati to Mel Brooks, Heiser is able to theoretically consider these moments and provide substantiation for many of the categories listed above.

Winter's chapter on John Landis's *Trading Places* (1983) identifies the manner in which Elmer Bernstein's score, which borrows extensively from Mozart's *The Marriage of Figaro*, creates a series of satirical inter-relations with both individual sequences and with the film's overarching narrative. Winter's careful analysis teases out the nuances of the score's interaction and enhancement of the film's dramatic theme. The manner in which allusions to and excerpts from works as diverse as Elgar's *Land of Hope and Glory* and the Silhouette's 1957 doo-wop song 'Get A Job' provide further comic nuances to what might, superficially, be perceived as a relatively uncomplicated role-reversal comedy. Complementing Winter's study, Heine analyses the manner in which Elmer Bernstein effectively parodied his own score for John Sturgis's 1960 mercenary western *The Magnificent Seven* for John Landis's comedy feature ¡*Three Amigos!* (1986), and the manner in which the inclusion of two original song compositions, both by Randy Newman, voiced in the film by a vocal trio implicitly that of the protagonists indicated in the film's title, contains comic elements that satirize any serious qualities the trio may initially be thought to possess. Heine's study emphasizes the intertextual qualities of the score for ¡*Three Amigos!* and the manner in which its effect derives from subtle allusions to popular culture, akin to those allusions to opera present in Landis's earlier feature *Trading Places*.

Following on from Heine's study, Giuffre and Evans consider the heavy use of intertextual sonic references in the Austin Powers series of films. Moreover, they look at the key song sequences at work in the films, especially the opening numbers and the comic songs choreographed into the films. What the chapter highlights is the way Mike Myers and director Jay Roach - as lead creative visionaries behind the films - construct the Powers films as 'musicals', without ever having to put that label on them. They then manipulate these musical and music theatre devices to construct sonic intertextuality to produce their comedy. While the Austin Powers films are frequently read as spy movie (most notably James Bond) spoofs, Giuffre and Evans unpack the films' use of musical spectacle and demonstrate how elements of the musical remain popular and relevant outside of the genre itself.

Fitzgerald and Hayward consider the music of *Ghostbusters* (Ivan Reitman, 1984), holistically, analysing the manner in which distinct musical aspects drawn, in the main, from horror/suspense cinema scoring traditions and from 1970s and 1980s American popular music, serve to switch the moods and generic modes of the film. Equally, their chapter emphasizes the extratextual functions of the film's theme song as a device that effectively captured the zest of the production and was successfully deployed as a promotional single and as the music track for a highly successful promotional video. Their study considers the film's comedy and musical enhancement of comic elements as part of the film's overall textual operation rather than as discrete elements within the production, emphasizing the manner in which the comedic element of contemporary cinema is often a component within a more diverse fictional entity. In a similar manner, Butkus and Fitzgerald identify how elements of horror/suspense scoring are deployed in the low-budget spook exploitation film *Lesbian Vampire Killers* (Philip Claydon, 2009) and are contrasted with musical incongruities to create subtle colourations to the film's somewhat less-than-subtle parodic 'romp' through a sub-genre of lesbianesque vampirism derived from early 1970s Hammer Horror productions.

In an important contribution that considers not only the sonic but also physical gesture and dance, Westover makes a detailed comparison of the songs 'Make 'Em Laugh' and 'Be A Clown'. Using a variety of analytical tools, Westover draws out objectively the oft-cited similarities between the two songs. Westover also shows how Donald O'Connor's athletic, physical performance combines movement and music to form a new comedic moment, one that continues to be referenced and revered by performers decades later.

The next two chapters provide studies of important historical European comedy films, the first from Finland and the following from Spain. Laine and Juva base their study on the Finnish auteur Matti Kassila, who was known for his belief in audio to produce the richest cinematic effect. They focus their attention of Kassila's film *Kaasua, komisario Palmu!*, and find that the key aspects of surprise and playfulness are arrived at sonically, more than visually or even verbally. In their analysis they also examine how modernist films, in particular historical contexts, are not necessarily averse to touches of comedy. Using distinctly Finnish examples, Laine and Juva are able to demonstrate how these historical films pushed the boundaries of their genres, and used sonically produced comedy to do it. Following on from this, Miranda provides a study of two scores written by Manuel Parada for 1940s Spanish comedy films, *El Camino de Babel* (Jerónimo Mihura, 1944) and *El Destino se Disculpa* (J.L. Sáenz de Heredia, 1945). Her study identifies the manner in which the scores embody aspects of musical modernity and incongruity that serve to identify and satirize the class positions and aspirations of the films' key protagonists and, in particular, those male characters that aspire to upwards socio-economic mobility. In her study, jazz (and musical modernity more generally) is understood to be disruptive to the hegemony of Franco-era cinema by dint of suggesting other socio-cultural mores and modes.

Moving to Asia, Hayward's detailed analysis of use of traditional Okinawan songs in Yuji Nakae's Japanese film *Nabi no koi* (*Nabbie's Love*) provides a case study of how a repertoire of vernacular material can be deployed within a film's diegesis to comic effect through subtle manipulation of the contexts of performance, the nature and character of performers and of the interaction between performers. Indeed, so dense is this level of textual operation and affect in Nakae's film that Hayward characterizes it as offering a distinct mode of *musicalized drama*, in this case deployed for comic purposes. As he also discusses, within this overarching musical framework the deployment of other musical material, such as excerpts from Bizet's *Carmen* and Anglo-Celtic fiddle melodies sourced from Atlantic Canada, serves to enhance and diversify the nature of comic effect and incongruity involved. Booth also considers the use of vernacular techniques to produce comedy, this time considering the musical instances, specific sounds, and carefully choreographed moments that produce comedy in Hindi film. Yet Booth also pulls back his lens to consider more holistically how Hindi film, and in particular the comic song sequences within them, provides respite from the tension of the central narrative. He also scrutinizes their ability to play with notions of gender and social class, noting how the songs themselves produce an 'other' to be laughed at. Booth suggests that "the comic song scenes shift back-and-forth between laughter as a subjective and dramatic representation which the audience experiences sympathetically and as an objective incongruity to which the audience responds by laughing."

The final chapter in the anthology provides a neat link to a previous volume in the series, Rebecca Coyle's *Drawn To Sound* (2010). In his chapter, Morris provides a detailed analysis of the structural framework underpinning the music in the famous Tom and Jerry animated movie, *The Cat Concerto* (1947). Morris demonstrates how the flexibility of the score, particularly its ability to be compartmentalized in various ways, underpins the comedy achieved through visual and physical humour.

Taken collectively, the chapters in this volume work to showcase the various categories of sonic humour used in film as listed above. What they show is that comedy film is not merely the sum of its parts, but rather the unique, enjoyable moment produced at the intersection of carefully crafted sonic and visual texts. While sound illuminates all film texts (and even silent films were simply live sound pieces, rather than completely without sound), sound in comedy film is absolutely paramount in developing and defining genre. 'Sounding funny' is a reference to the practice of creators, as well as appraisal by audiences. 'Sounding Funny' is also an example of quite a bad pun, something almost all editors of books about comedy have been unable to resist.

References

Aristotle (1996). *Poetics*. (M. Heath, Trans.). London: Penguin Books.
Bennett, M.P. (2008). 'Humor and Laughter May Influence Health: III. Laughter and Health Outcomes'. *Evidence-Based Complementary and Alternative Medicine*, 5(1), 37–40.

Bore, I.-L.K. (2011). 'Laughing Together?: TV Comedy Audiences and the Laugh Track'. *Velvet Light Trap: A Critical Journal Of Film and Television*, 68(1), 24–34. http://dx.doi.org/10.1353/vlt.2011.0011

Coyle, R., & Morris, P. (2010). DreamWorking Wallis and Gromit. In R. Coyle (Ed.), *Drawn to Sound: Animation Music and Sonicity* (pp. 191–208). London: Equinox.

Ferguson, T. (2010). *The Cheeky Monkey: Writing Narrative Comedy*. Melbourne: Currency Press.

Freud, S. (1960). *Jokes and their Relation to the Unconscious* (J. Strachey, Trans.). London: WW Norton.

Gray, Tim (2013). Golden Globes Comedy Race Is a Two-Way 'Street'. *Variety*, 22 November 2013, variety.com/2013/film/news/golden-globes-comedy-race-is-a-two-way-street-1200869876/, accessed 12 December 2013.

Keltner, D., & Bonanno, G.A. (1997). 'A Study of Laughter and Dissociation: Distinct Correlates of Laughter and Smiling During Bereavement'. *Journal of Personality and Social Psychology*, 73(4), 687–702. http://dx.doi.org/10.1037/0022-3514.73.4.687

Kilday, G. (2013). Golden Globes: '12 Years a Slave,' 'American Hustle' Dominate Film Noms. *The Hollywood Reporter*, 12 December 2013, http://www.hollywoodreporter.com/news/golden-globes-12-years-a-665271, accessed 12 December 2013.

King, G. (2002). *Film Comedy*. London: Wallflower Press.

Lawson, T., Downing, B., & Cetola, H. (1998). 'An Attributional Explanation for the Effect of Audience Laughter on Perceived Funniness'. *Basic and Applied Social Psychology*, 20(4), 243–249. http://dx.doi.org/10.1207/s15324834basp2004_1

Leggatt, A. (Ed.) (2002). *The Cambridge Companion to Shakespearean Comedy*. Cambridge: Cambridge University Press.

Mera, M. (2002). 'Is Funny Music Funny? Contexts and Case Studies of Film Music Humour'. *Journal of Popular Music Studies*, 14(2), 91–113. http://dx.doi.org/10.1111/j.1533-1598.2002.tb00039.x

O'Connell, D., & Kowal, S. (2004). 'Hilary Clinton's Laughter in Media Interviews'. *Pragmatics*, 14(4), 463–478. http://dx.doi.org/10.1075/prag.14.4.03con

Proyer, R., et al. (2009). 'Breaking Ground in Cross-Cultural Research on the Fear of Being Laughed at (Gelotophobia): A Multi-National Study Involving 73 Countries'. *Humor: International Journal of Humor Research*, 22(1–2), 253–279.

Sideridis, G. (2006). 'Coping Is Not an "Either" "Or": The Interaction of Coping Strategies in Regulating Affect, Arousal and Performance'. *Stress and Health*, 22(5), 315–327. http://dx.doi.org/10.1002/smi.1114

Smith, J. (2008). Recorded Laughter and the Performance of Authenticity. In J. Smith, *Vocal Tracks: Performance and Sound Media* (pp. 15–49). Berkeley & Los Angeles, CA, London: University of California Press.

Stott, A. (2005). *Comedy*. New York: Routledge.

Sully, J. (1902). *An Essay on Laughter: its Forms, its Causes, its Development and its Value*. London: Longmans, Green, and Co. Online at http://ovidsp.tx.ovid.com/sp-3.10.0b/ovidweb.cgi, accessed 12 December 2013.

Sutton-Spence, D. et al. (2012). 'Deaf Jokes and Sign Language Humor'. *Humor: International Journal of Humor Research*, 25(3), 311–337.

Symons, A. (2013). 'The Problem of "High Culture" Comedy: How Annie Hall (1977) Complicated Woody Allen's Reputation'. *Journal of Popular Film and Television*, 41(3), 118–127. http://dx.doi.org/10.1080/01956051.2012.755489

Szameitat, D., Darwin, C.J., Wildgruber, D., Alter, K., & Szameitat, A.J. (2011). 'Acoustic Correlates of Emotional Dimensions in Laughter: Arousal, Dominance, and Valence'. *Cognition and Emotion*, 25(4), 599–611. http://dx.doi.org/10.1080/02699931.2010.508624

Szameitat, D., Alter, K., Szameitat, A.J., Wildgruber, D., Sterr, A., & Darwin, C.J. (2009). 'Acoustic Profiles of Distinct Emotional Expressions in Laughter'. *Journal of the Acoustical Society of America*, 126(1), 354–366. http://dx.doi.org/10.1121/1.3139899

Weeks, M. (2002). 'Laughter, Desire, and Time'. *Humor: International Journal of Humor Research*, 15(4), 383–400.

Weisfeld, G.E. (1993). *Ethology and Sociobiology*, 14(2), 141–169. http://dx.doi.org/10.1016/0162-3095(93)90012-7

Wolosin, R. (1975). 'Cognitive Similarity and Group Laughter'. *Journal of Personality and Social Psychology*, 32(3), 503–509. http://dx.doi.org/10.1037/h0077083

Dr **Liz Giuffre** is a Lecturer in Communication at the University of Technology Sydney, as well as an arts and music journalist.

Mark Evans is the Executive Editor of *Perfect Beat: The Pacific Journal of Research into Contemporary Music and Popular Culture* and author of the book, *Open Up The Doors: Music in the Modern Church* (Equinox Publishing, London). He is Series Editor for *Genre, Music and Sound* and Executive Editor of *The Encyclopedia of Film Music and Sound* (Equinox Publishing) and is Head of the School of Communication at the University of Technology, Sydney.

2 The Soundtrack as Appropriate Incongruity

Marshall Heiser

The idea that instances of humour depend upon the perception of an incongruity is by no means a new idea (Morreall, 1989). Incongruity theories form a major strand of humour studies and have in common a (primarily) cognitive approach to the phenomenon. Oring's *appropriate incongruity* theory states that humour depends on relationships that are paradoxically right and yet not-right (2003). This collision of seemingly "incompatible matrices" (Koestler, 1964) need not be limited to one sensory mode however. As an audio-visual medium, cinema has the potential to articulate humour by playfully synchronizing sight and sound in an appropriately incongruous fashion. In these cases, humour may arise as an emergent property of the synthesis rather than belonging to either of the texts independently. Case studies from comedy cinema of the post-war period are examined to demonstrate a variety of ways this humorous synthesis can occur.

Humour studies

Agreement among scholars regarding how to adequately define and limit the concept of humour has still not been met today, despite a continued growth of interest in the topic in recent times. Roeckelein (2002) consulted the database PsychINFO and found that psychological studies of humour increased dramatically decade by decade during the previous 100 years (compare 171 in 1961–1970 with 464 in 1971–80, and 945 between 1981 and 1990). Humour studies as a whole, however, stem from a wide variety of disciplines, resulting in a far from standardized body of literature, and contributing to a "hodge-podge of diverse and often conflicting findings that are not easily integrated with one another" (Martin, 1998: 57). Adding further confusion is the fact that humour is a multidimensional construct, therefore making redundant attempts to formulate 'global' theories that might tie up all concerns together with a 'one-size-fits-all' approach (McGhee, 1972). Whereas the development of a uniform theory of humour might be problematic, the *experience* of the phenomenon itself is easily detected, and even unmistakable for anything else (Berlyne, 1972).

Despite this heterogeneity, humour studies can be arguably seen as consisting of three general approaches to the topic: 'psychoanalytic', 'superiority', and 'incongruity' theories. The basis for such groupings relates to which aspects of the phenomenon they focus on primarily. For example, emotion, motivation, social context, physiology and cognition (Martin, 1998). Of these three approaches, incongruity theories focus most strongly on the role cognition plays and state that humour may result from a manipulation of an audience's expectations. This strand of humour scholarship, therefore, provides the most useful analytical framework(s) for exploring the role film soundtracks play in articulating humour.

Incongruity theories

The notion that the awareness of an incongruity informs humour can be traced back to Aristotle and on through to, for example, Kant and Schopenhauer (Morreall, 1989). It was Arthur Koestler's *The Act of Creation* (1964) however, that most famously argued the role incongruity plays in not only humour, but also in scientific discovery and art. Koestler calls his model the *Triptych* – a conceptual continuum whereby the three domains of humour, science and art share a common creative process of *bisociation*; that is, the bringing together of seemingly incongruous 'universes of discourse' (*matrices*).

Koestler argues that it is *how* they make these associations that distinguishes them from each other. Humour, he says, involves the sudden *collision* of matrices, whereas scientific discovery forms an *integration* of supposedly incompatible concepts. Art/aesthetic experience, on the other hand, achieves its synthesis through the more subtle *juxtaposition* of perceptions. Koestler proposes that the fundamental theoretical basis underlying all instances of humour is 'bisociative':

> The humorist has solved his [sic] problem by joining two incompatible matrices together in a paradoxical synthesis. His audience, on the other hand, has its expectations shattered and its reason affronted by the impact of the second matrix on the first; instead of fusion there is collision; and in the mental disarray which ensues, emotion, deserted by reason, is flushed out in laughter. (ibid: 94)

Necessary but not sufficient

As humour is a multidimensional construct, incongruity alone cannot explain the difference between a situation that evokes laughter and one that merely confuses or bewilders. Some theorists claim that the presence of incongruity is a necessary but not sufficient condition for humour to occur (Ziv, 1984; Oring,

2003). Therefore, other dimensions of humour need to be explored in order to explain these sufficient conditions. What unifies various incongruity theories is not so much their level of agreement, but merely that incongruity receives the main focus, within what are otherwise often quite divergent models.

Although primarily concerned with cognition, many incongruity theories nonetheless take into account additional elements within the humour experience, such as motivational, psychophysiological and emotional aspects. Koestler (1964) states that motivation is an ever-present element of humour. This he illustrates by contrasting *bathos* with *pathos* – personified by the jester and the artist respectively. The former always has the element of derision present (no matter how subtle), allowing would-be jesters to look down upon their object of laughter, and in so doing asserting themselves. This concept echoes Herbert Spencer's theory that laughter results only from *descending* incongruities (http://www.t.hosei.ac.jp/~hhirano/academia/laughter.htm; accessed 26 August 2009). By contrast, the *artist's* subtler juxtaposition of incongruous elements within a new work is informed by a more 'self transcending' disposition. In this case, the identification with the plight of another is more likely to result in tears.

Other humour theorists and researchers point to the importance of context as a way of setting the stage for incongruity to be experienced as fun, rather than threat. The humour researcher Avner Ziv (1984) gives the example of tickling to demonstrate that what might be the source of laughter in one context – such as a parent tickling their child – would most likely result in fear or anger in another (e.g. if one were to attempt to tickle a stranger in the street). He explains that in the former situation, a pre-existing, positive social relationship acts as the cue that this isn't a real attack.

Michael Apter's *reversal theory* (1982) links humour and play together by stating that a playful attitude creates a psychological frame upon which the harsh realities and limitations of the 'real world' can't impinge. This is a concept common to many play theorists, but Apter interprets the relationship in terms of psychophysiological stimulus patterns. His theory states that a playful frame of mind dictates how arousal stimulus will be experienced by an individual. In the present-oriented *paratelic* state, arousal generated by the perception of an incongruity will be experienced as pleasurable (exciting), whereas low arousal is experienced as unpleasant (boring). In the future-oriented *telic* state however, the situation is reversed (hence *reversal* theory). In this state, high arousal produces feelings of anxiety, whilst low arousal is experienced as relaxing. Apter agrees with Ziv that humorous incidents themselves (or other cues such as smiling and laughter) can trigger the perceptual switch into a paratelic state: a frame of mind that Ziv simply calls 'fun mood' (1983).

The second part of Apter's theory deals with the cognitive aspect of incongruity. Unlike 'incongruity-resolution' theorists such as Suls (1972), whose ideas address narrative forms of humour only (like jokes and cartoons with captions), Apter argues that the simultaneous recognition of conflicting viewpoints regarding a single object are experienced as synergic in the paratelic state. Therefore no strictly logical resolution is desired. Apter's model can therefore account for examples such as physical slapstick, caricatures or gestural humour, all of which rely on a simultaneous Gestalt-style ground/foreground tension. Not surprisingly, he refers to such paradoxical incongruous perceptions as *synergies*, whilst Ziv labels this openness to the incongruous as a kind of *local-logic* (1984). Approaching the same concerns from a philosophical perspective, Morreall simply uses the term *amusement* (1989).

Appropriate incongruity

Another theorist who sees no need for the resolution of paradox within his own humour theory is Elliot Oring. In his book *Engaging Humour*, Oring revisits his earlier claim that humour "depends upon the perception of an *appropriate incongruity*; that is, the perception of an appropriate relationship between categories that would normally be regarded as incongruous" (2003: 1). The paradoxical coexistence of something that is simultaneously both right yet 'not-right' is here interpreted as constituting a "psychologically valid rather than logically valid relation" (*ibid*: 2).

Oring goes on to distance his theory from that of incongruity-resolution theorists by pointing out two key differences: first, his theory maintains that despite a connection of sorts being discovered between the incongruous categories present in humorous instances, the incongruity or paradox nonetheless remains (in a strictly logical sense). Second, he states that appropriate incongruity theory presumes no particular temporal order of recognition. That is, the realization of an 'appropriate' relation between seemingly incongruous categories need not necessarily follow the initial awareness of the incongruity itself. In some cases it may actually precede it – for example, in comic instances where what seems logical enough at first, suddenly 'turns upside-down'.

As Martin states: "Theories are a way of organizing information ... [and should not be] judged so much on the basis of whether they are right or wrong, but on the basis of their usefulness ..." (2007: 31). It was therefore decided to name this chapter after Oring's 'appropriate incongruity' theory as the phrase most succinctly and eloquently sums up the playful tolerance of paradox claimed to be so essential to humour appreciation by theorists such as Apter (1982), Ziv (1984) and McGhee (1972).

Post-war comedy cinema

The filmmaker Peter Greenaway claims that cinema is dead. Well, at least cinema as we know it, and most definitely films based on narrative forms. The present day formulaic world cinema monoculture made in Hollywood's image goes hand in hand with storytelling. The narrative *is* the Hollywood dream. The boy gets the girl or the good guy kills the bad guys and saves the world. The variations are numerous but the plots are nonetheless *essentially* similar (Vogler, 1992) and linear (or keep referring back to the linear). Anything that gets in the way of the film's dramatic flow must be sacrificed to the god of pacing. Greenaway states that narratives belong in the bookshop, not in twenty-first-century film (http://www.youtube.com/watch?v=-t-9qxqdVm4&feature=related; accessed 24 September 2010).

If Greenaway is right about the death of cinema, then The Three Stooges must have been trying to kill it since 1934. Stooges short subject comedies do indeed have narratives – but only begrudgingly so. Unlike their contemporaries the Marx Brothers, the Stooges didn't have to suffer the indignation of taking backseat to the 'love interests' that carried the plot in their feature-length films (at least not until the late 1950s when they were well past their prime). The Stooges' pratfalls and gags were thereby freed to take centre stage as they annihilated all and sundry between plot points A, B, and (at most) C.

The short subject format was tailor-made for the Stooges' slapstick schtick originally honed in vaudeville as sidekicks to comedian Ted Healy. Their films' *modus operandi* was contrary to that of Hollywood features of the time; a two-reel Stooges plot was never in danger of getting in the way of the gags. The same can be said for the wildly unpredictable cartoon shorts directed by Tex Avery during the 1940s and 1950s. Whereas the ever-ambitious Walt Disney craved recognition as a 'serious' and innovative producer (taking to feature-length animated films like a duck to a sailor's suit), neither Avery nor the Stooges aspired to the same Hollywood myth or status quo. They preferred instead to ambush it, as if waging filmic guerrilla warfare from the fringes of cinema. That is, from the seemingly inconsequential position of the short subject.

At approximately 16 minutes each, a typical Stooges film has no need for any great character arc. Larry (Larry Fine), Moe (Moses Howard), Curly (Jerome Howard) and, later, Shemp (Samuel Howard) were in no need of development anyhow. They were already fully realized: enlightened, at peace with their lot. Stooges shorts, therefore, don't finish with any real sense of resolution, as much as just stop ... the way a vehicle 'stops' when it hits a streetlamp. In *Visions of Cody* (1972) Jack Kerouac describes Larry's character as a 'saint in disguise' and goes on to use the Stooges and their goofy pranks as a metaphor for all that's sacred in the dusty, bustling, imperfect and mundane.

The Soundtrack as Appropriate Incongruity   19

The Stooges aren't heroes. They are no Luke Skywalkers, they are comic Obi Wans, obscurely shrouded in laughter cloaks, and going about their scams as impoverished monks go about with their begging bowls. They are *schnorrers*, but only in the most beatific sense. Larry, Moe, Curly and Shemp keep things real by disrupting the flow of all that is fake – and society is better for it.

There is no shortage of *visual* cues within an average Stooges film to suggest to the audience that what they're witnessing should be taken with 'a grain of salt'. Take for instance, each character's distinct clown-like *coiffure*: Larry's Einstein-esque bird's nest, Moe's pudding bowl cut, and Shemp's long dishevelled fringe. Yet it is arguably the sound effects (or more specifically, their synchronization with the visuals) that provide the greatest indication of how to interpret the action. A brief analysis of a typical Stooges gag and its separate audio-visual components will clarify their comedic interaction.

In the short subject film *Hold that Lion!* (Jules White, 1947), a textbook Stooges routine occurs in the opening scene when they meet in the offices of "Cess, Poole and Drayne – Attorneys at Law" to discuss their swindled inheritance. Soon enough, Larry interrupts the flow of the story and sets up a slapstick gag by asking why his palm is itchy. The following dialogue indicates nothing particularly amusing, at least not worthy of a paying audience over the age of five:

> Larry: "My right palm itches. What's that a sign of?"
> Moe: "Your hand's dirty."
> Shemp interjects: "Why don't you leave him alone!"
> Moe: "Quiet!"
> (transcribed by the author)

So the dialogue isn't responsible for my eruption of laughter. The visuals likewise, when viewed without audio, are decidedly lame. The action is unrealistic (in a theatrical sense), though rather workman-like and lethargic in its execution, therefore unconvincing as being threatening. The sound effects consist of a string of short staccato events and are widely varied in texture. When heard out of context, they can be more easily discerned as an array of disjointed percussion instruments played in succession. It could easily be a recording of an orchestral percussionist earnestly stepping through a demonstration of the various ratchets, horns and drums in the *batterie*. The resulting impression when considered out of context is a disjointed one, but again, not necessarily *funny*. Nonetheless, the excruciating *combination* of sight and sound compels one to wince as much as laugh (even on successive viewings).

This is no acrobatic slapstick in the silent tradition of Buster Keaton or Harold Lloyd. This isn't humour transmitted by and large through a visual medium, and merely augmented by an optional piano accompaniment. Neither does it resemble Abbott and Costello's 'Who's on first?' as a routine that could work equally as well on radio as on the screen. Using Koestler's bisociation model, we can see how this Stooges gag owes its funniness to the collision of two universes of discourse with seemingly incompatible logics. What is seen and heard simultaneously shouldn't belong together (in a strictly logical sense) and yet, when we experience them as one, they seem to have a *synthetic* validity. They seem somehow right, but in a funny way.

Why should the cue that this situation isn't for real be of such importance to the audience's interpretation of the action? Apter's 'paratelic state' or Ziv's similarly incongruity-tolerant 'fun mood' both allow for the interpretation of unresolved paradoxes in a manner very much at odds with traditional logic or a more serious frame of mind. In these states, paradox is not only tolerated but is actually enjoyed. Ziv calls this kind of cognition *local-logical* (or *paralogical*) *thinking*: "Local-logical thinking uses and enjoys both logic and fantasy without confusing them, and offers solutions that involve one or the other as required by the context" (1984: 98). In plain words, if the audience were encouraged to see (and hear) the action as real, it wouldn't be funny: it'd be pathetic.

Jacques Tati's movies are another example of comedy cinema that relies more on strings of gags than plot development to propel the action, but this time in the context of the feature film format. Watching Tati's features in chronological order is a little like witnessing one of your favourite wilderness areas being progressively developed. These films portray a post-war France that is, at first, merely starstruck by the American dream, but later overrun by it. All that is initially slow, gnarled and knotted or inscrutable soon gives way to the coolness of rationality, utopian straight lines and ideal geometric shapes. French Adam eats the fruit of knowledge and it is his ultimate undoing. It is as if the quaint villages of *Jour de Fête* (Jacques Tati, 1949) are bulldozed to make way for the nightmarish ultra-modern dreamhouse of *Mon Oncle* (Jacques Tati, 1958), that in turn becomes overshadowed by *Playtime*'s (Jacques Tati, 1967) labyrinth of Babel-esque office blocks and towers. The buildings get more numerous, bigger, blander, whilst natural space, and liberty along with it, can do little but contract.

In *Jour de Fête* the satire is gentler than in Tati's later films, with the provincial French world of 1949 being affectionately lampooned as a toddler taking its first wide-eyed steps towards mummy Hollywood. Juxtapositions of the fake and the real in ludicrously stark contrast allude to the deceptive nature of what is being coveted: carnival horses confused with the real thing, or a clumsy real-world French seduction played out against the Hollywood myth of heroic courtship.

This film starts with the idyllic image of a tractor steadily pulling a small caravan and trailer along a winding countryside lane. It weaves past field

The Soundtrack as Appropriate Incongruity 21

workers bailing hay, and soon enough, the approaching village is visible in the background. The carnival has come to town! The corresponding score by Jean Yatove is not unlike those featured in whimsical Disney short subject cartoons of the era, albeit with a continental twist. A nimble celeste melody is accompanied by a light, carefree, *andante*-paced rhythm section of snare (played with brushes), mellow jazz guitar and double bass, further augmented by pizzicato strings, flutes and clarinet, and later, accordion, xylophone and muted trumpet. The resulting atmosphere is relaxed and playful.

The first gag of the film approaches seconds later: a cock is heard crowing, a German Shepherd barks at the passing vehicle – but what follows is surprising. The shot focuses on six white wooden carousel horses secured to the back of the trailer, as a loud (and extremely realistic) 'neigh' rings out. The result is initially confusing, but makes sense moments later, as two very real horses are revealed standing in a field as the trailer moves past, and they gallop off. An unlikely 'coincidence' is responsible for the audio-visual incongruity, which logically resolves as suddenly as it happened. The audience is left to contemplate the irony of our attraction to things that simply imitate what is already on our doorstep.

Another gag using a similar technique soon follows, but this time without need for a strictly logical resolution. The driver of the tractor, Roger (Guy Decomble) and his long-suffering, ever-watchful wife (Santa Relli) have arrived at the town square and reacquaint themselves with the townsfolk, before setting up the carnival. As Roger starts unloading the trailer with the help of hordes of eager children, the beautiful young Jeanette (Maine Vallée) watches from her window – all the time pouting and preening. Roger looks up with predatory interest, and belatedly tips his hat as she closes the shutters. Meanwhile, a town-crier beats his drum and announces to the village that a movie will be shown tonight: a Hollywood western starring the 'lovely' Gloria Parson and 'daring' Jim Parker (and his horse Dixie!).

As the makeshift cinema tent is being finished off, faint gunshots, hooves and trumpets can be heard softly seeping out into the square – the projection equipment is, no doubt, being tested inside. This is followed with dialogue consisting of typically chivalrous sweet talk from a cowboy action-hero as he introduces himself to his romantic foil. Meanwhile, Jeanette is wheeling her laundry items across the town-square, stopping momentarily to stare at the movie poster. Roger, dressed in his workman dungarees and wide-brimmed hat, seizes his opportunity and casually saunters over from behind his caravan (which curiously resembles a stagecoach from this angle). All the while, he swivels his trusty spanner around one finger as a cowboy would his gun.

"It's time you and I got to know each other ..." is delivered in a broad, American accent. But Roger doesn't move his lips; it is the movie's soundtrack speaking. For the next 30 seconds, the actions of Roger and his potential paramour, silently and unwittingly, mimic the kind of gestural cues that precisely match the romantic dialogue of the western. Even references to the hero's gun coincide with Roger suavely placing his black, Colt-like workman's spanner into his pocket. All goes well until the words "I love you ..." droop down in pitch to a deflated, impotent halt. The projector falters and Roger's wife spies the two lovebirds from the window of the caravan. The jig is up!

In this scene, the humour is less startling and more poetic than the previous example. Koestler (1964) would say that both 'bathos' and 'pathos' are present here, as the audience is encouraged to identify with the would-be lovers in their failed attempt at infidelity, rather than to simply judge or mock them. In contrast to the provincial setting and (initial) pace of *Jour de Fête*, both *Mon Oncle* and *Playtime* chronicle a modernization of France that is, at first, well under way and finally, 'over the top'. The warm, clumsy, whimsical spirit of provincialism that Monsieur Hulot embodies becomes increasingly marginalized, not only in terms of the situations and landscapes that befuddle and dwarf him, but also in terms of his diminishing screen time.

A brave new world of a different kind is the target of the comedy in *They're a Weird Mob* (Michael Powell, 1966). It is easy to dismiss this British–Australian co-production headed by Michael Powell and Richard Imrie (A.K.A. Emeric Pressburger) – both of *Black Narcissus* (Michael Powell, 1947) and *The Red Shoes* (Michael Powell, 1948) fame – for its dated exploitation of culture clash, crude racial stereotypes (that paint all Australian males as lovable chauvinistic scallywags), and the patronizing message that tolerating the lesser of equals is *fair dinkum*. What is more, there is clearly a kind of cultural hierarchy at work here. The English filmmakers tolerate the quirky Antipodean characters they lampoon, just as these colonials in turn tolerate the even quirkier 'dagos' (i.e., provided they're polite and try to 'fit in' with the Aussie way of life by being ... well, *less* dago). This perspective is cemented, in no unsubtle way, at the end of the film with a visual pun where the camera swings upside down to illustrate Sydney Harbour's *downunderness*. The reference alludes to Australia as being yet another tossed aside colonial curio: a distorted fairground mirror of the 'mother country'.

They're a Weird Mob begins with the Italian Nino (Walter Chiari) emigrating to Australia to work as a sports journalist for his cousin's Sydney-based Italian-language publication. Upon arrival, he finds that not only has the magazine folded, but his cousin has run off leaving a considerable debt unpaid. Nino feels obliged to honour the liability and soon enough finds menial work as a builder's labourer to raise funds. Though inexperienced and unprepared for the arduous task before him, Nino gives it his best.

The gag starts with Nino meeting up with Pat (Slim de Grey) at the worksite on the first day. They chat briefly before Pat unceremoniously hands Nino a shovel and tells him to follow behind, digging out the earth that's been broken up with a mattock. They start off. Nothing extraordinary occurs visually at first (with perhaps the exception of Nino's child-like, nervous attempts to dodge Pat's swinging hoe), but the musical underscore by Alan Boustead and Lawrence Leonard is unexpected. The style is reminiscent of a symphonic ode to truly epic struggles, its grandeur worthy of the building of nations. And herein lies the paradox: Nino and Pat are indeed helping to build a young (suburban) nation in their own ramshackle way – hence the score's appropriateness – yet clearly not in such dramatic form as the famous 'Battle of the Ice' sequence from *Alexander Nevsky* (Sergei Eisenstein, 1938), complete with its Sergei Prokoviev score. Boustead and Leonard's music seems to allude to this work, but any comparison of the scenes they accompany is obviously ludicrous.

Fifteen seconds after the 'glorious' rolling timpani introduces the first musical cue, the reference is reinforced visually, with the camera turning to a set of work tools randomly scattered on the ground including a hammer and sickle. If the joke hasn't sunk in yet, then the large, red garment on the Hills' hoist (an iconic Australian clothes line) billowing in the breeze, and photographed from below for impact, will clarify things.

This scene clearly depends on the general public's ability to associate a particular style of music with specific dramatic themes – or at least, their corresponding emotional cues. David Huron in his book *Sweet Anticipation: Music and the Psychology of Expectation* (2006) explains how a certain style of music might become associated with certain dramatic themes or genres in time:

> In general, research has shown that whenever we experience a strong emotion, the brain has a tendency to associate the emotional state with whatever salient stimuli exist in the environment. The net is cast quite widely. (2006: 136)

The humour here results in part from the descending scale of the comparison: from the truly grand to the homely. Nino's small, personal struggle seems silly and insignificant when set to music more befitting the battle of countless patriots and martyrs-to-the-cause. In this way, it has much in common with the seduction scene in *Jour de Fête*. They both amount to a synthetic audio-visual caricature.

The smug and condescending – rather than truly disparaging – humour in *They're a Weird Mob* represents comic film-as-empire, however: an antithetical stance to Tati's *Jour de Fête* (where the fear of Yankee cultural imperialism in the face of the Marshall Plan was justifiable). Although Nino finally proved himself worthy of acceptance by the Aussies (the monkey cousins), he could never be British. That would be just *too* ludicrous! That this so-called Australian film needed a proven director-writer team from Britain likewise speaks volumes about the 'cultural cringe' that existed in Australia at the time. It would be another six years before English language cinema was liberal enough for an Australian filmmaker to (literally) regurgitate these stereotypes back on England's doorstep in *The Adventures of Barry McKenzie* (Bruce Beresford, 1972), and in the process show what a weird mob the 'poms' were as well.

Since the early 1930s, the American social institutions of family, *faux* egalitarianism, religion and nationhood were staunchly protected from the threat of over-long kisses, drugs and double-beds by the Motion Picture Production Code (or Hays Code, as it was also known). In the eyes of pre-code cinema, America looked something like the boozy Pottersville in *It's a Wonderful Life* (Frank Capra, 1946), but afterwards was transformed into a picket-fence-lined Bedford Falls. Life was no longer portrayed as wildly complex, but rather more like some outdated morality play. Temptations and sordidness in films were all well and good, provided the earnest pilgrim progressed through the mire with his (gender intentional) halo intact. Hence the ubiquity of the narrative form, with endings looming as large as Judgment Day. 'Film noir' sprung up just as quickly to give voice to America's shadow. But even then, somebody had to take the fall in the end (usually the femme fatale, as in the witch burnings of old) if they didn't 'get wise'.

By 1968, with the code's demise, American filmmakers could again deal explicitly with taboos such as sex, drugs and violence, just like the good old days. Anti-establishment sentiment had been growing steadily against the backdrop of a still-rising youth culture, the Vietnam War, student riots in Paris and the assassinations of Robert Kennedy and Dr Martin Luther King. Hollywood responded by redrafting the archetypal hero as a morally ambiguous (but again male) *anti-hero* figure, as featured in satirical films like *Catch 22* (Mike Nichols, 1970) and *M.A.S.H.* (Robert Altman, 1970).

Widespread scepticism and a lack of faith in authority were so prevalent in America by the time of the Watergate scandal, that comedian Mel Brooks was backed by a variety of major studios to deconstruct code-era Hollywood genre by genre. He did so with five films in a row: a western – *Blazing Saddles* (Mel Brooks, 1974); then a horror film – *Young Frankenstein* (Mel Brooks, 1974); a silent movie – *Silent Movie* (Mel Brooks, 1976); a Hitchcockian suspense thriller – *High Anxiety* (Mel Brooks, 1977); and an epic – *History of the World Part I* (Mel Brooks, 1981). Brooks' America is ruled by sex, power, greed, xenophobia ... and sex. But *Blazing Saddles*, for example, succeeds mostly because it parodied a far-off 'home on the range' rather than hitting the audience head-on. Moviegoers felt they weren't laughing so much at themselves as at the genre, and *its* antiquated, redundant values. Brooks was then free to deal with thorny issues like racial prejudice directly, and in doing so, make them seem as outdated as the Wild West itself.

The gun-slingin' Sheriff Bart (Cleavon Little) is an inspired comic creation. He is quite the western anti-hero, if only for the colour of his skin. His role is perfectly plausible as an example of 1970s 'affirmative action' but the rest of the typically '70s *Blazing Saddles* characters (1870s, that is) might not be so tolerant of the anachronism. Mounted on his steed and resplendent in dazzling attire, Bart beams proudly as a swing jazz tune provides a stylishly appropriate African-American soundtrack. As he rides off, he tips his hat to someone in the distance. The camera pans left, revealing the Count Basie Big Band playing on a gleaming white bandstand in the middle of the desert! Bart and Basie give each other some 'skin' and he trots off. In this way, Brooks turns the tables on the concept of the underscore. Whereas a musical score might normally follow the lead of the visual text, the visuals in this case are now under the direct influence of the music – following it logically enough to a most illogical conclusion. To add insult to injury, the tune might *sound* appropriate enough for a post civil-rights western, but its title 'April In Paris' most definitely isn't.

Brooks sets up a similar gag three years later in his Hitchcock spoof *High Anxiety* (Mel Brooks, 1977). The movie opens with a dramatic score by John Morris intended to reinforce Dr Richard H. Thorndyke's (Mel Brooks) fear of heights. The action shows the doctor landing and disembarking at an airport where his interior neuroses and paranoia seem to distort everything he sees. The score is crucial in establishing the film's mood and conveys an unrelenting sense of urgency and foreboding. Eventually, Thorndyke emerges from the departure lounge unscathed and exclaims "What a dramatic airport!" as the automatic doors slam shut behind him.

This emphatic score spoofs the music of Bernard Hermann, composer of many of Hitchcock's most famous suspense scores, such as *Vertigo* (Alfred Hitchcock, 1958) and *Psycho* (Alfred Hitchcock, 1960). Many of Hermann's stylistic markers meant to signify fear and paranoia are present: an urgent use of ostinati, syncopated staccato rhythms, (at times) discordant harmonies, dizzily swirling, high-pitched, chromatic strings and sweeping horns, even a theremin. The latter instrument is a reference to Hermann's eerie score for the landmark science fiction film *The Day the Earth Stood Still* (Robert Wise, 1951). The audience is now primed for a memorable gag with the next musical piece we hear.

The psychoanalyst Thorndyke has arrived to take up a position as head of the Psycho-Neurotic Institute for the Very *Very* Nervous. He finds his new driver Brophy (Ron Carey) awaiting him at the airport. *En route* to the asylum, Brophy recounts the suspicious circumstances surrounding the recent death of Thorndyke's predecessor, eventually blurting out: "If you ask me, I think

Dr Ashley was a victim of ... foul play!" Immediately, a long, loud, sustained note rings out (tremolo strings and trilled woodwinds) with emphatic bursts of flammed timpani, anxious upward galloping horns, and climaxing with dizzyingly, chromatically-falling, unison spirals of sound. The effect is entirely apt (if not heavy-handed) for just such a key plot moment, and is in keeping with the mood of the main titles score. However, as the doctor looks around in stark bewilderment, the audience is made aware that he's searching for the source of music that should lie outside the narrative's diegesis! The line between cinematic illusion and disbelief has again been crossed ... or has it? The gag starkly resolves with the sight of the rehearsing Los Angeles Symphony Orchestra as they pass by in their tour bus. Tricked again ... the narrative wasn't compromised after all. But as one paradox is scuttled, an even stranger conundrum begs consideration. How many symphony orchestras have full dress rehearsals in their moving tour bus?

Summary and conclusion

The case studies analysed in this chapter have in common a type of humour that depends upon the dual modes of sight and sound incongruously colliding together to form a surprising synthesis. The humour in all cases constituted an *emergent* property. Not a mere combination of the separate audio-visual elements to amplified affect, but a far more complex and irreducible phenomenon resulting that is qualitatively distinct from the parts. Any playful cues given in a single medium to establish a fun mood (such as the Stooges' hair styles or lame dialogue) should be considered contextually and not mistaken for the joke itself. They are the catalyst, but not the reaction. These cues are present to ensure that audiences realize the situation isn't to be taken seriously. The incongruous-yet-appropriate pairing of sight and sound in each is fantastic. That is, they are psychologically valid rather than logically so. In short, the sound and vision components, when experienced separately might be fun, but aren't exactly *funny*.

Analysis can be a deceptive practice however. Simply dissecting frogs doesn't necessarily bring us any closer to understanding frog-ness. Life's complexities resist reduction. Despite being a universal experience among cultures of the world, and receiving great academic interest in recent times (Martin, 2007), humour, too, continues to resist reduction to a simply-defined construct. The true common denominator between all of the cases examined is not so much a specific technique as a willingness by the filmmakers to misbehave. A spirit of *playfulness* is the key: the filmmakers simply played around with the very 'serious' parameters of cinema in a ridiculous manner. Consider the following:

> ... *ridiculing the world of letters, numbers, dates and alphabets is what they deserve, given the way the world pressures us into accepting them. Making nonsense is making belief that we count for as much as the sense from which it temporarily delivers us.* (Sutton-Smith, 1979: 319)

But from exactly what are we being delivered? Looking back over the last 20 years of cinema, it seems that Tati's fear of a planet remade in Hollywood's image was well founded. The world outside is looking more and more the same, and films the world over reflect this trend. Instead of a vibrant and genuinely diverse world cinema existing today, we have merely a plurality of demographics and niche markets. Low-budget 'indie' films are aimed at 'arthouse' cinemas strategically placed in high-income locales, while megaplex theatres the world over pump out 'economies of scale' flicks (crammed with computer-generated imagery) in new suburbs looking every bit as sterile as *Mon Oncle's* dreamhouse. But indeed, films must be marketed as well as made. And nothing is easier to market than 'brand new platitudes' acted out by stars who look surprisingly like that other star, who looked just like another big name, who was reminiscent of ...

There's a saying that nothing stands in the way of progress, but most certainly, humour does. Ideals of progress are the stuff of the great cinematic narrative franchise, a convention that railroads audiences' perceptions into 'obvious' conclusions. The camera tells us *where* to look, while the underscore tells us *how* to feel. In the end, we have no option but to buy into the illusion. Humour, at its best however, playfully upturns our expectations and questions the tacit assumptions of cinema. Humour is digressive rather than progressive. It interrupts the flow of linear thought and all the sundry identifications/ illusions that go with it, bringing us back with a jerk to moment-to-moment awareness (Capra, 1982). Maybe Mel Brooks had this in mind when the big, butch, brawling cowboys of *Blazing Saddles* smash through a wall into the adjacent soundstage, only to start beating the crap out of the cute Busby Berkeley guys in top hats and tails. Or maybe – as one of the characters might say – I'm just full of shit. Either way, it was a pretty funny scene.

References

Apter, M.J. (1982). *The Experience of Motivation: The Theory of Psychological Reversals.* London, New York: Academic Press.

Berlyne, D.E. (1972). Humor and Its Kin. In J.H. Goldstein & P.E. McGhee (Eds.), *The Psychology of Humor: Theoretical Perspectives and Empirical Issues* (pp. 43–60). New York: Academic Press. http://dx.doi.org/10.1016/B978-0-12-288950-9.50008-0

Capra, F. (1982). *The Tao of Physics*. London: Flamingo.

Huron, D.B. (2006). *Sweet Anticipation: Music and the Psychology of Expectation*. Cambridge, MA: MIT Press.

Kerouac, J. (1972). *Visions of Cody* (1st ed.). New York: McGraw Hill.
Koestler, A. (1964). *The Act of Creation*. New York: Macmillan.
Martin, R.A. (1998). Approaches to the Sense of Humor: A Historical Review. In W. Ruch (Ed.), *The Sense of Humor: Explorations of a Personality Characteristic* (pp. 15–60). Berlin, New York: Mouton de Gruyter. http://dx.doi.org/10.1515/9783110804607.15
Martin, R.A. (2007). *The Psychology of Humor: An Integrative Approach*. Amsterdam. Boston, MA: Elsevier Academic Press.
McGhee, P.E. (1972). On the Cognitive Origins of Incongruity Humor: Fantasy Assimilation versus Reality Assimilation. In J.H. Goldstein & P.E. McGhee (Eds.), *The Psychology of Humor: Theoretical Perspectives and Empirical Issues* (pp. 61–80). New York: Academic Press. http://dx.doi.org/10.1016/B978-0-12-288950-9.50009-2
Morreall, J. (1989). 'Enjoying Incongruity'. *Humor: International Journal of Humor Research*, 2(1), 1–18. http://dx.doi.org/10.1515/humr.1989.2.1.1
Oring, E. (2003). *Engaging Humor*. Urbana, IL: University of Illinois Press.
Roeckelein, J.E. (2002). *The Psychology of Humor: A Reference Guide and Annotated Bibliography*. Westport, CT: Greenwood Press.
Suls, J.M. (1972). A Two-Stage Model for the Appreciation of Jokes and Cartoons: An Information-Processing Analysis. In J.H. Goldstein & P.E. McGhee (Eds.), *The Psychology of Humor: Theoretical Perspectives and Empirical Issues* (pp. 81–100). New York: Academic Press. http://dx.doi.org/10.1016/B978-0-12-288950-9.50010-9
Sutton-Smith, B. (1979). *Play and Learning*. New York: Gardner Press.
Vogler, C. (1992). *The Writer's Journey: Mythic Structures for Storytellers and Screenwriters*. Studio City, CA: M. Wiese Productions.
Ziv, A. (1983). 'The Influence of Humorous Atmosphere on Divergent Thinking'. *Contemporary Educational Psychology*, 8(1), 68–75. http://dx.doi.org/10.1016/0361-476X(83)90035-8
Ziv, A. (1984). *Personality and Sense of Humor*. New York: Springer Pub. Co.

Marshall Heiser is a classically trained musician, songwriter, sound engineer and writer. He has recently completed a PhD at the Queensland Conservatorium of Music, Griffith University, with his area of expertise being the intersection between record production, play/humour theory and creativity studies. He has presented papers internationally and is published in the peer-reviewed *Journal on the Art of Record Production*. As well as lecturing in audio/music at a multidisciplinary creative media institute in Brisbane, Australia, Marshall is currently developing computer music applications designed to facilitate creative flow for musicians of all skill levels.

3　The Sound of Satire; or, *Trading Places* with Mozart

Ben Winters

Trading Places (John Landis, 1983) is a money-fuelled 1980s comedy of conflicting cultural and social values. Updating Mark Twain's *The Prince and the Pauper* to contemporary Philadelphia, it sees spoilt business executive Louis Winthorpe III (Dan Aykroyd) and street-smart beggar Billy Ray Valentine (Eddie Murphy) swap places in an elaborate experiment by the Duke Brothers (Ralph Bellamy and Don Ameche) to test the nature versus nurture debate. In its fish-out-of-water approach to characterization, then, it might seem to offer plenty of opportunities for satirical social and political critique of Reagan's first-term America. But this is not how the film has often been read. Christopher Beach, for instance, argues that while Eddie Murphy's comedies of this period may contain counter-ideological potential, they are essentially conservative in their treatment of race and class (2002: 228). Similarly, Chris Jordan has noted that although the film is a kind of screwball comedy that "criticizes capitalism's uneven distribution of rewards on the basis of birthright and privilege rather than meritocratic deservedness," it nonetheless eventually turns to such a system to "resolve the principal characters' class and gender conflicts" (2003: 86). Michael Ryan and Douglas Kellner, on the other hand, offer us a rather different perspective:

> Trading Places *(1983) does assume as natural a distinction between black poverty and white wealth, and it seems to promote the values of capitalism. But it also enacts the illogical scenario of a black having economic power, and it thus offers both an enabling image and an implicit critique of the fact that blacks do not have such power.* (Ryan and Kellner, 1988: 128)

A promoter of Reaganite conservative capitalism? Or a satire that threatens to upturn the existing socially unjust order? The answer to these questions, or at least a way to reconcile some of the contradictions of the film, might lie in the music. The thematic content of Elmer Bernstein's score for the film relied extensively on Mozart's *Le nozze di Figaro* (*The Marriage of Figaro*), itself based on Beaumarchais's satirical play *La Folle Journée, ou Le mariage de Figaro*

(*The Follies of a Day*, or *The Marriage of Figaro*). An investigation of the way in which Bernstein's score, the Mozart opera that inspired it, and the other parody musical elements interact with the film's narrative and characters may thus result in a more nuanced reading of the film. After examining some of music's uses, and the contexts provided by contemporary concerns about class and race, I will suggest that there may be a subtler satirical process occurring here that largely sidesteps issues of social injustice to make a point about the overdrawn opposites inherent in Reagan's social policy – a satirical task that is aided by the film's music. My conclusion will, however, balance this position by highlighting the continued relevance of eighteenth-century *opera buffa*[1] – and its emphasis on entertainment values over political satire – as an interpretive lens through which to view the film.

* * *

John Landis, the film's director, noted in an interview that Elmer Bernstein's score "was ironically nominated for an Academy Award, because most of it is variations on Mozart's 'Marriage of Figaro'!"[2] Clearly, Mozart's opera plays an important role in the film's soundtrack, but a number of other classical and popular references are present that also play their part in the film's cultural discourse: these range from further Mozartean references to pastiches of Elgar, Brahms and Mendelssohn to a song by the doo-wop group The Silhouettes. The *Figaro* citations are, however, the most striking, and are introduced from the film's outset.

The opening titles sequence is underscored with a version of *Figaro*'s overture, and is noteworthy in presenting us with images of great social contrast. It juxtaposes the preparations of Winthorpe's manservant, Coleman (Denholm Elliott), with working (white) men and unemployed blacks (see Figure 1). These contrasts were of contemporary significance in an America that had only just begun to recover from its worst period of economic turmoil since the 1930s, and might therefore be assumed to carry some implied social critique of the divisions still inherent in 1983 American society. Although unemployment had peaked in the autumn of 1982 at 10.8% and the economy seemed to have pulled itself out of recession, it was far from obvious that the recovery would last (Ehrman, 2005: 63). Income inequality was increasing dramatically (Ehrman, 2005: 63) and poverty rates peaked at 15.2% in 1983, far above their levels in the 1970s. Moreover, one of the chief losers seems to have been the black working man, whose tremendous economic progress from the 1940s to the 1970s slowed markedly, triggering concerns about a growing black underclass that was unemployed, uneducated and trapped in urban poverty. This is certainly a picture that *Trading Places* portrays, at least in its opening sequence. We are also presented, however, with contrasting cultural symbols in the form of statues and architecture: 'high' cultural values are embodied in Philadelphia's commemorative monuments to American history, such as the Tomb of the Unknown Revolutionary War Soldier and Independence Hall (images that match the historicism of Mozart's music), along with a statue erected by the freemasons. The presence of a revolutionary monument that declares "Freedom is a light for which many men have died in darkness," bracketed by the images of black poverty seen in Figure 1, certainly carries strong satirical overtones. Contrasted with these, we also see a theatre advertising a sex show, and the 'Rocky' statue (an image of the fictional boxer with his arms aloft), commissioned by Sylvester Stallone for the filming of *Rocky III* and exhibited at the Spectrum arena (see Figure 2). In featuring this statue, *Trading Places* may be satirizing an agenda that Jordan sees outlined in *Rocky* (John G. Avildsen, 1976): that "interracial harmony stems from minority self-help and marketplace talent rather than affirmative action or welfare" (2003: 61). Things seem to stack up neatly, then: on one side of the 'divide' is a vision of an uncaring white elite social class, defined by a wealthy and historicist culture whose revolutionary values they seem to have betrayed; on the other is a black social underclass, whose only cultural icons are Hollywood tales of minority self-help.

Mozart, with his high-culture associations, stands ostensibly for this uncaring social elite – a viewpoint that, at first glance, seems to be reinforced by the other Mozartean references heard later in the film. These include the selection of the *Andante cantabile* of K.465 to serve as background music to Winthorpe's private dinner with his fiancée, Penelope, and a piece of Mozartean pastiche as Coleman performs his duties in the opening scene. Furthermore, following a temporary softening of Winthorpe's attitude (particularly towards Ophelia, the prostitute who helps him up from the gutter in return for the promise of future riches),[3] his reading of Valentine's exploits in the paper reignites his class warfare instincts, and with it his Mozartean 'voice': we hear an allusion to the 'Kyrie' from the *Requiem* K.626. Mozart (and particularly *Figaro*), however, functions as more than a general indicator of high culture and the social elite. Clearly, in its concern with the servant characters of Figaro and Susanna and their challenging of the feudal rights of Count Almaviva through disguise and cunning, *Figaro* presents a typically *opera buffa* reversal of power relations that chimes with the *Trading Places* narrative – though Da Ponte's opera libretto undoubtedly toned down many of the politically controversial elements of Beaumarchais's play (Carter, 1987: 26) and lost a great deal of the satire directed against the judicial system, the treatment of women and gambling (Steptoe, 1988: 113). As Melanie Lowe has pointed out, the perceived irony of hearing what American audiences would presumably associate with 'elitist' culture in conjunction with images of poverty and a social underclass "*isn't* ironic if one recognizes the overture and knows the opera from which this main-title

Figure 1 Images of social inequalities
a) White working class

The Sound of Satire 33

b) Black poverty

34 Sounding Funny

c) White upper class

Figure 2 Cultural contrasts
a) Superposition of classical architecture and sex show

b) Statues of Commodore John Barry and Rocky

music comes" (2002: 116). The presence of Mozart in the film, then, may stand in part for those revolutionary values contemporary with the opera and its source material, values that led to the play being banned by Louis XVI (Carter, 1987: 34). The references to Mozart, far from simply standing for an uncaring social elite, may thus act as a constant reminder throughout the film of the social inequalities that the opening segment introduces.

In addition to the subsequent occasional nod to the themes of the overture, there are two other *Figaro* references in the score, which gain some interpretive currency as a result of their intertextual links with the opera. Early on in the film, for example, Winthorpe whistles an extract from Figaro's Act 1 aria 'Se vuol ballare', the text of which suggests Winthorpe has assumed the mantle of the underclass hero (certainly in his relationship with his social superiors, the Duke brothers). Simultaneously, though, it anticipates Winthorpe's impending fall from society's elite, and his revenge on the Dukes. Thus, part of the text of the aria reads:

> Saprò ... ma piano
> meglio ogni arcano
> dissimulando
> scoprir potrò.
>
> L'arte schermendo,
> l'arte adoprando,
> di qua pungendo,
> di là scherzando,
> tutte le macchine
> rovescierò.
>
> [I'll know ... but soft, / better every secret / by dissembling / can I discover. Acting by stealth, / acting openly, / thrusting here, / teasing there, / all your plans / will I overthrow (Carter, 1987: 77)]

Winthorpe, though, cannot get past the first few phrases of the aria, and does not reach this section of text: he is not yet ready to occupy the role of Figaro (and the scheming that this aria announces), and the orchestra take over to bring the theme to an enforced (and un-Mozartean) close on a half-cadence. The score's references to Figaro's 'Non più andrai', from the end of Act I, benefit less obviously from an intertextual reading, though the prominence of the thematic references to this aria when Winthorpe and Valentine prepare to do battle at the New York Board of Trade Exchange near the film's close ("In this building it's either kill or be killed. You make no friends in the pits and you take no prisoners ...") are mirrored by Figaro's enthusiastic advocacy of military life to the reluctant Cherubino at the end of the aria. Because the use of Mozart – and particularly the class-crossing agenda of *Figaro* – is associated most closely with one of the film's heroes, both Winthorpe and Mozart escape the more stinging satirical swipes directed at other characters or composers in the film. These other characters are associated far more obviously with an uncaring upper-class establishment, and therefore trigger a musical language that is deliberately parodic in referencing the classical canon.

The Duke brothers, for instance, are given a thinly disguised version of Elgar's *Land of Hope and Glory* to emphasize their old world associations (see Example 1). They are openly, and shockingly racist: Mortimer (Don Ameche) describes Valentine using the n-word, and, using only a slightly less offensive n-word, notes "of course there's something wrong with him. He's a Negro! He's probably been stealing since he could crawl"; Randolph (Ralph Bellamy), too, rejects the idea of a black man running the family business, and articulates a common prejudice when noting of Valentine's singing, "they're very musical people, aren't they?" Similarly, the Heritage Club, of which the Dukes are prominent members, is a bastion of old world (racist) values: all the Club's servants are black (as is the Dukes' driver); and Ezra, the Dukes' personal drinks waiter, is given the derisory sum of $5 as a Christmas 'bonus', prompting him to muse, "maybe I'll go to the movies – by myself." Both the Heritage Club and the commodities brokers firm Duke & Duke are associated with a deliberately pompous piece of Brahms-pastiche academicism (see Example 2), reminiscent of the *Academic Festival Overture* and its quotation of the *Guadeamus igitur*.[4] When Valentine violates the club's interior, chased by police who wrongly believe he has attempted to rob the payroll, he is accompanied by yet more parody – this time of the opening of Mendelssohn's 'Italian' *Symphony No. 4*. Classical music parodies are thus associated with something out of place – either an uncaring social attitude, or an injustice – and signify characters or institutions to be ridiculed.

Aligned with this vision of an uncaring and racist establishment is the character of Clarence Beeks (Paul Gleason), the Dukes' right-hand man. In bribing a police officer (Frank Oz) and framing Winthorpe, he is the instrument of the Dukes' social experiment. It is clear, however, that the film sees Beeks as a kind of shadowy political operative.[5] He is shown reading Gordon Liddy's autobiography *Will*, and is thus associated with the secret (and yet bungling) operations of Nixon's 'plumbers' – intelligence-gathering activities that came to light with the Watergate break-in and led to the fall of the previous Republican administration in 1974. Yet, in the same way that Liddy and his fellow 'plumbers' were engaging in the Nixon administration's dirty work, so is Beeks operating on behalf of the Dukes: Mortimer Duke even has a photograph of Nixon on his desk to emphasize this connection; his brother, significantly, has a signed photograph of Reagan. Beeks's musical theme is also evidently a parody, however – one that emphasizes his inflated opinion of his own importance and stealthiness (Example 3). For all his use of trench coat

38 Sounding Funny

Example 1 The Duke brothers' theme

Example 2 The Heritage Club theme

Example 3 Beeks's 2-part theme

and sunglasses, and his melodramatic meetings in car parks (another clear reference to Watergate),[6] Beeks is ultimately undone by an amorous gorilla, and left to an ignoble end.

Yet, despite the critical attitude to racial persecution and social inequality that these characters and their 'pompous' music might signal, commentators have often been troubled by the film's treatment of race. Jordan notes that *Trading Places* relates black experience exclusively from a white point of view, isolating an African-American character (Valentine) in a largely white cultural setting, with only a token insight into his background (2003: 78). As a bi-racial buddy movie, it seems, *Trading Places* represents the common (white) fantasy of blacks and whites teaming up to overthrow conspiratorial forces of racial and ethnic others who threaten the ideal of racial equality and classlessness (Jordan, 2003: 80). Evidently, the racial equality and classlessness that Valentine's ascent ostensibly reveals is threatened by the Duke brothers and the establishment they represent; and while the comic lampooning of their old-fashioned prejudices and the elevation of Murphy's character to a prominent role might suggest a colour-blind approach, Jordan notes that the bi-racial buddy pair's "overthrow of the threat [of the other] implies that black integration into white society is predicated on the former's assimilation of white cultural norms" (2003: 82). Certainly, Valentine becomes racially invisible once he's ascended the corporate ladder: he is coerced into denying his identity in a way that moves far beyond his ascent out of poverty. Moreover, where Winthorpe is given the love interest (Ophelia), Valentine is forced to go it alone (Paul, 1994: 126). Then there are the troubling scenes aboard the New Year's Eve train, where Murphy and Aykroyd are given the opportunity to dress up in a kind of Saturday Night Live double-act as a pair of 'Africans' (Naga Eboko from Cameroon and Lionel Joseph, supposedly from Ethiopia, but actually sounding more Caribbean). While Denholm Elliott's impersonation of an Irish priest (obsessed with his whiskey) and Jamie Lee Curtis's blond Austrian stereotype (with Swedish accent) are equally problematic – and Murphy's buffoonish character is disturbing to say the least – there seems absolutely no narrative justification for Aykroyd to black up and play the part for laughs. In many ways it undoes all the more subtle racial commentary that is evident in the first half of the film.

In contrast to the Mozartean language of Winthorpe, or the parodic treatment of the Duke brothers, references to popular culture are associated primarily with Valentine's former life and Winthorpe's temporary existence at the bottom of society. Valentine's frame of reference when Randolph Duke introduces himself, for instance, is to invoke popular music ("Randy? That's like Randy Jackson from The Jackson Five"). By contrast, the only 'songs' associated with the social elite are of the type that allow the close harmony singing of Winthorpe's former friends (in a style reminiscent of the Yale Whiffenpoofs)[7] or classical arrangements of Christmas carols. As Valentine learns to deal with his sudden climb up the social ladder, then, it seems these popular cultural associations must be thrown off, rather like Tom Canty in *The Prince and The Pauper*, who is able to adjust to his new situation after finding a book on etiquette. Shortly after his sudden social and economic ascent, Valentine returns to his old neighbourhood and invites his old 'friends' to his new house in a party scene that Pauline Kael called "nasty and humorless" (1987: 13). Throwing his 'guests' out (including the only other prominent African-American characters in the film) for putting out their cigarettes on his floor, spilling drinks on his Persian rug, and not using drinks coasters, he appears to suffer a temporary identity crisis. He rejects the music of his former life (he'd gleefully sung in the style of James Brown while taking a jacuzzi, but now angrily silences 'Do You Wanna Funk' by Sylvester), and instead appears to embrace the manners of his 'new' social class: we see him happily socializing to the sound of a string quartet playing waltzes and ländlers in a restaurant. With this new role, he even adopts the uncaring attitude of a social elite. At perhaps the film's satirical highpoint, he refuses to sympathize with Winthorpe's bungling attempts to frame him with drugs, and thus completes his change of identity: "It's no excuse [Winthorpe's poverty and unemployment] ... you can't be soft on people like that." Only when learning of the Duke brothers' experiment is his apparent sense of justice restored, and he seeks to right the wrongs inflicted upon Winthorpe.

Many of the *Trading Places'* musical choices and allusions (*Figaro* aside) thus appear to line up in a very straightforward manner, suggesting simple divisions that map onto the film's opening images:

'High' Class (white)	'Low' Class (black)
1. The Dukes' 'Elgar' theme	1. Valentine's singing in the Jacuzzi
2. The music of the Heritage Club	2. 'Out Of the Sheets – Into the Streets' (heard in the bar that Valentine visits to flaunt his new wealth)
3. References to Puccini's *La bohème* (Winthorpe's opera tickets)	3. 'Do You Wanna Funk' (Valentine's selection of party music)
4. Close harmony singing of Winthorpe's friends at the club	4. Blues – playing in the pawnbrokers
5. The string quartet texture (used as diegetic background music in the Restaurant scene)	5. Ophelia and Louis's love theme ('easy listening')
6. Classical arrangements of Christmas songs (at Duke & Duke's Christmas party)	6. 'Jingle Bell Rock' (played in Ophelia's apartment)
	7. 'The Loco Motion' (heard on the New Year's train)
	8. 'Get A Job' (heard over the closing credits)

Moreover, the uncaring attitudes of the privileged seem to be associated specifically with 'high' cultural values. It would be far too simplistic to claim, though, that Winthorpe and Valentine's contrasting social trajectories can be represented as a journey from one side to the other (whereupon each learns the values of the other, and perhaps moves on to a more enlightened space that rejects such binary opposites). For one thing, the social critique implicit in the film's opening scenes is gradually lost. This is perhaps why the film has been read so often as Reaganite in its message: the illumination of social inequalities is soon forgotten in the rush to make money (for the filmmakers, perhaps, as well as the characters). Ophelia, for example, is initially portrayed as a strong businesswoman with a head for figures ("I've saved forty-two grand and it's in T-Bills earning interest ... I'm talking about a business proposition, Louis. I help you get yourself back on your feet, and you pay me, in cash, five figures."), but discussion of the social inequalities that have forced her into prostitution are notably absent, and she is shown in the film's final scene to slot back into the traditional conservative female role (bikini-clad decoration for Winthorpe's yacht). Unlike the characters in *The Prince and The Pauper*, who seem to benefit from the chance to experience life from another perspective (we are told that Edward becomes a more enlightened king on account of his experience), Winthorpe seems to have re-embraced his return to the elite. Though the final scene reveals that he has chosen the company of Ophelia, Valentine and Coleman over his former friends, it feels entirely forced as an ending. The racial divide between Winthorpe and Valentine is almost as wide as before: as Alan Nadel points out, even in their success they are separated by a quarter of a mile and cannot have a plausible face-to-face relationship (2007: 86). Furthermore, the presence of the comedy waiter (Dimitri), who is now Coleman's willing servant, suggests that attitudes towards social hierarchies remain firmly entrenched.

Yet, might there not be a subtler process occurring here? Might the satire be predicated not on the highlighting of social and racial injustices, after all, but on complicating Reagan's simplistic conservative social policies – which identified clear-cut distinctions between moral and immoral blacks and ethnics, the individual and the collective, and men's and women's roles (Jordan, 2003: 16)? As Nathan Glazer points out, the underlying ideological force of the incoming administration's attitude to social policy

> *was provided by a vision of how societies grew economically and what makes them strong. Individual action, unhampered by government, spurs an economy. Consideration for the poor, in the form of special programs, tends to undermine the incentives that move the poor into economic action and out of poverty.* (1984: 78)

Social and cultural mobility was thus associated with a moral force of individual action. These simplistic distinctions – which Betty Glad (1983) also identifies as a feature of Reagan's contemporary thinking on issues of foreign policy, and which are arguably set up in the overture sequence – are revealed to be increasingly problematic throughout the film. For example, not only are we encouraged to admire Valentine's role as 'immoral' Vietnam veteran impersonator and would-be pimp, and Ophelia's entrepreneurial spirit as a prostitute (in clear contradistinction to the moralistic thrust of Reagan's traditional attitudes), but we also find ourselves cheering on the scheme hatched by Winthorpe and suggested by Coleman to exact revenge on the Dukes and *to commit fraud while doing so*. They steal a top-secret report and use the information to make a fortune in frozen concentrated orange juice futures, bankrupting the Duke brothers in the process. It is also ambiguous whether Valentine's desire to team up with Winthorpe is motivated by knowledge of the Dukes' social engineering, or by the certainty that he is about to lose all that he has gained, and be "returned to the ghetto". Similarly, the simplistic portrayal of the Dukes as racist (and thus worthy of social punishment) is problematized by the blackface make-up and casual racism of our supposed hero, Winthorpe (who claims of his predicament: "It was all because of this terrible, awful Negro"). In short, none of these characters is an example of the moral or immoral Hollywood hero or villain that might have helped shaped Reagan's view of social policy. What we are presented with, then, is a film in which the one acknowledged supporter of Reagan, Randolph Duke, for all the apparent worthiness and egalitarianism of his views (that nurture is more important than nature, and his claim that his social engineering is "for a good cause"), is ultimately shown to be a morally bankrupt racist, and his views merely in the service of an establishment whim (expressed as a bet). We are also presented, however, with a pair of heroes who ascend to riches not through hard work but by immoral means. Moreover, their entrepreneurial spirit – the very embodiment of the American dream – is motivated by an act of revenge rather than a sense of social betterment.

It is here, then, that *Figaro*'s role in the soundtrack makes its presence felt. Aside from its intertextual social satire – which in referencing ideals of social equality is also supported by the allusions in the score to the French national anthem and the revolutionary-era song 'Yankee Doodle' – *Figaro* is never associated with the Duke brothers, and can thus function as a neutral musical language that also escapes the simple divisions outlined above, for all its ostensibly 'high art' status. The clear cultural associations of Mozart's music as 'elitist' thus gradually unravel alongside the realization that economic (and cultural) progress is not the simple result of a morally-driven individualism. Indeed, the fissures in these simple social distinctions, and the space in which satire may be found, arguably have their musical corollary as early as the manipulation of the overture in the film's titles sequence. Its subversion of the overture's structure, through elisions and fractured repetitions in the coda (see Example 4), hint that the divisions in society and culture that the images suggest may not only be turned upside down and intermixed in the narrative that follows but may also be revealed to be more complicated than this simple binary suggests. Moreover, the titles might seem to present Coleman as the film's principal character (since he is aligned overtly with Figaro's status as Count Almaviva's servant): the camera follows him up the stairs with his breakfast tray, and over the last few chords of the overture we see Winthorpe awaken from his sleep. Knowledge of the overture's source might then set up the expectation that Winthorpe's social class will be challenged by Coleman's cunning. Right from the beginning, insider knowledge of 'high culture' (in this case, the plot of a Mozart opera) is revealed to be something of a red herring – the elitism that Lowe argues is necessary to understanding the references to the overture also misleads with regard to the film's intentions.

Exposition (bars 1–138)
    1st subject: cuts bars 18–34
    Transition to 2nd subject: cuts bars 67–74
Recapitulation (bars 139–235)
    Transition to 2nd subject: cuts bars 180–187
Coda (bars 235–294)
    Repeats bars 266–279; cuts bars 280–283

Example 4 Manipulation of *Le nozze di Figaro* overture

Appearances can be deceptive with characters, too: Valentine, for instance, is not the cultural ignoramus the Dukes assume him to be (they claim they run a programme for "culturally disadvantaged individuals"). Though he does not reference the high cultural world of Mozart or Puccini, admittedly, he is capable nonetheless of invoking the plot of Gershwin's *Porgy and Bess* when attempting to chat up a passing woman. Similarly, Ophelia is aware of the Shakespearean heritage of her name (to Winthorpe's evident surprise), while Winthorpe's choice of music in his private moments with Penelope (a tango) is in marked contrast to his use of Mozart when Coleman is present. Indeed, when we look at Winthorpe's actions in *Trading Places*, he appears to betray many of the features of the class-anxious individual, namely the average middle-class American in 1983 (Fussell, 1983: 16). In other words, he is not the uncomplicated representative of white upper-class culture that the titles sequence seems to suggest. He is evidently not in the same class bracket as the Duke brothers, who are quite obviously an old East Coast family with ties to tradition ("A

Duke has been sitting on this exchange since it was founded. We founded this exchange. It's ours. It belongs to us!"). Fussell argues that the force of class envy – the result of disillusion over the official myth of the classless society – should never be underestimated, noting: "It's a rare American who doesn't secretly want to be an upper-middle class" (1983: 34). Although Winthorpe *is* clearly upper-middle class, he still feels the need to boast to Ophelia of his credit cards "I can charge goods and services in over 86 countries around the world." Moreover, although his possession of opera tickets alone is enough to indicate a higher social class, Winthorpe also asserts his cultural superiority over Frank Oz's corrupt police officer by correcting in a condescending way his pronunciation of Puccini's *La bohème*. Winthorpe's attitude to possessions is also particularly revealing in this regard. Though he hides his television set away in a piece of furniture – in a typically upper-middle class way (Fussell, 1983: 91) – when attempting to pawn his watch to a sceptical pawnbroker (Bo Diddley), Winthorpe proudly states: "this is a Rochefoucauld, the thinnest water-resistant watch in the world ... This is the sports watch of the '80s ... It tells time simultaneously in Monte Carlo, Beverly Hills, London, Paris, Rome, and Gstaad!" Fussell's class rule of thumb with regard to the wristwatch is:

> the more 'scientific,' technological, and space-age, the lower. Likewise with the more 'information' the watch is supposed to convey, like the time of day in Kuala Lumpur ... (1983: 65)

While Winthorpe's pride in his watch may simply be a sales pitch in the pawnbroker's language, he seems to be a character that embodies many of the class concerns of 1980s American society.

Stylistically, too, what might be regarded as a simple anti-elitist beginning to the film – highlighting cultural divisions and associations between classical music and an uncaring social elite – leads to a postmodern embracing of all musical styles. Thus, the cross-societal love between Winthorpe and Ophelia allows Bernstein's score to assume temporarily a Burt Bacharach-esque, easy-listening musical language (the scene in Philadelphia's 30th Street Station), before Mozartean references return to the underscore. Indeed, the use of Mozart in the latter part of the film as the heroes rush for New York functions as an indicator of the kind of ideal classless position temporarily occupied by both Winthorpe and Valentine; as a result, it can be combined much more easily with other musical elements. The film's gag reel, for instance, which puts actors' names to faces at the film's close, is underscored with a version of 'Non più andrai', and can both follow the Caribbean steel-drumming of the final scene and be succeeded by The Silhouettes singing 'Get A Job' with no discernable cultural dislocation; in fact, the distinctive beginning of the song dovetails with a held string chord from the end of the Mozart. Cultural opposites, it seems, have been undone to a degree, even if social inequalities remain.

The choice of this final musical number ('Get a Job') may have been motivated by The Silhouettes' origins in 1950s Philadelphia (the song was recorded in 1957 and was the group's first single), but its satirical significance for a film released at a period of high unemployment is striking. Having witnessed Valentine ascend socially and economically through hard work (he is clearly good at his job at Duke & Duke), only to see him threatened with a return to the 'ghetto' once the establishment figures – the personification of Reagan's social policy – have 'won their bet', an audience would surely find it difficult to hear this song as a serious affirmation of Reaganite values. Although the triumph of the characters, through the manipulation of commodities markets, does not make a case for affirmative government action on social and racial inequalities, Valentine's economic triumph at the film's ending is certainly not the image of Reaganite capitalism that many have taken it for. Rather, it suggests that economic advancement is best achieved through breaking the rules and working outside the system, rather than through hard work and personal advancement. The Silhouettes singing 'Get A Job' cannot be taken at face value, then, as a Reaganite *command*, and when one listens to the rest of the lyrics, it becomes clear that there is a final satirical swipe at America's economic problems, and the Reagan administration's notion of individual action as the solution:

Every morning about this time
She gets me out of my bed a-crying
Get a job
After breakfast every day
She throws the want ads right my way
And never fails to say
Get a job ...

And when I get the paper
I read it through and through

And my girl never fails to say
If there is any work for me
And when I go back to the house
I hear the woman's mouth
Preaching and a-crying
Tell me that I'm lying
About a job
That I never could find

For the song's narrator, no amount of individual effort can secure a job if there is no job to be had, and the idea that poverty or economic inequality is the result of moral choice is thus revealed by this choice of song to be a fallacy.

Although this last song provides a final satirical punch, there can be little doubt that the film's attitude to aspiration and wealth is complicated (to say the least), and that many may take from it the mantra uttered by a character from another 1980s film: "greed is good".[8] The film's poster, after all, showed Valentine and Winthorpe surrounded by money. Its subtler satirical points, which are aided by the music, are to some degree battling against the trajectory suggested by the Hollywood narrative, the need for a feel-good ending, and the desire for entertainment. Thus, Jordan argues that inherent in *Trading Places* is an "agenda of striving for the broadest possible appeal by promoting multiple readings of the relationship between race and class mobility" (2003: 16). Even here, though, the score's references to *Figaro* suggest a further way to think about the film: namely, within the context of the *opera buffa* genre. As such, *Figaro* offers us a way to sidestep some of the contradictions and tensions that the film's treatment of social inequality suggests, a few thoughts about which I offer in conclusion.

* * *

Opera buffa in Mozart's Vienna, as Mary Hunter and James Webster point out, was a genre "located squarely between 'art' and 'entertainment'" (1997: 5). For all its satirical possibilities, and although many *opera buffe* were profoundly political, the primary function of the genre was to entertain (Hunter, 1999: 19). Hunter, in examining this tension, notes that many works are characterized by complex and contradictory sets of social values that represent conservative notions of hierarchy, while simultaneously presenting reversals of this conservative order in a carnivalesque manner (1999: 20–21). Although a conservative frame ultimately contains these social reversals, the 'progressive' social content witnessed leaves what she calls "a residue of irritation" (1999: 21). Thus, she argues "[i]n any given opera, and in any particular circumstances, one pleasurable reversal may seem like the licensed excess of carnival, and another like constructive social criticism" (1999: 73). In *Figaro*, after the confusions and disguises of Act IV that allow characters to act as equals, and which are facilitated by the pastoral world of darkness (rather like the world of Shakespeare's *A Midsummer Night's Dream*), the final scene restores the social order. Certainly such a reading can be applied to *Trading Places*, which likewise seems to present a social reversal within a largely conservative frame: although Valentine's economic wealth at the end of the film might suggest that the old order has been overturned, his separation from Winthorpe, and Winthorpe's own journey back to prosperity, can be seen as a return to a conservative order that ignores social problems. Significantly, it also occurs after the carnivalesque scenes of disguise on the New Year's train, though these are not essential to the reversal theme of the film's narrative. Clearly, though, the social satire provided by the film's first half (and the reminder provided by the final satirical punchline of 'Get A Job') ensures that *Trading Places* also provides that 'irritant' about which Hunter writes.

Other aspects of the film respond to the frame of *opera buffa* implied by the use of Mozart's *Figaro*. The names of the Duke brothers clearly reference the noble characters that populate the eighteenth-century genre, while Ophelia's Shakespearean heritage suggests the supposedly low-born character who is actually of high birth, and thus fit to marry the hero (see, for example, Giannetta in Anfossi's *L'incognita perseguitata* of 1773; or the similar characters in Goldoni and Piccini's *La buona figliuola* of 1760, and Puttini and Anfossi's *La vera costanza* of 1776). Similarly, the numerous servant characters found in *opera buffe* are paralleled by *Trading Places*' use of a valet-butler character (Coleman) – though Pauline Kael saw his presence as indicative of the movie's heritage in a rather different theatrical tradition, namely Broadway plays of the 1930s and 40s (1987: 13). Even the film's visual language – in which Eddie Murphy's looks to camera dissolve the fourth wall (see Figure 3) – could be said to have its basis in the comic asides found in *opera buffa*, as in Figaro's turn to the audience in 'Aprite un po' quegli occhi'. Performers of *opera buffa* were also in the habit of speaking outside their roles: Hunter points out that in Petrosellini and Paisiello's *Il barbiere di Siviglia*, Nancy Storace and Francesco Benucci "imitated the German-speaking actor Friedrich Ludwig Schroeder and the singer Johann Valentin Adamberger, much to the delight of Joseph II" (1999: 5). Certainly, much of the comedy of *Trading Places* relies on seeing the activities of Winthorpe and Valentine as a series of comic performances by Dan Aykroyd and Eddie Murphy, and the troubling dressing-up scenes aboard the train are really an excuse for Aykroyd and Murphy to perform outside the roles that have been established for Winthorpe and Valentine – particularly in the case of Aykroyd, whose character is never previously shown to have the comic/acting abilities that are displayed on the train. As Hunter argues, the "process of instigating, and then directing the audience's attention to, an immediate and almost involuntary response [to the breaking of the narrative frame] is a crucial part of *opera buffa*'s rhetoric of pleasure" (1999: 51). Seeing *Trading Places* operating on these terms, then, ensures the references to Mozart's *Figaro* function intertextually not only on a plot level but also in terms of genre.

Evidently, for all *opera buffa*'s social satire and political overtones, the primary function of the genre was to give pleasure. Thus, Da Ponte's removal of much of the satirical bite of Beaumarchais's play, when writing the libretto for *Le nozze di Figaro*, was motivated not by political timidity but by theatrical pragmatism (Steptoe, 1988: 113). In a similar way, the inability of *Trading Places* to carry through its overt social satire in quite the manner that is suggested in the film's opening half, might be seen as less the expression of an innate conservatism, or a fundamentally Reaganite agenda, and more an example of the same pragmatic approach to a dramatic form. While *Trading Places* (for all its subtle satirical deconstruction of Reagan's social policy) may ultimately fall short of the standards for satire set by Nicolas Boileau-Despreux in 1668 – "fertile in lessons and novelties", uniting "the pleasing and the instructive"

Figure 3 Eddie Murphy dissolves the fourth wall, highlighting the patronizing attitude of the Duke brothers

and releasing "minds from the errors of their times" (Goulbourne, 2007: 139) – its invocation of one of the most beloved *opera buffe* might be seen as an appeal to not to take its message too seriously. The concluding gag reel (to the music of Mozart), suggests that, like the operatic genre *Trading Places* references, entertainment is likewise the film's primary aim.

Notes

1. *Opera buffa* (or 'comic opera') is an Italian genre that appeared in the eighteenth century in opposition to *opera seria* (or 'serious opera'). It tended to use contemporary rather than mythological characters, and to make extensive use of duets, trios, quartets and larger ensembles.
2. http://www.soundtrack.net/content/article/?id=156, accessed 19 November 2009.
3. Ophelia is a character that fulfills a similar role to that of Miles Hendon in Mark Twain's novel, *The Prince and The Pauper*.
4. The film is perhaps tapping into the overdrawn nineteenth-century critical portrayal of 'Brahms the conservative', in contrast to the overt modernism of the New German School of Wagner and Liszt.
5. When referring to 'the film', I am referencing Daniel Frampton's idea of a 'filmind' (Frampton, 2007), to avoid suggestions that these are necessarily the intentions of John Landis, or 'the filmmakers'.
6. When working with Carl Bernstein on their exposé of the Watergate cover-up, *Washington Post* reporter Bob Woodward used to meet his secret source, 'Deep

Throat' (later revealed to be the acting associate director of the FBI, W. Mark Felt), at 2 am in a car park.
7. The Whiffenpoofs is a long-standing, all-male, *a cappella* singing group, consisting of undergraduates from Yale University.
8. Gordon Gekko in *Wall Street* (Oliver Stone, 1987).

References

Beach, C. (2002). *Class, Language, and American Film Comedy*. Cambridge: Cambridge University Press. http://dx.doi.org/10.1017/CBO9780511606342

Carter, T. (1987). *W. A. Mozart Le nozze di Figaro*. Cambridge: Cambridge University Press.

Ehrman, J. (2005). *The Eighties: America in the Age of Reagan*. New Haven, CT: Yale University Press.

Frampton, D. (2007). *Filmosophy*. London: Wallflower Press.

Fussell, P. (1983). *Class: A Guide Through the American Status System*. New York: Summit Books.

Glad, B. (1983). 'Black-and-White Thinking: Ronald Reagan's Approach to Foreign Policy'. *Political Psychology*, 4(1), 33–76. http://dx.doi.org/10.2307/3791173

Glazer, N. (1984). 'The Social Policy of the Reagan Administration: A Review'. *Public Interest*, 75, 76–98.

Goulbourne, R. (2007). Satire in Seventeenth- and Eighteenth-century France. In R. Quinto (Ed.), *A Companion to Satire* (pp. 139–160). Oxford: Blackwell. http://dx.doi.org/10.1002/9780470996959.ch9

Hunter, M. (1999). *The Culture of Opera Buffa in Mozart's Vienna: A Poetics of Entertainment*. Princeton, NJ: Princeton University Press. http://dx.doi.org/10.1515/9781400822751

Hunter, M., & Webster, J. (Eds.) (1997). *Opera Buffa in Mozart's Vienna*. Cambridge: Cambridge University Press.

Jordan, C. (2003). *Movies and the Reagan Presidency: Success and Ethics*. Westport, CT: Praeger.

Kael, P. (1987). *State of the Art*. London: Marion Boyars.

Lowe, M. (2002). 'Claiming Amadeus: Classical Feedback in American Media'. *American Music*, 20(1), 102–119. http://dx.doi.org/10.2307/3052244

Nadel, A. (2007). 1983 Movies and Reagnism. In S. Prince (Ed.), *American Cinema of the 1980s: Themes and Variations* (pp. 82–106). Oxford: Berg.

Paul, W. (1994). *Laughing Screaming: Modern Hollywood Horror and Comedy*. New York: Columbia University Press.

Ryan, M., & Kellner, D. (1988). *Camera Politica: The Politics and Ideology of Contemporary Hollywood Film*. Bloomington, IN: Indiana University Press.

Steptoe, A. (1988). *The Mozart-Da Ponte Operas: The Cultural and Musical Background to* Le Nozze di Figaro, Don Giovanni, *and* Così fan tutte. Oxford: Clarendon Press.

Twain, M. (1996). *The Prince and the Pauper*. Oxford: Oxford University Press.

Ben Winters is Lecturer in Music at The Open University, UK. His research – which focuses on Hollywood film music of the studio era, *fin-de-siècle* Vienna and the works of Erich Korngold – has been published widely in journals including *Music & Letters*, *Cambridge Opera Journal* and *Music, Sound, and the Moving Image*. He is the author of *Erich Wolfgang Korngold's* The Adventures of Robin Hood: A Film Score Guide (Scarecrow Press, 2007), and *Music, Performance, and the Realities of Film: Shared Concert Experiences in Screen Fiction* (Routledge, 2014).

4 Parody, Self-Parody and Genre-Parody
Music in The Magnificent Seven and ¡Three Amigos!

Erik Heine

Elmer Bernstein's music for ¡*Three Amigos!* is a unique example of a composer parodying his own genre for a film that is a parody of its own genre. Bernstein's score for *The Magnificent Seven* (John Sturgis, 1960) largely helped to codify the 'sound' of the American western film, as noted by several scholars (Buhler and Neumeyer, 2001; Timm, 2003). Bernstein's sound was an appropriation of "concert composer Aaron Copland's distinctive style", which was used "in the 1950s to signify American nostalgia and, later, the American West" (Buhler, Neumeyer and Deemer, 2009: 356). This codification occurred long after the creation and development of the western genre, which dates back to silent film and early sound film, particularly in the films of John Ford.[1] Despite the newness of the music, the story in *The Magnificent Seven* was one that had already been told in *Seven Samurai* (Akira Kurosawa, 1954). The story in *The Magnificent Seven* is simple: a small Mexican farming village is annually terrorized by Calvera, the leader of a gang of bandits, played by Eli Wallach, so three villagers travel just north of the border and hire seven men to rid the village of Calvera and his gang. At one point, the Seven are defeated by Calvera's men and must leave the village, but ultimately return to defeat Calvera despite sustaining losses in personnel. ¡*Three Amigos!* (John Landis, 1986) is the story of three Hollywood actors who play wealthy landowners in the movies and drive out those that would repress the poor and helpless; ¡*Three Amigos!* is a comedic retelling of *The Magnificent Seven*. When the Amigos are forced in the real world to become the characters they play in the movies, they must defeat El Guapo, the leader of a gang of bandits, played by Alfonso Arau, and his men, and drive them out of the village of Santa Poco forever. In the book *Parody as Film Genre*, Wes Gehring specifically names ¡*Three Amigos!* as an example of parody of the American western genre, specifically, a "Saturday matinee variety" (Gehring, 1999: 3). ¡Three Amigos! was also scored by Elmer Bernstein, who figured out how to parody his own music while staying within the codified constraints of the genre. Bernstein's music not only had to fulfil its stylistic role of the western genre, it also had to provide aural cues in order to inform the audience that the film is a comedy, and not an action/drama film.

The music used in ¡Three Amigos! is related to the music in The Magnificent Seven through character themes, general setting, orchestration and style. However, Bernstein's music also adds a humorous tone to ¡Three Amigos!. Several cues between the films, both in location and style, can be compared to show the similarities between the two films. In addition, significant moments in ¡Three Amigos! can be shown to be humorous without a reference to The Magnificent Seven. The roles of the songs in ¡Three Amigos!, written by Randy Newman, will be analysed to show how they function within the appropriate confines of the genre. First, the relationship of the title song to other western title songs, specifically 'Do Not Forsake Me' from High Noon (Fred Zinnemann, 1952) will be investigated, followed by an analysis of how 'Blue Shadows' operates both as fulfilling its function within the genre and also as parody.

Elmer Bernstein's music in *The Magnificent Seven* and *¡Three Amigos!*

In the liner notes to the CD re-release of the soundtrack to ¡Three Amigos!, Jeff Bond, a regular contributor to the journal Film Score Monthly, wrote:

> By treating the plots of characters of [comedy] films with straight-faced seriousness, Bernstein was able to have it both ways: his music became part of the joke as it played against the often outrageous comic behavior onscreen, and he was able to write the kind of full-blooded orchestral scores that were falling out of favor with producers of contemporary dramas and action films. (Bond, 2006)

After Bernstein's western scores in the 1960s and 1970s[2] he began to grow weary of the genre, and found a new home composing film scores for comedies, such as Animal House (John Landis, 1978), Airplane! (Jim Abrahams, David Zucker, Larry Zucker, 1980) and Ghostbusters (Ivan Reitman, 1984). Because of his previous work with John Landis, the director of Animal House, Bernstein agreed to compose the score for ¡Three Amigos!. Bond also states the composer "chose not to specifically parody any of his famous Magnificent Seven music" (Bond, 2006). Bond's statement indicates that Bernstein did not compose a complete score that satirized his Magnificent Seven score, however Bernstein did parody elements of the Magnificent Seven score, specifically the main titles and the more 'romantic' cue, 'Petra's Declaration'.

Regarding The Magnificent Seven, Elmer Bernstein said:

> The Magnificent Seven *score really benefitted from the fact that for years I'd wanted to do an American type of theme as it was something I knew a great deal about, partly because of my own interest in American folk music, and also because of my relationship with Copland. He invented American music to a great degree – a certain style, a certain sound, and I always found it very attractive ... By the time I got to do* The Magnificent Seven *all of this stuff that had been in my head for years and years had a chance to be set free, and I think that accounts for the tremendous amount of energy and rhythmic intensity in that score. The influence was Tex Mex, and I also brought in a lot of characteristically Mexican percussion instruments, and guitar. However, I wasn't drawing on folk themes – I was drawing on feelings.* (Bernstein, 2000: 40)

From this quote, particularly the word 'feelings,' it is obvious that Bernstein was giving a sympathetic voice to the farmers and the village through his music. The majority of the music refers to the farmers, even though the most popular theme from the film relates to the title characters. Bernstein used a similar orchestration for ¡Three Amigos!, particularly with the guitar and percussion, as well as the brass, especially the mariachi-sounding trumpet, and once again provided a sympathetic voice to the villagers of Santa Poco. In both films, the villagers need help, and the music sympathizes with their respective plights, and in both films, the music for the villagers is syncopated, but lacks the presence of the snare drum, which creates a more 'heroic' feeling by doubling the orchestral accompaniment. El Guapo and his gang continually harass the villagers of Santa Poco. When a young woman, Carmen, played by Patrice Martinez, sees a film starring the Three Amigos, she sends a telegram to Hollywood requesting their presence. The music, with the snare drum in the accompaniment and the heroic-sounding brass and string melodies for the title characters, emphasizes the plight of the villagers of Santa Poco through the lack of syncopated percussion and absence of the heroic melodic brass.

The most obvious place to compare music between the two films is in the main titles sequence for each film. The opening music from The Magnificent Seven is well known, and appears below as Example 1.

This opening theme music is one of the ways in which Bernstein helped to codify the genre of western films. One important aspect of this theme is the rhythmic subdivision of the two-measure phrase, which, in eighth notes, is a pattern of 3+3+3+3+2+2. Scott Murphy, in a presentation entitled 'Western Rhythms and Wild Western Rhythms' noted that Bernstein, as an arranger for Glenn Miller, would have been keenly aware of this rhythm, as well as the 3+3+2 one-measure rhythm (Murphy, 2002). Murphy also pointed out later applications of this rhythm in additional film scores of Bernstein's such as The Sons of Katie Elder (Henry Hathaway, 1965) and Wild Wild West (Barry Sonnenfeld, 1999).

Example 1 Author transcription of melody from the main titles of *The Magnificent Seven*, mm 5–26

In addition to the 'theme,' the 'introduction' also shows typical characteristics of the genre, such as syncopation and mixed metre. Finally, the opening leap of a third corresponds to the word 'seven', the title characters from the film, a trait that Bernstein would repeat in *¡Three Amigos!*. Later in the main titles from *The Magnificent Seven*, those two notes are preceded by syncopated rhythms that syllabically correspond to the word 'magnificent.'

Unlike in *The Magnificent Seven*, the main titles in *¡Three Amigos!* function similar to an opera overture, introducing several elements of themes that will be used later in the film, but focusing on the music of the village of Santa Poco. The cue in *¡Three Amigos!* that Bernstein originally composed is different than the cue ultimately used in the film. The version used omits the music for El Guapo, the villain. The opening melody from the main titles appears in Example 2.

The opening demonstrates how the name of the title characters in *¡Three Amigos!* is realized in the music, similar to the syllabic setting of the word 'seven' in *The Magnificent Seven*. In *¡Three Amigos!*, the opening measure of the theme is a 3+2+3, a variation on the 3+3+2 (and 3+3+3+2+2) rhythms. The rhythmic similarities between the two films, in that neither film contains a straight subdivision of 2+2+2+2, show that Bernstein conceived of both films

Parody, Self-Parody and Genre-Parody 55

Figure 1 Main title credit from *The Magnificent Seven* (Sturgis, 1960)

Example 2 Author transcription of melody from the main titles of *¡Three Amigos!*, mm 1–8

as belonging to the western genre, but the variation in the rhythm in *¡Three Amigos!* indicates that the film is going to be different from *The Magnificent Seven*. The orchestration in *¡Three Amigos!* is similar to *The Magnificent Seven*, once again indicating the genre of western film. In addition, the name of the title characters appears rhythmically at the beginning of the music, as shown in the musical example, and this displays another similarity, but not necessarily a parody, between the two films. Bernstein's "title music is heroic, with a five-note fanfare that by accident or design has the same number of notes as 'The Three Amigos' has syllables", supporting the idea that the title characters are syllabically realized in the main title sequences in both films (Bond, 2006).

A deeper connection can be made between the music for the two main title sequences. The descending syncopated gesture in the titles to *The Magnificent Seven* is very closely related to the opening gesture in the titles to *¡Three Amigos!*[3] Example 3a shows the gestures from *The Magnificent Seven*, while Example 3b adds an additional note to the main titles from *¡Three Amigos!* so that the scale degrees exactly correspond. The solfege syllables (in the moveable do system) are marked above the pitches.

Example 3a Author transcription of melody from the main titles of *The Magnificent Seven*, mm 10–12

Example 3b Author transcription of melody from the main titles of *¡Three Amigos!*, mm 1–5

Even if Bernstein did not intentionally relate the two films' main title sequences, the similarity between the gestures in both films is undeniable. The word choice of 'parody' is not the correct term in this instance, but musically, the material in the opening of the main titles in *¡Three Amigos!* is clearly derived from the main titles of *The Magnificent Seven*.

Figure 2 Main title credit from *¡Three Amigos!* (Landis, 1986)

A comparison of the pictures of the main title credits from the two films shows that the films are focusing on very different elements. In *The Magnificent Seven*, the picture is of the unnamed Mexican village, indicating that the village is the emphasis; the village is where the significant action will be located. In *¡Three Amigos!*, the picture is of the title characters, indicating that the film will focus on the journey of these three men and how they develop over the course of the film. The font used in *The Magnificent Seven* is very large but plain, covering most of the screen, thus indicating that the film will be highly dramatic. Even though the village is the primary location of the action, the title characters are strongly emphasized through the text. The font used in *¡Three Amigos!* is much smaller, but appears in 3-D with a line painted across the middle of every letter. The appearance of the letters is akin to the appearance of a child's maraca, emphasizing the lack of depth to the personalities of the actors and the overall film, as well as a certain amount of innocence. Ned Nederlander, played by Martin Short, is shown to possess childlike qualities such as naivety and fear of the dark. The font shows the 'Saturday matinee' quality of the film, intended for children and families, and even though it does not overtly emphasize the comedic quality of the film, it greatly diminishes the seriousness of it.

The music that represents the villains in both films is also similar. In *The Magnificent Seven*, the villain's name is Calvera. In the *¡Three Amigos!*, the villain's name is El Guapo, Spanish for 'The Handsome Man', the irony of which sends the message that this is a comedy, and should not be taken too seriously. The music for Calvera accompanies his arrival in the nameless village just after the main title sequence is complete. The short four-measure motif is shown in Example 4, and log drums and other 'indigenous' percussion instruments accompany this motif.[4]

Example 4 Author transcription of melody from 'Calvera' from *The Magnificent Seven*, mm 5–7

Although the main titles begin in E♭ major, they conclude in F major. When Calvera's motif enters, it sounds as though it begins in D Phrygian or D minor, the relative minor of F major, indicating a clear distinction between heroes and villains. As more of Calvera's music is heard, it becomes obvious that the key is G minor; Calvera's music begins on the dominant pitch. The motive for El Guapo is presented after he chases the Amigos away from the village of Santa Poco and declares that it is no longer under his protection.

His music was intended to be heard during the main titles of ¡Three Amigos!, as Bernstein composed it, but did not make the film's final cut. El Guapo's music is shown in Example 5.

Example 5 Author transcription of melody from 'Ridden Out' from ¡Three Amigos!, measures unknown

Once again, it appears as though the cue is in D Phrygian or D minor, and only after additional music is heard does it become clear that G minor is the tonality. The similarities are obvious between the music for El Guapo and Calvera. Both leitmotifs begin with the pitches D and E♭, and both seem to tonicize D initially, with the presence of E♭ indicating a D Phrygian scale. But based on the complete gesture, the note D is actually the dominant pitch and G is the tonic pitch in both instances. Calvera's music ends with a Picardy third, so that the final melodic interval heard is a minor third; this allows the cue to avoid any sense of major mode tonality. In addition, Calvera's music is accompanied by a non-triadic harmony, the pitches G, A♭, C, and D, and a bass line that outlines a tritone; both harmonic and bass dissonances encourage the audience to hear Calvera as a villain because of the lack of consonance in his music, as well as the melodic tonal ambiguity. In contrast, El Guapo's music ascends, and is accompanied by tertian harmonies, indicating that although he is a villain, he is not to be feared in the same fashion as Calvera. Indeed, as the Amigos note when receiving the telegram requesting their presence in Santa Poco, El Guapo is 'infamous'; Ned Nederlander says, "Infamous is when you're more than famous. This man, El Guapo, is not just famous, he's *infamous*." A traditionally evil villain would not have an adjective misconstrued in such a humorous fashion. The Amigos completely misunderstand the nature of the telegram. They believe that they will be doing a personal appearance with El Guapo, who they believe to be the biggest actor in Mexico. Instead, they will be asked to fight El Guapo for real.

Bernstein highlights moments of beauty in both films, but does it in very different ways. A second, more lyrical theme appears in the main titles in ¡Three Amigos! In this version, the music is stated twice, and on the second statement, the orchestration becomes more lush, adding glockenspiel and a mariachi-style trumpet line, and becomes even more grandiose and sweeping. The first melodic statement of the Santa Poco music, after the main titles, is shown in Example 6.

Parody, Self-Parody and Genre-Parody   59

Example 6 Author transcription of melody from 'Donkey' from ¡*Three Amigos!*, mm 1–24

This music appears later as the music for the Amigos' travels to the village of Santa Poco with the same two musical statements of the theme. Of course, the sweeping, lush music that corresponds to Santa Poco is playing against the image. The village is in disrepair, the villagers are poor, the location and inhabitants are similar to those in *The Magnificent Seven*, but in ¡*Three Amigos!*, the music intentionally misleads the Amigos. The Amigos believe that they are 'on location', acting with El Guapo, so they believe that they are headed to a Hollywood-like film set in Mexico.

Even the title of the cue is misleading. The music begins while the Amigos travel with Carmen back to Santa Poco and continues when they arrive, somewhat in awe of the amazing 'sets'. One might believe that the cue title is not particularly important, but in this instance, it is. The cue title is 'Donkey', in reference to the donkey upon which the Three Amigos ride into the village. Seeing three grown men riding a donkey is certainly not as spectacular as seeing the Magnificent Seven riding individually on horses. But on a deeper level, the cue title of 'Donkey' is not nearly as romantic as the parallel cue in *The Magnificent Seven*, entitled 'Petra's Declaration,' where she declares her love for Chico.

On the topic of this phenomenon, Dan Harries writes, "Spectatorial misdirection is often generated through the misleading use of setting in parody films. A viewer of parody is presented with a setting which looks very similar to the one in the prototext, yet turns out to be a complete fabrication" (Harries, 2000: 62). Harries' theory applies to this music. The Amigos believe the village of Santa Poco to be a set, which would explain the lush music. In this instance, however, the music is misdirecting both the audience and the Amigos because the village is not a set, it is real. Based on the telegram they received earlier in the film requesting their help, the Amigos fully believe that they are doing a personal appearance, and when the arrive in the village of Santa Poco, they think that they are on the set, or 'on location.' This belief is furthered by the fact that Dusty Bottoms, played by Chevy Chase, asks, "Do you have anything besides Mexican food" while eating dinner. Dusty believes that a catering kitchen is nearby, and isn't in the mood to eat Mexican food. It is only during the encounter with El Guapo, after initially driving two bandits out of town, when Lucky Day, played by Steve Martin, is shot, that the Amigos' beliefs begin to unravel. The exchange begins with Lucky whispering to El Guapo, "It's a pleasure working with you", and later in the exchange, they instruct El Guapo to tell them that they will die like dogs so that they can state their famous slogan.

Naturally, El Guapo has no idea that the Amigos are movie stars, and instructs his right-hand man Jefe, played by Tony Plana, to only shoot one of them because "they are funny guys". After being shot, Lucky confronts Jefe, takes his gun, and announces, "Oh great! Real bullets!" When Lucky tells Jefe that he is "in a lot of trouble, mister", and Jefe smiles, only then does Lucky realize that the entire encounter – the food, the fiesta, the poverty of the village, and the imminent peril that they are in – is real. El Guapo asks them, "Don't you want to die like dogs?" and the Amigos respond, "Well, if there's any way that can be avoided ..." The music serves to confirm the misdirection, and allows the Amigos to keep thinking that they are simply acting the part rather than living it for real.

The Santa Poco music does not return until the conclusion of the film, after El Guapo has been defeated and his forces dispersed, because it is only at that point that the village has become what the Amigos originally believed it to be. A full statement of the Santa Poco music, similar to the music from the main title sequence, does not appear until the end credits of the film, and those are at a much faster tempo than when it first appears.

Bernstein wrote a similarly lush cue in *The Magnificent Seven*. There the more romantic theme is given to a young woman named Petra, played by Rosenda Monteros, as opposed to the village of Santa Poco. In a cue called 'Petra's Declaration', she admits to Chico, played by Horst Buchholtz, that she has fallen in love with him, but not in so many words, nor quite so overtly. Petra tells Chico that her father has admonished her for acting so shamelessly, but she does not care. Interestingly, the cue begins earlier than the scene, creating an overlap, and also possibly including the previous scene with the music. The previous scene shows Vin, played by Steve McQueen, speaking with one of the villagers. Through learning how to defend himself and the village, the villager has become empowered, and says to Vin, "That's a feeling worth dying for. Have you ever felt something like that?" Vin replies, "Not for a long, long time", which is followed by a long pause, and the music begins. Vin then states, "I envy you", and the villager smiles. The camera cuts to Chico hunkered down at his post. The presence of this cue is to signify emotion, specifically love, the love that Petra has for Chico, and potentially the love that Vin has for the simplicity of life that the villagers have. Through the scene overlap, in

Parody, Self-Parody and Genre-Parody   61

which music "smooths discontinuities of editing within scenes and sequences" (Gorbman, 1987: 89) and "bridges gaps between scenes or segments" (*ibid*), the emotion extends to Vin, and it is clear that he is sympathizing with the villagers regarding their lives, and is longing for that life.[5] This romantic music, like in ¡*Three Amigos!*, also returns at the end of the film when the village elder, played by Vladimir Sokoloff, states that "only the farmers have won". Clearly, this life of the land is romanticized by Bernstein's music, so much so that Chico decides to stay to help rebuild and revitalize the village.

Figure 3 Chico and Petra in *The Magnificent Seven* (Sturgis, 1960)

The majority of the overtly musically-comedic moments in ¡*Three Amigos!* occur in scenes where the dialogue and action are intending to be humorous. Two of the most prominent instances are when the Amigos are retrieving their outfits from the studio in Hollywood, and when Lucky Day is giving his speech about defeating El Guapo. In the scene where the Amigos retrieve their costumes from the studio, each one is shown donning his hat. When this occurs, a heroic gesture, synchronized to the image, sounds. This gesture is a filled-in ascending perfect fourth. The cue, entitled 'Suits' and shown in Example 7, contains an opening marking of 'Religioso'. The marking of 'religiously' indicates a certain reverence, or irreverence, for the situation. The Amigos believe that they are about to resurrect their career in Mexico, and the music indicates a heroic 'rebirth' of the actors.

Example 7 Author transcription of 'Suits' from the main titles of ¡*Three Amigos!*, mm 1–5

Each gesture is a minor third higher than the previous one, showing both a chromatic mediant relationship, as well as the traditional "heroic" gesture, that of the key of E♭ major, a minor third higher than C. The designation of E♭ major as the 'heroic' key comes from Beethoven's *Symphony No. 3 in E♭ major*, 'Eroica', and this designation has been applied since the early nineteenth century. After all three Amigos are wearing their complete costumes, the music ascends once more, but this is a leap of a perfect fourth rather than a filled-in fourth, and the same pitches as in the main titles, D to G, showing that the Amigos are now ready to head to Mexico. However, for all of the heroism in this music, the Amigos are anything but heroic at this point. Despite the chromatic mediant relationships, none of the gestures arrive on E♭, so none of the Amigos can actually be considered heroic, especially because they do not realize what they have been asked to do, which is defend Santa Poco for real. As they swing across the storage room on ropes, a brief 'Amigos' thematic statement is sounded, and they head for Mexico.

The second prominent instance of overtly humorous music is used after the Amigos have retrieved Carmen from her captivity in El Guapo's compound, and they return to Santa Poco with a fanfare based on the opening song. They declare to the people of Santa Poco that the village of Santa Poco must stand up to El Guapo. Lucky Day begins a speech about how everyone has an El Guapo in his or her life, and how eventually, each person must rise up and defeat their own personal El Guapo.

Figure 4 Lucky's Speech in ¡*Three Amigos!* (Landis, 1986)

The cue that underscores this speech, which is untitled but marked as '12/1AR' in the manuscript, is reminiscent of Edward Elgar's *Pomp and Circumstance March No. 1*, which immediately invites comparisons to a (lacklustre) graduation speech:

> For some, shyness might be their El Guapo. For others, a lack of education might be their El Guapo. For us, El Guapo is a big dangerous guy who wants to kill us. But as sure as my name is Lucky Day, the people of Santa Poco can conquer their own personal El Guapo who also happens to be the actual El Guapo.

According to the parameters of this speech, any type of obstacle is a 'personal El Guapo', and everyone can conquer their own personal El Guapo, a statement that sounds ridiculous when spoken aloud.[6] The musical examples from Elgar's *Pomp and Circumstance*, and *¡Three Amigos!* are shown in Examples 8 and 9.

Example 8 Author reduction of Elgar, *Pomp and Circumstance March No. 1*, rehearsal [J], beginning of Trio

Example 9 Author transcription of 'Untitled' (12/1AR) from the main titles of ¡*Three Amigos!*, mm 1–9

Songs in ¡*Three Amigos!*

The songs in ¡*Three Amigos!*, 'The Ballad Of The Three Amigos' and 'Blue Shadows', contain music and lyrics by Randy Newman, who also voiced The Singing Bush in the film. As might be expected, the 'Ballad' occurs only once in the film, and that is at the outset before the main title sequence. The full song, as composed, did not make it into the final cut of the film, just like Bernstein's 'Main Titles'. The lyrics of the song invoke a sense of the Three Musketeers between the Amigos as evidenced by the "One for each other and all for one" lyric, the lyrical emphasis on 'brotherhood', 'amigos forever we'll be', and the sense of destiny about which they sing. It also helps that all three Amigos are singing in unison; no one adds harmony until the conclusion of the song, and no one adds additional lyrics. The Amigos sing as a tightly constructed unit. It is undeniable that the function of this song is primarily narrative, designed to introduce the characters of the Three Amigos as banded together, as an unbreakable unit, and also as entertainers, singing cowboys. One significant point in the song is where three-part harmony occurs on the lyrics "We are the Three Amigos", sung three times in a row at the end of the song. Each instance gets progressively higher and more unrealistic for three men to sing, and the held note on the syllable 'A' in "Amigos" gets harmonized and progressively longer. All three instances use borrowed chords (bIII, bVII, I; bIII, IV, I; bVI, bIII, I), and these chords are highlighted by the absence of a dominant functioning chord, resulting in a lack of authentic cadence, which only occurs on the final words of the song, "and forever Amigos we'll be", sung by the Amigos in thirds. Although they may be singing different parts, they are still a tightly constructed unit. It also showcases their abilities as entertainers by singing more than just one melodic line; they are simultaneously brothers and entertainers.

Figure 5 'The Ballad of the Three Amigos' in ¡*Three Amigos!* (Landis, 1986)

The function of this song is similar to 'Do Not Forsake Me' from 1952's *High Noon*, but the two songs realize their respective functions in significantly different ways. 'Do Not Forsake Me', with music by Dmitri Tiomkin and lyrics by Ned Washington, is sung in the film by Tex Ritter. This song is purely narrative, but in a strange twist, the lyrics are sung in first person. It is obvious that Will Kane, played by Gary Cooper, is not singing the song, but the unseen narrator is singing from Kane's perspective. The lyrics essentially provide a synopsis of the film, and ultimately how it will end; *High Noon* is a realization of the title song's lyrics. Over the course of *High Noon*, the verses are individually sung in order to prepare the viewer for the upcoming action. As Roger Hickman writes, "The ballad is not restricted to the opening credits. During the film, Ritter's voice sings parts of the ballad seven times. The sound of the solo voice with its sparse accompaniment serves as a constant reminder of Will Kane's isolation" (Hickman, 2006: 203). The first-person lyrics of the song contribute to Kane's isolation, and also continue to remind the viewer of the impending action.

While both songs concern bravery, 'Do Not Forsake Me' realizes this on a personal level, with lines such as "If I'm a man I must be brave" and "I can't be leavin' until I shoot Frank Miller dead." In the 'Ballad', bravery is realized at a group level, with the line "The three brave amigos are we." This particular line, and slight variations, is written seven times in the song, and sung four times in the film because of the cuts made to the song in editing. The effect of singing so overtly about bravery so many times is that bravery becomes a farce; the Amigos are brave, but the actors themselves are not.

Several film and film music scholars have noted the significance of 'Do Not Forsake Me' and its impact on Hollywood film music during the 1950s and 1960s.[7] Mark Evans writes, "Commercial success went to several songs that had appeared originally in motion pictures, most particularly Dimitri Tiomkin's theme from *High Noon*. By the mid-1950s, the composer of a musical score for an important film (artistically or financially) could be assured of consideration for commercial recording" (Evans, 1979: 191). Buhler, Neumeyer and Deemer note, "Ritter's version was only one of six recorded and released at or near the time of the film's premiere. By releasing it in different versions, the thought was that the song would sell more copies and garner more radio airplay because it would appeal to different audience tastes" (2009: 353–4). Roy Prendergast writes that "The title song of this film, 'Do Not Forsake Me Oh My Darlin'', sung by the late Tex Ritter, became a popular hit in its own right and unknowingly rang the death knell for intelligent use of music in films" (Prendergast, 1992: 102). Later, discussing what he feels is the negative impact of the theme song on film music, Prendergast writes:

> *The aesthetic effect on film music was immediate and devastating. Every producer, in order to help assure the financial success of his film, now wanted a film score with a song or instrumental number of a type that would 'make the charts.' No longer did producers care if the music written for their films was the best possible music for that specific picture. The artistic problems for the composer were obvious. He was now asked to impose a strictly musical form and style, the pop song, onto a film whether it was appropriate or not.* (ibid: 103)

It is interesting that ¡*Three Amigos!* begins with the equivalent of a theme song, similar to *High Noon*. Of course, multiple reasons exist for this. The first is that since *High Noon*, it has been exceedingly typical to begin a western with a theme song, although *The Magnificent Seven* is a notable exception. Even the great western parody *Blazing Saddles* (Mel Brooks, 1974) contains a title song,

'Blazing Saddles', performed by Frankie Laine. It is not a coincidence that Laine sings the title song in *Blazing Saddles*, as Laine was one of the several recordings available of 'Do Not Forsake Me', although his version was not used in *High Noon*. The lyrics of 'Blazing Saddles' follow a path similar to 'Do Not Forsake Me' in that the audience learns a great deal about the ensuing plot: a man named Bart, a sheriff, will "conquer fear and hate" and will rid the town of the bad guys. The audience knows that this will happen over the course of the film because the lyrics are written in the past tense, as though the events have already occurred and the film itself is a flashback.

The second reason for beginning with a theme song is that the Amigos are supposed to be portrayed as 'singing cowboys' or entertainers, an idea that is mentioned multiple times over the course of the film, so naturally, the audience's first introduction to the characters is through song. In his liner notes, Bond writes that Newman's songs are "affectionate parodies of the type of lightweight numbers that might have actually appeared in a singing cowboy movie of the Thirties or Forties". The third reason is that contemporary films of all genres often used 'theme songs' that were successful examples of popular music, such as *Footloose* (Herbert Ross, 1984) and *Top Gun* (Tony Scott, 1986), as well as the James Bond film *A View to a Kill* (John Glen, 1985). Unlike those films just mentioned, the theme song from *¡Three Amigos!* was not intended to reach the Top 40 charts in the United States and never released as a single to radio.

A more significant reason is at the root of opening *¡Three Amigos!* with a song. Bernstein believed that 'Do Not Forsake Me' was one of the main causes for the decline of the classical film score. In his own 1972 essay, 'What Ever Happened to Great Movie Music?', Bernstein wrote:

> The events of the past few years in the field of film score seem to indicate that any discussion on this great art may indeed have to be a historical summary at the end of its era of greatness ... I find it inconceivable that this sophisticated area has in such a short time degenerated into a bleakness of various electronic noises and generally futile attempts to "make the pop Top 40 charts."... Two innocent events in the early and middle Fifties, it seems to me, signaled the beginning of the end of the golden age of film music. The first of these was the extraordinary commercial success of the title song by Dimitri Tiomkin for the 1951 motion picture *High Noon*. How fresh and exciting that main title seemed then! But the free advertising resulting from the song – not to mention the enormous money that the song itself made – led to an instant demand by movie producers for similar title songs in almost every picture that followed ... The second event was the success of my own *Man with the Golden Arm* in 1955, which was compounded by Henry Mancini's TV success with *Peter Gunn*. With the commercial bonanza of these 'pop' sounds in two perfectly legitimate situations – my score was not a jazz score, but a score in which jazz elements were incorporated towards the end of creating specific atmosphere for that particular

> film – producers quickly began to transform film composing from a serious art into a pop art and more recently into pop garbage ... Today the once proud art of film scoring has turned into a sound, a sensation, or hopefully a hit. How ironic that in an era in which music enjoys its greatest popularity as an art, film producers are demonstrating the greatest ignorance of the use of music in films since the beginning of that medium's history. (Bernstein, 1972: 55–58)

Bernstein himself had difficulty finding a place for his large scores in the early 1970s until he began scoring comedies so that the large orchestra often played against the image track. Prendergast wrote that film composers became compromised in terms of what music they were allowed to write. So, what better way for Bernstein to proverbially thumb his nose at the established order than by opening a western parody with a song whose lyrics and performance are so tongue-in-cheek that they become absurd, and a song for which he was neither the lyricist nor composer? 'The Ballad Of The Three Amigos', based on its lyrics, performance and lack of authentic cadence at the apex of the song, is used as a parody of typical western theme songs in a parody of a typical western film.

'Blue Shadows' occurs approximately half way through the film. After El Guapo has run them out of Santa Poco, the Amigos return to collect their belongings, but discover that everything is gone, and Carmen has been kidnapped by El Guapo. At that point, they decide to become the Three Amigos for real. Then they begin the journey to El Guapo's hideout. On the first night of their journey, as the they are enjoying their meal of cooked bat, Ned becomes sleepy, but is quickly awoken by the sound of a coyote howl in the distance. He is behaving in a childlike manner by being afraid of the dark and the outdoors, and both Lucky and Dusty treat him in this fashion. Lucky instructs Dusty to play a song that will allow Ned to relax and fall back asleep. Unlike the 'Ballad', this song's function is not narrative. The lyrics of the song assist Lucky and Dusty in their attempt to put Ned at ease and allow him to sleep. In fact, all three Amigos prepare for sleeping at the end of the song. Following the preparations for bed, the screen fades to black and the following scene picks up in a desert with the sun blazing overhead.

Rick Altman's book *The American Film Musical* describes three different 'dissolves' during songs that move the action from the diegetic to something beyond the diegetic world (Altman, 1987). The first type is what Altman calls the 'audio dissolve'. He creates an opposition between the diegetic track and the music track, and writes, "By convention, these two audio tracks have taken on a quite specific sense: the diegetic track reflects reality, while the music track lifts the image into a romantic realm far above this world of flesh and blood" (Altman, 1987: 62–3). Altman continues:

> The most common form of audio dissolve involves a passage from the diegetic track to the music track through the intermediary of diegetic music. This simple expedient, perhaps more characteristic of the musical than any other style trait, has long been sensed as a typical – and somewhat unrealistic – musical technique. (ibid: 63)

The song 'Blue Shadows' begins with only diegetic sounds from the guitar, but immediately begins incorporating accompaniment from nondiegetic and unseen sources. While this is not an audio dissolve as Altman describe it, the song shows characteristics of the audio dissolve by incorporating nondiegetic music into the diegetic song, and the song moves from an exclusively diegetic space to a more romanticized space.[8]

The third and final type that Altman discusses is the 'personality dissolve'. In the personality dissolve, motivating factors associated with characters are present, but hidden, and music has the power to unlock those hidden features (ibid: 80–1). In 'Blue Shadows', Ned is portrayed as extremely nervous and childlike with his fear of sleeping outside. The song is performed in order to calm him. Once he begins singing, he instantly matures, and is shown to have the best singing voice of the Amigos. At the conclusion of the song, Ned immediately falls asleep as soon as he lies down. The song draws the maturity out of Ned and the childlike personality that he previously displayed dissolves.

In addition, 'Blue Shadows' operates as a typical song within a Hollywood musical, moving from the mundane diegetic world to the enchanted world. Altman writes, "In leaving normal day-to-day causality behind, the music creates a utopian space in which all singers and dancers achieve a unity unimaginable in the now superseded world of temporal, psychological causality" (ibid: 69).

In the sheet music to Randy Newman's 'Blue Shadows (from the motion picture ¡Three Amigos!)' the attribution states "Words and Music by Randy Newman", indicating fresh lyrics and a new melody and harmony, both of which are unrelated to Roy Rogers' earlier song of the same title. The tempo marking, however, clearly relates to Rogers, as it is marked "Easy shuffle, 'Happy Trails' feel ♪ = 84" (Newman, 1986/2006). 'Happy Trails' was the ending song to Rogers' radio and television shows. Although Newman's lyrics and melody were written specifically for the film, it is clear that the song, and its performance in the film, is a gesture to Rogers' earlier performance. Roy Rogers' 'Blue Shadows' was performed in the Disney animated/live-action hybrid film *Melody Time* (1948, dir. Clyde Geronimi, Wilfred Jackson, Jack Kinney, and Hamilton Luske). In *Melody Time* the majority of the song is animated, with animals scurrying about in the desert, and then finding their way to the musical performance. Once the animation 'pans' to the live actors, the cowboy performers are sitting around a campfire with an obviously painted backdrop behind them, and they perform the conclusion of the song. The reference to this performance in ¡Three Amigos is largely related to the film performance of the song. While no animation is present, the Amigos are sitting around a campfire, and they do perform the song with an obviously painted backdrop. Various desert creatures do appear in the song, gathering around the Amigos. Even the horses participate in the performance, with their part marked into the sheet music: "(Horses): Bom-ba, bom-ba, bom-ba, bom-ba" etc. This, of course, adds to the humour and outrageousness of the film. At the conclusion of the song, the Amigos wish each other good night, with Ned being the final Amigo wished good night. After Ned is wished good night by Lucky and Dusty, the turtle, previously an audience member to the song, also wishes Ned good night, anthropomorphizing the animal in much the same way as would occur through animation, and adding further to the humorous nature of the performance and the film.

The lyrics of both songs deal with the idea of worrying about sleeping outdoors. In ¡Three Amigos!, Ned is very worked up about sleeping outdoors, and the function of the song is to calm Ned's nerves. At one point, Lucky sings the line, "Little cowboys, close your eyes and dream, All of the doggies are in the corral, All of your work is done, Just close your eyes and dream, little guy, Dream of someone." Ned sings the final verse and accepts the idea when he sings, "All the other little cowboys, Back in the bunkhouse now, So close your eyes and dream." Rogers' song also deals with the same concept, as those lyrics contain the passage, "Move along, blue shadows, move along, Soon the dawn will come and you'll be on your way." Unlike ¡Three Amigos!, Rogers' song does not appear to have the same functionality or purpose within the film. Instead, it appears to act as just a campfire cowboy song performance instead of contributing to the narrative.

The 'enchanted' world of ¡Three Amigos! operates as a parody of 'the enchanted' in other Hollywood films. It is necessary for Ned to act as a child because children use their imaginations, and only in one's imagination could the elements of the Amigos world exist, even though they are absurd and silly – albeit comedically.

Conclusion

Elmer Bernstein's music for The Magnificent Seven and ¡Three Amigos! shares many similar traits. Both scores make significant use of the title music throughout the film, both contain musical motifs for the villains, and they both contain at least one lyrical cue. Both films are composed in the same style with similar instrumentation, and both contain music that would be considered appropriate for the genre. However, the music used in the two films differs in significant ways. ¡Three Amigos! contains multiple instances where the music is overtly trying to be humorous, such as Lucky's speech, with Bernstein's music channelling Elgar's *Pomp and Circumstance*. The lyrical theme in *The Magnificent Seven* is associated with a relationship between Petra and Chico, while the lyrical theme in *¡Three Amigos!* is associated with the village of Santa Poco, which the Amigos believe to be a Hollywood-style set. The subdivision of metre in each of the main title sequences is different, and the opening gesture in the 'Main Title' for *¡Three Amigos!* is only one note different from a similar gesture in the 'Main Titles' for *The Magnificent Seven*. Claims have been made that Bernstein did not directly parody any of his music from *The Magnificent Seven*, but through the analysis of cues, it is clear that he did. Bernstein was not mocking his own music, but was successfully reusing and reworking it for humorous effect, a technique he had been using since the mid-1970s.

Randy Newman's songs also assist in defining *¡Three Amigos!* as a comedy film, while still having the songs function appropriately within their specific genre. The title song 'The Ballad of the Three Amigos' introduces the title characters as brothers as well as entertainers. The song also serves as a good example of a title song within the American western film genre, particularly when compared with *High Noon*'s 'Do Not Forsake Me'. The other song by Newman, 'Blue Shadows', operates as a song might within the confines of the American musical. Ned, childlike at the beginning, provides the opportunity for the campsite and all of the Amigos to move from a mundane diegetic space to an enchanted one. But since the film is a parody, the song fails to return the Amigos to the mundane space at the conclusion, leaving the Amigos enchanted so that they can find the Invisible Swordsman.

The music of Elmer Bernstein helped to codify an entire genre of film, the American western, with its sound based on the music and orchestration of American composer Aaron Copland. Bernstein became a master of the genre, but sought out new challenges, specifically in the comedy genre. Bernstein's orchestrator Patrick Russ recalled that originally Bernstein was unavailable to score *¡Three Amigos!* and was not particularly interested. Through email correspondence, Russ stated:

> Landis persisted, and said that like *Animal House*, he wanted a serious score, which he felt would make the scenes even funnier. The relationship between *The Magnificent Seven* and *¡Three Amigos!* understandably created a link between their musical scores as well. Those similarities were intentional on the part of the composer. (Email to the author, 25 October 2009)

When it came time to compose a western comedy, he was up to the task, parodying some of his most famous music, and adding new humorous cues. Elmer Bernstein's music for *The Magnificent Seven* and *¡Three Amigos!* demonstrates his ability to compose music in the western style, both to codify, and to create laughter.

Acknowledgments

Portions of this article were presented at the ECHO Conference in Los Angeles, 5-6 June 2009. I would like to thank several people for their assistance at various stages in my research including Ed Bryant, Ned Comstock, Andrew Dell'Antonio, Robert Fink, David Neumeyer, and Patrick Russ.

Notes

1. For a detailed discussion of music in the films of John Ford, please see Kalinak (2007).
2. These films include *The Tin Star* (Anthony Mann, 1957), *Saddle the Wind* (Robert Parrish, 1958), *The Comancheros* (Michael Curtiz, 1961), *Hud* (Martin Ritt, 1963), *The Hallelujah Trail* (John Sturgis, 1965), *The Reward* (Serge Bourguignon, 1965), *The Sons of Katie Elder* (Henry Hathaway, 1965), *Return of the Seven* (Burt Kennedy, 1966), *The Scalphunters* (Sydney Pollack, 1968), *Guns of the Magnificent Seven* (Paul Wendkos, 1968), *True Grit* (Henry Hathaway, 1969), *Cannon for Cordoba* (Paul Wendkos, 1970), *Big Jake* (George Sherman, 1971), *The Magnificent Seven Ride!* (George McCowan, 1972), *Cahill: United States Marshall* (Andrew V. McLaglan, 1973), *From Noon Till Three* (Frank D. Gilroy, 1976) and *The Shootist* (Don Siegel, 1976).
3. I would like to thank Robert Fink for pointing out this relationship between the two main titles.
4. The four distinct pitches in Calvera's motif, in order of appearance, form the DSCH motif, the musical monogram of Russian composer Dmitri Shostakovich. Whether there is any relevance to Shostakovich or not is the subject of further research.
5. When this film clip was shown at the 2009 ECHO conference, it solicited a significant amount of unintentional laughter for the stiffness of the acting and for the somewhat dated style of the music that accompanied the clip. In 1960, the scene was highly effective, but nearly fifty years later, it appears to have become ineffective and unintentionally humorous.
6. Bernstein was familiar with this technique and used it in *Animal House* to underscore Bluto's speech about the Germans bombing Pearl Harbour. Bernstein also applied this same technique in *Airplane!* after Ted Striker lands the plane safely.
7. Jeff Smith, in *The Sounds of Commerce* (1998: 59-60) notes the significance that theme songs gained through the popularity of 'Do Not Forsake Me' and musical cross-promotion of film, both domestically and abroad.
8. The second type of dissolve that Altman discusses is the 'video dissolve', which moves the physical space to a different time. This particular type of dissolve is not used in 'Blue Shadows', since the Amigos never leave the campsite.

References

Altman, R. (1987). *The American Film Musical*. Bloomington, IN: Indiana University Press.
Bernstein, E. (1972). What Ever Happened to Great Movie Music? *High Fidelity*, July, 55–58.
Bernstein, E. (2000). Interview. In M. Russell & J. Young (Eds.), *Film Music: Screencraft* (pp. 32–43). Boston, MA: Focal Press.
Bond, J. (2006). ¡*Three Amigos!*. Collector's Choice Music, Liner notes, CCM-696-2.
Buhler, J., & Neumeyer, D. (2001). Analytical and Interpretive Approaches (I). In K.J. Donnelly (Ed.), *Film Music: Critical Approaches* (pp. 16–38). New York: The Continuum International Publishing Group.
Buhler, J., Neumeyer, D., & Deemer, R. (2009). *Hearing the Movies*. New York: Oxford University Press.
Evans, M. (1979). *Soundtrack: The Music of the Movies*. New York: Da Capo Press, Inc.
Gehring, W. (1999). *Parody as Film Genre: Never Give a Saga an Even Break*. Westport, CT: Greenwood Press.
Gorbman, C. (1987). *Unheard Melodies*. Bloomington, IN: Indiana University Press.
Harries, D. (2000). *Film Parody*. London: British Film Institute.
Hickman, R. (2006). *Reel Music: Exploring 100 Years of Film Music*. New York: W.W. Norton and Co.
Kalinak, K. (2007). *How the West was Sung: Music in the Westerns of John Ford*. Berkeley & Los Angeles, CA, London: University of California Press.
Murphy, S. (2002). Western Rhythms and Wild Western Rhythms. Conference on Popular Music and American Culture, Austin, TX, November 20–23, 2002.
Newman, R. (1986/2006). *Anthology: Music for Film, Television, and Theater* (Vol. 2). Van Nuys, CA: Alfred Publishing.
Prendergast, R. (1992). *Film Music: A Neglected Art* (2nd ed.). New York: W. W. Norton and Co.
Smith, J. (1998). *The Sounds of Commerce*. New York: Columbia University Press.
Timm, L. (2003). *The Soul of Cinema: An Appreciation of Film Music*. Upper Saddle River, NJ: Prentice Hall.

Erik Heine is Professor of Music at the Wanda L. Bass School of Music at Oklahoma City University. He has presented and published on music in films as diverse as ¡*Three Amigos!*, *The Magnificent Seven*, Grigori Kozintsev's adaptations of *Hamlet* and *King Lear*, *Signs*, *Fearless*, and *The Truman Show*. He currently teaches Music Theory and Aural Skills and courses in Classical Era Form and Music Since 1900. In his spare time, he is an avid runner.

5 Austin Powers: Intentional Music Man

Liz Giuffre and Mark Evans

Comedian Mike Myers achieved international success with his franchise of Austin Powers films in the late 1990s and early 2000s. The success of the franchise has generally been attributed to Myers' formulation of the character of Austin Powers as a parody of the British spy James Bond, associated 'Bond girls' and ensemble players, and, of course, the archetypal Bond villain represented by Dr Evil. The look and feel of the films are read mostly as a "myriad of references to spy films past" (Feldman, 2009: 64) and "irreverent parod[ies] of just about every popular spy film and television series produced over the last forty years" (Linder, 2003: 76). But it is the Bond films that make the ultimate reference points for Powers to engage with and, as a result, the "intertextual humour positively demands an audience armed with an intimate knowledge of the secret agent genre from the early Bond films onwards" (Linder: 2003: 77).[1] Linder playfully sums up the relationship by noting "James Bond's licence to kill is what gives Austin Powers his licence to shag" (*ibid*: 78). However, as the analysis below will show, there is far more to the Austin Powers franchise than Bond parody, so this "intimate knowledge" might not be as essential as Linder suggests.

Myers himself has noted the similarities between Powers and Bond, providing the following narrative summary of the Austin Powers films:

> [It is] *the same as in the James Bond films. You see him finishing his last mission; then he's given a new mission; he meets with his mentor figure who gives him a special amulet; he crosses over the threshold to an exotic locale where he meets two girls, one of them a protector, one a destroyer; then he's taken to the legitimate face of the evil empire and he changes his identity and infiltrates; then two assassins come, on one, he uses his secret amulet, the second, he uses whatever instrument that they have against themselves; then he's taken prisoner and left for dead, and he's put in an easy escapable death situation in which the bad guy never actually checks; then he and the girl escape; rally, reattach again, using superior numbers in forces; they overcome*

> *the guy but the guy escapes; then they end up in a raft. That's the movie. So to that extent it's a noble and finite structure. Then we just insert the jokes.*
> *(Myers quoted in Baldassarre, 2003: 89-90)*

Aside from merely adding jokes however, Myers uses a raft of nuanced musical and sonic elements that move the Powers films beyond mere spy genre parody.[2] By drawing on conventions of musical parody the films are able to critique and draw from wider sections of cultural and filmic history. Through extensive intertextuality and allusion to historic scenes from the musical canon, Myers makes his films attractive to an older demographic, namely those with the cultural capital to recognize, and be amused by, the parodic musical re-settings. In drawing from these additional genres, the Austin Powers films demonstrate Gehring's argument that "parody embraces the first and still most controversial axiom of modern art: get away from the limitations of a single perspective" (1999: 5). By diversifying his approach and the film genres he parodies, Myers has diversified his potential audience by drawing on the broad cultural history of the musical.

Music is an important part of how the Austin Powers franchise was delivered and developed during its initial release and since. In a press release supporting the soundtrack for *Goldmember*, 'Music From the Motion Picture: Austin Powers In Goldmember', President of Warner Music Group Soundtracks, Danny Bramson, described how "a team that included Maverick Records' Guy Oseary and Music Supervisor and Co-Producer John Houlihan, who has overseen music for all the 'Austin Powers' films," worked with Myers in making music for and beyond the film (Maverick Records, 2002). Bramson suggests that as part of the production:

> *What was emerging was really closer to a musical comedy than a just a movie with music ... The songs we picked, and the artists who performed them, became an integral part of telling the story and creating the world that Mike [Myers] and his cast of characters lived in. (ibid)*

While the selection of music could be focused on the collaboration of Maverick, Houlihan and Myers, or between Myers and Houlihan solely, this chapter will show that the Austin Powers films can be considered as part of the musical and musical comedy traditions. In drawing this focus we move beyond industrial discussions (and larger debates over the franchise as a cross-promotional opportunity), to instead explore more expressly how the creator/performer Mike Myers engaged music and comedy primarily. Particular attention will be paid to the characterizations created in the films, and their respective connection to musicals, dance performance and music video styling. Of course, the work of specialist screen sound personnel like Houlihan has contributed to these outcomes, but for the purposes of clarity here we are focusing on Myers as a key creative force.

Connecting musicals and comedy

There is a strong connection between comedy and music, a connection that can be traced back to the origins of the term 'comedy' itself, as "the word comedy comes from the kind of singing associated with revelling (Greek komoidos: komos = revel + aiodos = song)" (Altman, 1999: 51). While this relationship is not always exclusive, and initially in early cinema the "the term 'musical' was always used as an adjective, modifying such nouns as comedy, romance, melodrama, entertainment, attraction, dialogue and review" (Altman, 1999: 32), the term 'musical' soon became tied to a specific type of film. The year was 1933, when "with the merger of music-making and romantic comedy, the term 'musical' definitively abandon[ed] its adjectival, descriptive function and assume[d] its identity as a generic form" (*ibid*: 33).

The connection between the musical and romantic comedy was solidified during what has often been called "the 'golden age' [of the American Musical Comedy], starting in the late twenties and lasting until around 1960" (Hornby, 1988: 182). While comedies, and specifically romantic comedies, continued to develop during and after this time[3] using different styles of performance and different filmic devices, the musical's use of comedy was distinct. As part of a description of the three main types of musical, the fairy tale musical, the show musical, and the folk musical, Altman argues that comedy performs an important function in each, noting that "comedy ... appears as a strategy to domesticate myth, to reduce it to the level of social laughter-producing device" (1989: 316). Specifically, the film musical also engaged comedy during a specific time to answer a specific audience need: "The 1930s musical [evolved as] an escapist response to the Depression condition ... [as] films which involve the spectator to a greater extent than many other Hollywood films" (Collins, 1981: 134). Often this spectator involvement in the musical is tied to the suspension of disbelief and the audience's acceptance of the genre's conventions, the often apparent spontaneity of characters singing and dancing.[4] In an examination of the film musical, Wood argued that this aspect is designed for comedic interpretation:

> bursting into song on screen is both the delight and difficulty of the screen musical genre ... what is it about that moment where song takes over from speech that when treated with skill and finesse can seem like the most natural thing in the world, yet when carelessly done is jarring and comedic in the extreme? ... We could only find these comic renditions amusing if we accepted, at least in part, the artificiality of someone breaking into song in the ultimate medium of documentary realism: film. (Wood, 2008: 306)

Wood's denial of the role of comedy in film is itself problematic. He also fails to acknowledge that musical comedy is far from careless, but indeed, very carefully constructed in order to function successfully. Furthermore, to ignore the musical set pieces in films such as the Austin Powers trilogy is to ignore a major part of their appeal. That appeal is based around a style of comedy that draws not just on one genre or character, but on an intricate suite of references that crosses various genre conventions and numerous decades. The importance of exploring the use of music in the Austin Powers films, and extending this to explore the use of the conventions of the film musical in these comedies, is acknowledging that, as Wright argued, "music is the primary instrument for emotional direction in film ... critical to the emotive power of music in general, but especially in film, is this ability to evoke – to subtly call to the viewer's mind a related or comparable situation, to act as a shorthand to steer the viewer emotionally" (Wright, 2003: 10-11). Given that a successful comedy film relies on the ability to draw an audience's emotions (specifically, to draw laughter), it is logical that a study of comedy should include an emphasis on the use of music.

A musical comedy rather than just a spy spoof

The film musical has recently been defined "not so much [by] a question of music or the number of songs, but rather [in terms] of approach" (Wood, 2008: 308). Wood here continues to reference Mast, who argued that "a play or film is a musical if its primary entertainment value and investment lie in the musical numbers themselves" (Mast in Wood, 2008: 309) and by this definition, we assert here that the Austin Powers films can indeed be considered as musicals as well as spy parody comedies. The advantage of considering these films in this way is that it allows for a greater perspective to be gained on how these draw in audiences (with the musical scenes in all three, particularly the 'introduction' sequences and later the 'Dr Evil/Mini Me' serenades, drawing significant audience and critical acclaim).

As a performer and writer who notably began in sketch television on America's *Saturday Night Live* (*SNL*) programme, Mike Myers' style of film comedy takes in a variety of genre components not always considered part of standard film comedy. Myers' use of musical performances as key comedic devices can be compared to Mel Brooks' (who began on television with *Your Show Of Shows*), Monty Python (who began with their Flying Circus),[5] and even Belushi/Aykroyd/Landis with *The Blues Brothers* film (1980) (and who were also *SNL* alumni). In Myers' films previous to the Powers trilogy, most notably *So I Married An Axe Murderer* (Thomas Schlamme, 1993), *Wayne's World* (Penelope Spheeris, 1992) and *Wayne's World 2* (Stephen Surjik, 1993), music was also used as a key comedic device. In these cases, however, narrative causality allowed Myers to introduce comedic musical moments. For example, *Wayne's World*'s leads Wayne (Myers) and Garth (Dana Carvey) are two music enthusiasts who are shown performing to music and interacting with musicians while trying to organize a major music festival. Myers' use of music in *Wayne's World*, specifically the sing-a-long to Queen's 'Bohemian Rhapsody' (1975), cleverly drew in audiences with a variety of experiences, including those younger viewers who first experienced the song via the film and "had no idea about the subtext of it" as well as those drawn to the scene who "are old enough to remember 'Bohemian Rhapsody' at its time of release (Buhler *et al.*, 2003: 77). Similarly, with the main character in *So I Married an Axe Murderer*, the main character Charlie's (Myers) part-time indulgence as a beat poet allows him to deliver key plot and comedic moments via musical performances. It also allows the construction of larger musical set pieces, notably serenading his girlfriend Harriet (Nancy Travis) by bringing his band to her house to perform a musical apology to her.

By considering the Austin Powers trilogy in terms of the musical, we are also able to examine the role, and success, of these films as romantic comedies or stories of courtship. Unlike the spy genre, and specifically Bond films, which feature many 'Bond girls' but which inevitably see Bond as the hero triumph as the eternal bachelor, in the Powers films there is a movement towards courtship and eventual marriage (in *International Man of Mystery* (1997)), then commitment (in the *Spy Who Shagged Me* (1999)) and at least monogamy (in *Goldmember* (2002)). As Mellancamp argued in her much respected examination of the musical (where 'musical' refers to 'musical comedy'), "the narrative of musical comedy coincides with classical narrative ... musicals virtually re-enact the ritual of re-creation/pro-creation of the privileged heterosexual couple" (Mellancamp, 1977: 29).[6] In addition to this, the Powers trilogy also developed examination of other types of personal relationships, such as that of father and son in *Goldmember*, and used musical pieces to make them comedic.[7]

Parody and comedian comedy

In an analysis of Mike Myers' comedy films published just after the first *Austin Powers* film, Speed argued that Myers played particularly with recognizable media stereotypes of masculinity (1999), while Stott (2005) later described Mike Myers' film comedy style as built on "single-mindedness" and "automatism", specifically "the channelling of diverse thoughts and feelings through one overriding principle" (2005: 41–2). Most often the one principal or key masculine figure that has been observed in commentaries of Austin Powers is that of the Bond-like spy, and indeed there are many similarities between Myers' Austin Powers and associated characters and other established film spy and espionage films (King, 2002: 121). Myers himself has discussed the Powers films as "a parody of James Bond parodies", with noting in particular the influence of Peter Sellers' Bond spoof *Casino Royale* (1967).[8] Although a rather surreal spoof, with a truly fantastic narrative complexity, there are key features of the film that clearly have influenced Myers. Most notable is the scene with Peter Sellers as James Bond (there are numerous James Bonds in the film) prancing suggestively on a rotating circular bed in an effort to entice his female partner into further sexual activities. Combined with Sellers' thick-rimmed glasses,[9] the connection to the similar Austin Powers scene is clear.

The connection between Sellers' Bond spoof and Myers' work is most convincing with the use of Burt Bacharach's 1967 composition 'The Look Of Love' in both films. The track is used as the theme song to *Casino Royale* (and is the only recognizable song in the film), while Myers uses it as the theme for the Austin Powers' attempted seductions (notably in the first film, with the song sung by Susanna Hoffs). Myers has stated that this song was a strong inspiration for the musical elements in the Austin Powers films, and the sexualized nuances of Powers himself.[10] Bacharach himself also appears in the Powers franchise to provide a 'live' seduction soundtrack, first as part of a montage with Powers and Vanessa Kensington (Elizabeth Hurley), and in the second film as part of a montage with Felicity Shagwell (Heather Graham). He does appear in the third film, but only in the credits and not the feature narrative.

While the parody element is obviously strong within the Powers franchise, there is another way to examine the comedy. Mike Myers' work in Austin Powers can be considered alongside what Drake calls "a surge in the popularity of comedian comedy" in a "post-classical" comedy era (2003: 187). In this sub-genre definition, Drake mentions Myers alongside comedians Jim Carrey, Adam Sandler, Robin Williams and Eddie Murphy, noting that "all have performed in commercially successful films that have taken the bodily performance of the star as their primary focus rather than more conventional forms of narrative motivation" (*ibid*). Drake's work develops a theoretical framework to consider new types of performance during this time, in particular the development of "comedian comedy" through his observations of Jim Carrey's film work. With this comedian comedy as a film type, Drake notes that

> *performers are able to represent a character in a fictional narrative while at the same time signifying a star, outside the performance. Furthermore, in comedian comedy the stars can often refer to their performance, or change the framing of the performance (by addressing the audience, for example), without breaking the primary frame in which the performance takes place.* (2003: 191)

If we explore the Austin Powers franchise as a character comedy as Drake defines, rather than as merely a Bond parody or other genre parody, then we are able to focus on the diversity of Myers' performance with more depth than has previously been afforded. Adopting Drake's term is also useful as it allows us to consider the different types of performance Myers delivers during these films, specifically as he plays more than one character (notably Austin Powers and his nemesis, Dr Evil).

In this chapter we build on Drake's work to show the development of Myers as a maker of comedian comedy. However, while Drake tends to focus on physical and bodily comedy (2003: 193–6), with Austin Powers we argue that Myers has developed his comedian comedies differently. Specifically, audio markers have become important defining tools for the actor as he plays two characters (sometimes in the same scene). This begins most obviously with dialogue and his adoption of different accents but extends to adopting different types of audio-visual screen performance for each character. For example, Myers aligns the character of Austin Powers with more classic film musical performances and sequences, while developing the character of Dr Evil with televisual and music video-like performances.

Musical moments

Each of the Powers films features a musical performance sequence to initiate the film's opening titles and (re)introduce Austin Powers to the audience. These sequences function, as in film musicals generally, to capture the audience using "the core formal structure [of] the song and dance number" and an "intersection of distinct points of reference" (Frow, 2006: 114). As such, Myers borrows from an essential film musical convention, that of "self reflexivity" (Wood, 2008: 307), which "refers to those aspects of a musical that quote or allude to their own history – the history of musical theatre, the entertainment industry, or the process of making musicals" (*ibid*).

The first Austin Powers films, *Austin Powers: International Man of Mystery*, opens with an establishing scene that introduces Dr Evil's (Myers) "underground lair" and which sets up the narrative duel between himself and Austin Powers. Dr Evil's costume, and in particular his white cat (Mr Bigglesworth), is an almost exact replica of the persona for villain Ernst Stavro Blofeld in the Bond film *You Only Live Twice* (Donald Pleasence actor, 1967). While audiences might expect a Sean Connery-like Bond figure to appear as the antidote to this character, instead Austin Powers appears in a loud, blue-striped suit. The shot opens with the song 'Soul Bossa Nova'[11] (Quincy Jones, originally released in 1962) playing nondiegetically over a sequence of him dancing down the street, greeting and talking with girls in 1960s costume, and as the girls begin to dance to the theme song, the frame freezes and the film's titles appear. This theme functions in many ways like the Bond leitmotif created by John Barry, as a way to herald the character and establish mood, however, these functional aspects are where the similarity between the two themes end.

In the opening musical number from *Austin Powers*, we first see Powers' shoes, not walking but prancing down the street. Immediately we have here a nod to the film musical rather than the spy film, with this shot more akin to John Travolta's introduction in *Saturday Night Fever* (John Badham, 1977),[12] the opening shot of which stays on Travolta's feet as the Bee Gees' track 'Staying Alive' is played and the film's title is shown. Returning to *Austin Powers*, the text on screen indicates that the scene is set in London, something that is confirmed as Powers is greeted by a group of girls dressed as mods, and shots of the famous scooters associated with this subculture soon follow.[13] The girls and Powers dance in the street as the theme continues to play. This action can also be understood as the demonstration of another recognizable film musical convention, that being the demonstration of masculinity through dance. As Cohan argued, "the Hollywood musical routinely makes a spectacle of the male star" (2002: 94), and although Cohan's study focuses on Fred Astaire particularly, his argument that masculinity, and particularly desirability of the male performer, is demonstrated through song and dance in the musical spectacle remains applicable to Powers here.[14] For instance, we don't see Powers woo the women in the frame with anything other than his dancing, yet they, and others who are watching, are drawn into the spectacle through the projected power of his masculinity and end up following him down the street.

Following this shot of Powers dancing the Twist – another iconic 1960s cultural marker – with the women in the street,[15] Powers' appeal with women is then confirmed as we see him pausing to photograph three models, then being chased down the street by a large crowd of screaming women. Again, this references a film musical by mirroring almost exactly the opening to the Beatles' 1964 musical film *A Hard Day's Night* (Richard Lester, 1964). As with the Beatles' film, the shot freezes as Myers jumps in the air, then resumes with shots of him apparently hiding, first in a phone box while wearing a fake moustache, then hiding behind a magazine which has a picture of his face on the cover.

The scene concludes with Powers leading a marching band down the street, a reference to the finale reprise of '76 Trombones' from *The Music Man* (Morton DaCosta, 1962), and then leading a group dance in the street (including an unexplained flash mob of extras who join in, similar to the scene for 'Shake Your Tail Feather' in *The Blues Brothers* – it is so similar that it even starts with a dancer flipping in the frame for no reason. The dance itself also draws on the conventions of the film musical, with Powers' stance and animal-like gestures a combination of the Shake Your Tail Feather 'chicken and bird', and classic

Bob Fosse choreography with its crooked stance and cat-like hand gestures (particularly reminiscent of 'Rich Man's Rag' in his *Sweet Charity* (1969)).[16]

This type of referencing, mashing-up and part-recreation of iconic film musicals continued with the introductions/opening sequences of the two sequels, with *Goldmember* containing a direct reference to 'backstage' musicals. *Goldmember*'s opening takes place on a film set, where extras join in to dance with Powers, as happens during 'Make 'Em Laugh' in *Singin' In the Rain* (Gene Kelly and Stanley Donen, 1952).[17] Indeed, Myers takes the reference further by breaking into the *Singin' in the Rain* dance sequence. The quotations and references flow quickly from that point, as Powers breaks off-screen to join musician Quincy Jones with his orchestra, then moves to a music video shoot with Britney Spears, and then to a Busby Berkely/Esther Williams-style choreography set in a pool, and finishing with Powers rising away from the scene like Gene Kelly's conclusion of 'Broadway Melody' in *Singin' in the Rain*, or Danny and Sandy at the end of *Grease* (Randall Kleiser, 1978).

Relationships through time and music

While time travel and period setting is not exclusive to the musical film (other genres, notably science fiction, use this as a staple), its use in the musical has effectively created nostalgia, comedy and/or social commentary for its audiences. Many musicals use a form of 'period displacement' to help establish their content: *Grease* as a 1970s film looking at the 1950s, *Singin' in the Rain* as a 1950s musical looking at the 1930s, *The King and I* (Walter Lang, 1956) set in the 1800s, and *Cabaret*, made by Bob Fosse in 1972 but set in the 1930s, to name a few. By using this period commentary device, Myers is able to widen the appeal of his Powers trilogy. Myers deliberately plays with time (and cultural eras) by having Powers 'displaced' within the 1960s, 70s, 80s and 90s cultures he inhabits throughout the three films. This allows comedy to be derived from more complex avenues than costumes and hair design.

Much of the sonic comedic play related to the various time periods in the Powers movies is connected to Powers' relationship with his three separate female partners. In the first film, we see Vanessa Kensington (Elizabeth Hurley) introduced as Powers is cryogenically unfrozen. Kensington and Powers' first musical accompaniment occurs as Powers' (rather incriminating) personal effects are being re-issued to him by a cynical military officer. The music cue playing under the scene is a whimsical militaristic piece, with descending I-V crochet bassline and a light, playful flute melody replete with trills at the cadence points. The playful militaristic music works well with the dialogue to undermine any sense of Powers being a strong, masculine hero. The music cuts abruptly as Powers delivers the line "Danger's my middle name" hoping to impress Kensington, however the music restarts immediately and squashes any pretence Powers is hoping to claim. In a later scene Powers tries to seduce her as 'Call Me' by 1990s retro ensemble The Mike Flowers Pops plays, and although she denies his advances verbally she ends the scene smiling endearingly at him. Music is again used as he tries to seduce her, this time more successfully, promising to 'take her for on a night on the town'. This sees the two having dinner on top of a bus driving through the city with Burt Bacharach's 'What the World Needs Now Is Love' (1965) playing diegetically (and featuring Bacharach on the bus itself, with Powers talking direct to camera to introduce him, "Ladies and gentleman, Mr Burt Bacharach"). Powers and Kensington then leave their meals to dance, and with this spectacle the music changes, breaking into a more upbeat instrumental, while a montage of Powers and Kensington apparently travelling through the lit-up city visiting various clubs, shows and casinos takes place. An example of what McDonald describes as the "love montage", one of several "commonly employed romantic comedy troupes" (McDonald, 2007: 118), the scene concludes with Powers and Kensington back at their hotel, and although they do not have sex, their relationship is solidified during this spectacle and the musical period for their courtship established.

In *The Spy Who Shagged Me*, Powers is transported back from the 1990s into the 1960s to retrieve his lost mojo, and here he is first introduced to companion Felicity Shagwell (Heather Graham). The title "Austin's Pad 1969" flashes up on screen while 'Magic Carpet Ride' by Steppenwolf (1968) plays, immediately followed by a shot of Powers' time machine car smashing through a wall and disturbing a brightly coloured 1960s party. The dancing stops only momentarily as the car enters, then Powers gets out of the car and the screaming girls and his dancing with members of the crowd begins (much like that in the opening sequence of *International Man of Mystery*). We see Felicity Shagwell dancing with a group of go-go dancers on a top floor platform while other (mostly female) dancers perform on the floor and around the room. As the song moves from chorus to bridge it is faded down as Powers talks to Robin Swallows/Spits (Gia Carides). Following a brief discussion the music changes to 'American Woman' by The Guess Who (1970)[18] and the shot, and Powers' attention, moves directly to Shagwell. As the song's strong guitar introduction plays, we see her slide down a fireman's pole and onto the dancefloor to approach Powers, who turns from Swallows to face her. Powers begins an animal-like dance routine directed at her, and we see her move through the crowd (stopping to dance with another man to garner a reaction from Powers) before she reaches him and begins to dance for him directly. The music fades down as they have a brief exchange, then is turned up again as Swallows returns and tries to break Powers and Shagwell apart, again using dance to distract his and the audience's attention. Shagwell responds by whistling to four dancers to come join her and approaches him again in unison, finally taking his arm away from Swallows while her dancers literally block Swallows' path. This musical scene ends as Shallows is used as bait in an assassination attempt on Powers, with the diegetic music of the party replaced by nondiegetic 'action' music and the spectacle of the musical is broken. 'American Woman' returns as Shagwell arrives in a car to rescue Powers. It continues to play as they drive away and introduce each other, with this song serving as a theme for Shagwell (as the archetypal American woman – for Powers at least) and their relationship. As in the first film, this relationship is confirmed later in the film with a dance scene between the two leads, as Powers and Shagwell, like Powers and Kensington, dance to a Burt Bacharach performance, 'I'll Never Fall In Love Again' (1968). Bacharach again performs in the scene, this time joined by Elvis Costello, and Powers introduces them directly to the audience, "Ladies and Gentlemen, Mr Burt Bacharach and Mr Elvis Costello."

Finally, in *Goldmember*, Powers is introduced to the 1970s and Foxy Cleopatra (Beyonce Knowles) via a *Saturday Night Fever*-like disco sequence. Powers enters the 1970s using the car time machine as per *The Spy Who Shagged Me*, with the scene introduced textually on-screen "New York City 1975 – Studio 69", and a roller disco taking place. 'Shining Star' (Earth, Wind & Fire) is playing as Powers enters wearing huge platform shoes, a hat and large fur coat, and cane. He approaches a girl at the bar but the scene is interrupted with a shot of Cleopatra onstage singing 'It's Solid Gold' with two backing singers. Cleopatra, dressed in a blaxpolitation-like large afro and gold bikini continues to perform to the song 'Hey Goldmember'[19] as it moves into samples from 'Shake Your Booty' (K.C. and the Sunshine Band). The audience continue to dance and skate and she sings directly to Powers, gesturing to him to watch before introducing Goldmember himself (also played by Myers). Goldmember skates down the hall, leading a roller dance sequence as the Goldmember song lead by Cleopatra breaks into an adaptation of the title line from K.C. and the Sunshine Band's 1975 hit 'That's the Way I Like It', modifying it to "That's the way, uh huh, he likes it, Goldmember", and here Powers is upstaged as Goldmember dances while Powers stands still. Cleopatra leaves the stage to come to talk to Powers, doing this through an interpreter (David Lane mouthing because, as Cleopatra explains "we can't be seen talking to one another so I'm using this cat as a distraction"). Playing underneath the conversation is 'A Fifth of Beethoven' (made famous by *Saturday Night Fever*). She fills him in on his father's kidnapping, and with this the relationship between Cleopatra and Powers is restored.

The use of multiple time periods in the Powers films allows creator Myers to play with musical stereotypes and musical nostalgia for comedic value. It also affords him the ability to develop deeper characterizations for his brand of comedian comedy, whether that be through the disco trappings of Goldmember or the film musical leanings of Austin Powers. In developing the character of Dr Evil, Myers brings televisual stylings to complement his musical performances.

"Mini Me, you complete me"

Myers' comedian characterization is perhaps most developed in the character of Dr Evil. This begins with the quality of Dr Evil's voice, delivered with a snarl-like timbre and accent that sounds radically different to Powers' broad British accent, but is perhaps undefinable other than this. While there are clear American syllables at times, the vocal accent remains largely of unspecific origin. Myers accentuates Dr Evil's vowels by rolling them in an unusual way, and placing a slightly jarring emphasis on keywords like the names of other characters (notably 'Austin Po-wers') or his own plans for 'e-vil'). When creating musical spectacles for Dr Evil, Myers utilizes contemporary music video techniques and 'new musical' conventions rather than parodying classic film musical conventions as he does with Powers. As Dr Evil, Myers again breaks with the immediate preceding narrative, and again uses musical spectacle sequences for broader character development.

The first of these 'Dr Evil/Mini Me' musical pieces appears in the second film, *The Spy Who Shagged Me*. In this film Mini Me (Verne Troyer) is introduced as a character created as part of the experiment to clone Dr Evil. Following a slight technical glitch, the clone is created, as Number Two (Robert Wagner) explains to Dr Evil "exactly like you in every way, except one eighth your size." Following this introduction and a reveal of the clone (Troyer dressed exactly as Dr Evil and striking his trademark finger-to-mouth pose), Dr Evil responds, "Breathtaking. I shall call him [pauses for dramatic effect] 'Mini Me'." Spectacle is used to develop the relationship between Dr Evil and Mini Me soon after, first as a serenade from Dr Evil to his clone, and later as a duet. The serenade begins with Dr Evil apparently playing piano and singing Joan Osborne's 1995 single 'One of Us' (with a grand piano appearing in his 'evil lair' out of place, but unquestioned), and then breaks into a parody of Will Smith's 'Just the Two of Us' (1997). The Osborne track, a subtle nod to the idea of 'playing god' by creating a clone, soon diverts to the parody Smith track, which was originally a love song from father to son, and is now refashioned to be a rejection by Dr Evil of his actual son Scott (Seth Green), and approval of his clone.

Dr Evil's direct-to-camera performance of a few lines of Osborne's original (with Mini Me also playing along on a toy piano played on top of Dr Evil's grand), evokes music video conventions. The two play for a short while before Dr Evil apparently forgets the lyrics (descending into "blah blah blah" and "blue blue blue" as nonsense words to finish), and Mini Me leads a short round of applause. Soon after Dr Evil transitions into a version of 'Just the Two of Us', introducing the performance by saying "this is a very sensitive subject", and replacing parts of Will Smith's original rap with his own narrative of the film's story to date. Here the performance changes with Mini Me accompanying him on the 'stage' proper, including Mini Me as a partner in the sung duet (apparently returning the song's key lyric in a deep baritone, 'You and I'). Dr Evil's performance also features dancing extras in silver suits, and invites comparisons with other prominent music-video era musicians such as Devo and the Beastie Boys (particularly with the silver suits, dance style and miming spinning records). The performance's 'audience' of Frau (Mindy Stirling) and Number Two (Rob Lowe) are made more prominent towards the end, but the music video aesthetic is maintained as the camera pans, Number Two looks around confused, and Dr Evil and Mini Me dance awkward versions of 'contemporary' moves like The Robot.

In *Goldmember*, a similar music video-like spectacle is created as Dr Evil and Mini Me perform an adaptation of Jay Z's 'Hard Knock Life' (1999). Set in prison, the two engage the other inmates and perform for and with them, with the scene breaking to include parodies of rap music videos. This begins as the group, lead by Dr Evil and Mini Me, approach the camera in a 'gang-like' dance (reminiscent of the main routine in Michael Jackson's clip 'Smooth Criminal' (1987)), and confirmed as images of Dr Evil and Mini Me are superimposed over green screen images of dancing girls, cars and urban streets. The track keeps the song's original sample as its hook (from the musical *Annie*) as well as its defining staccato, relatively monotone keyboard base. Mini Me mimes the sample to camera, specifically the lyric 'it's the hard knock life', while Myers as Dr Evil performs a new rap over the top with lyrics specific to Dr Evil's character. Retelling key parts of the Austin Powers franchise story to date ("Austin caught me in the first act that's all backwards, what's with that?"), Myers as Dr Evil also acknowledges the parody for the audience by including the line "This is a shout out to HOVA, God MC ... You all know him, That's Jay Z!! I met him/Well I saw him a restaurant once ...".

This section also includes a parody of the music video broadcast context as well as music video itself. During the Dr Evil/Mini Me clip some lyrics are 'silenced' as if censored, similar to the way curse words in lyrics may be censored when shown on television. This audio/visual cue is particularly nonsensical given the context of performance is a film that already features curse words as part of its rating classification, therefore parodying the character's apparent desire to appear 'edgy' by being censored (rather than a practical need in the film). The original track, subtitled by Jay Z as a 'Ghetto Anthem' (1998), could not be further from this Dr Evil/Mini Me serenade, as the declaration of a

'Hard Knock Life' is ultimately about Dr Evil showing his relatively comfortable existence with his clone.

These serenades help Myers develop his character comedy in what Mundy called "a music video aesthetic" (Mundy, 1999: 224), that is, evidence of "a process of aesthetic, ideological, technological and industrial convergence between popular music and the screen" (*ibid*). With these serenades this convergence is clear and used to comedic effect, first as a way to draw audience attention to the scene by breaking the conventions of the film to date (as the characters break into song), but also with direct-to-camera address, close-ups and apparent backing singers. As such, comedy is delivered as Neale and Krutnik describe, though "a game of transgression and familiarity [as comedy] sets up deviations from 'rules' and 'norms' in order to replace them" (1990: 149). Myers' use of music video performance styles when developing and presenting Dr Evil also aligns with Drake's definitions of comedian comedy as noted earlier, particularly the comedian's ability to simultaneously perform in character in and beyond the film's immediate narrative (2003: 191). Given that Dr Evil doesn't perform in this way until the second Powers film, here it is reasonable to assume that Myers wanted to acknowledge the growing audience for Dr Evil as a character, as well as his own profile as a character comedian able to present more than one persona at once.

Conclusion: towards a complex understanding of the use of comedy and music

The Austin Powers franchise has been widely praised for its rich performances by Myers in particular; however there has been virtually no analysis of the complexity of comedic approach that allowed Myers to make the series so successful. The relationship between the Powers films and James Bond series is evident from Myers' film titles, however, by simply focusing on Austin Powers as a Bond parody, commentators overlook a huge part of Myers' performance, namely his influence (and evocation) of established markers of the classic movie musical and more contemporary screen music techniques like music video. As an interesting afterword (but also telling of Myers' wide palate of comedic and performance influence), reports in the press leading up to the release of *The Spy Who Shagged Me* noted that Myers originally wanted to call that film *Austin Powers 2: The Wrath of Khan*, which signalled a move away from Bond and towards *Star Trek*. According to Jenson reporting for *Entertainment Weekly* in 1999, it was only a potential copyright issue that prevented the franchise switch (http://www.ew.com/article/1999/07/09/austin-powers-identity-crisis, accessed 15 May 2015) away from Bond.

The musical aspects of Austin Powers have to date not been the prominent feature of the analysis and commentaries of the film. However, they are key features of the films themselves. As the franchise grew, so too did the scale of the musical introductions (by *Goldmember* the musical introduction was itself extended to 6 minutes), as well as the introduction of serenade sequences between Dr Evil and Mini Me, and musical spectacle sequences for each of the films' female leads (again, in the third this was heightened with Beyonce cast to sing as well as act). These spectacles had an obvious and immediate comedic intention and affect, but can also be understood as clear devices used by Myers to ensure character developments were clear and distinct (and funny). Musical performances were stylized to help advance the relationships between characters, as well as assist Myers as an actor playing more than one role.

This chapter demonstrated that musical comedy and the conventions of the musical remain appealing beyond the traditional bounds of the musical genre itself. Further, it has shown the complex way comedians like Myers approach not just visual performance, but also audio-visual performance.

Notes

1. See also Storey (2010: 66–67), who also explores the intertextuality present in Austin Powers, incorporating his own reading of the film as well as comments made by Myers.
2. For more on the differences between Austin Powers and James Bond, see Evans and Giuffre (2011).
3. For more information see McDonald (2007).
4. While this would change with the development of the 'integrated musical', a type of musical which tried to incorporate the musical performances more directly into the storytelling, the spectacle of the musical (and often accompanying dance) performance remained. For more details on the 'integrated musical' see Mueller (1984).
5. Myers has also noted how these artists inspired him, including Python and Mel Brooks in a list of "comedy heroes" (Myers in Brett, 2002).
6. See also Schatz, who describes "the musical as courtship rite" (1981: 196).
7. Specifically as Powers performs 'Daddy Wasn't There' on stage with Ming Tea as part of a concert in his apartment.
8. See Myers' speech from AFI's 'Night at the Movies' (14 January 2009) at http://www.youtube.com/watch?v=BE4UBmbMZwQ.
9. Myers has claimed that the glasses idea came both from Peter Sellers and Michael Caine's character in *The Ipcress File* (Sidney Furie, 1965), see https://www.youtube.com/watch?v=X54kMwzgH04.
10. Ibid.
11. It is not surprising that Myers selected 'Soul Bossa Nova' for the Austin Powers films. Even if not a fan of Quincy Jones, Myers would have known the song from

its use as the theme music to the long-running Canadian television game show *Definition* (1974–1989). Although Jones' original was altered in the latter years of the programme, the show used Jones' original version for many years.
12. Although, again, not strictly a traditional film musical, *Saturday Night Fever* can been considered as part of the film musical canon as part of the associated "dance film" genre (Vize, 2003: 24).
13. For more on the influence and evocation of Mod stylings in the Powers' films see Feldman (2009).
14. As Cohan explained, "the musical imagined an alternative style of masculinity, one grounded in spectacle and spectatorship … the Hollywood musical could produce this effect so easily because it was the one genre which, through its [performance] numbers, could take the performance of a star's masculinity to heart so completely, so seriously, and so openly as spectacle" (Cohan, 2002: 98).
15. Notably, in this scene Powers is about to be disciplined by a male police officer, who changes his mind and begins dancing with Powers and another male dancer. While Powers wears his heterosexuality prominently, throughout the trilogy there are several moments where the strength of his masculine sexuality also attracts male characters.
16. It should be noted that many of these intertextual filmic references were deliberately outlined in the production notes of the original script, see http://www.imsdb.com/scripts/Austin-Powers-International-Man-of-Mystery.html.
17. See Chapter 8.
18. While the version used in the scene is the original by The Guess Who, Lenny Kravitz also recorded a version for the film which became a huge hit on release in 1998. The music video for the track featured a sexually charged performance by Heather Graham, playing herself rather than Felicity Shagwell.
19. According to the film's credits, this song actually interpolates 'That's The Way (I Like It)', 'Get Down Tonight' and 'Shake Your Booty'. The song was written for the film by Harry Casey and Richard Finch, with "parody" lyrics by Mike Myers and Paul Myers.

References

Altman, R. (1989). *The American Film Musical*. Bloomington, IN: Indiana University Press.
Altman, R. (1999). *Film/Genre*. London: BFI.
Baldassarre, A. (2003). *Reel Canadians: Interviews from the Canadian Film World*. Toronto: University of Toronto Press.
Brett, A. (2002). Mike Myers in *Goldmember*. BBC Online, 17 July 2002, http://www.bbc.co.uk/films/2002/07/17/mike_myers_austin_powers_goldmember_interview.shtml, accessed 20 September 2010.
Buhler, J., Kassabian, A., Neumeyer, D., Stilwell, R.J., Barnett, K., Bowman, S.L., & Boa-Ventura, A. (2003). 'Panel Discussion on Film Sound/Film Music: Jim Buhler, Anahid Kassabian, David Neumeyer, and Robynn Stilwell'. *Velvet Light Trap*, 51(1), 73–91. http://dx.doi.org/10.1353/vlt.2003.0003

Cohan, S. (2002). 'Feminizing' the Song-and-Dance man: Fred Astaire and the spectacle of the Hollywood Musical. In S. Cohen (Ed.), *Hollywood Musicals: the Film Reader* (pp. 87-101). London: Routledge.

Collins, J. (1981). Toward Defining a Matrix of Musical Comedy: The Place of the Spectator Within the Textual Mechanisms. In R. Altman (Ed.), *Genre: The Musical* (pp. 134-146). London: Routledge.

Drake, P. (2003). Low Blows? Theorizing performance in post-classical comedian comedy. In F. Krutnik (Ed.), *Hollywood Comedians: The Film Reader* (pp. 187-198). London: Routledge.

Evans, M., & Giuffre, L. (2011). Groovy Baby! Disguising Musical Comedy in the Austin Powers Trilogy. Cattemole, J. (Ed.), *Instruments of Change: Proceedings of the International Association for the Study of Popular Music Australia-New Zealand 2010 Conference* (pp. 37-40). Sydney: Perfect Beat Publications.

Feldman, C. (2009). Austin Powers: Reinventing the myth of mod spies and swingers. In J. Packer (Ed.), *Secret Agents: Popular Icons Beyond James Bond* (pp. 52-76). New York: Peter Lang Publishing.

Frow, J. (2006). *Genre*. New York: Routledge.

Gehring, W. (1999). *Parody as Film Genre: 'Never Give a Saga an Even Break*. Westport, CT: Greenwood Publishing.

Hornby, R. (1988). The Decline of the American Musical Comedy. *The Hudson Review*, 41(1), 182-188. http://dx.doi.org/10.2307/3850853

King, G. (2002). *Film Comedy*. London: Wallflower Press.

Linder, C. (2003). Criminal vision and the ideology of detection in Fleming's 007 series. In C. Linder (Ed.), *The James Bond Phenomenon: A Critical Reader* (pp. 76-90). Manchester: Manchester University Press.

McDonald, T.J. (2007). *Romantic Comedy: Boy Meets Girl Meets Genre*. London: Wallflower.

Maverick Records (2002). Get Funky With 'Austin Powers' Sizzling Soundtrack. Press release, 2 July 2002, http://movies.about.com/library/weekly/aa062902a.htm, accessed 9 December 2013.

Mellancamp, P. (1977, Summer). 'Spectacle and Spectator: Looking Through the American Musical Comedy'. *Cine-Tracks*, 2, 27-35.

Mueller, J. (1984). 'Fred Astaire and the Integrated Musical'. *Cinema Journal*, 24(1), 28-40. http://dx.doi.org/10.2307/1225307

Mundy, J. (1999). *Popular Music on Screen: From Hollywood Musical to Music Video*. Manchester: Manchester University Press.

Neale, S., & Krutnick, F. (1990). *Popular Film and Television Comedy*. London: Routledge.

Schatz, T. (1981). *Hollywood Genres: Formulas, Filmmaking and the Studio System*. New York: Random House.

Speed, L. (1999). Millennium Man: Comedy and Masculinity in the Films of Mike Myers. *Metro Magazine*, 120, 56-64.

Storey, J. (2010). *Culture and Power in Cultural Studies: The Politics of Signification*. Edinburgh: Edinburgh University Press.

Stott, A. (2005). *Comedy: The New Critical Idiom*. Routledge: Milton Park.

Vize, L. (2003). Music and the Body in Dance Film. In I. Inglis (Ed.), *Popular Music and Film* (pp. 22–38). London: Wallflower Press.

Wood, G. (2008). Why do they start to sing and dance all of a sudden? Examining the Film Musical. In W.A. Everett & P.R. Laird (Eds.), *The Cambridge Companion to the Musical* (2nd ed.) (pp. 305–24). Cambridge: Cambridge University Press. http://dx.doi.org/10.1017/CCOL9780521862387.018

Wright, R. (2003). Score vs Song: Art, Commerce, and the H factor in Film and Television Music. In I. Inglis (Ed.), *Popular Music and Film* (pp. 8–21). London: Wallflower Press.

Filmography

A Hard Day's Night (Richard Lester, 1964)
Austin Powers: International Man of Mystery (Jay Roach, 1997)
Austin Powers: The Spy Who Shagged Me (Jay Roach, 1999)
Austin Powers in Goldmember (Jay Roach, 2002)
Casino Royale (Guest, Hughes et al., 1967)
Grease (Randal Kleiser, 1977)
Saturday Night Fever (John Badham, 1977)
Singin' in the Rain (Donen and Kelly, 1952)
So I Married an Axe Murderer (Thomas Schlamme, 1993)
The Blues Brothers (John Landis, 1980)
The King and I (Walter Lang, 1956)
The Music Man (Morton DaCosta, 1962)
Wayne's World (Penelope Spheeris, 1992)
Wayne's World 2 (Stephen Surjik, 1993)
You Only Live Twice (Lewis Gilbert, 1967)

Dr Liz Giuffre is a Lecturer in Communication at the University of Technology Sydney, as well as an arts and music journalist.

Mark Evans is the Executive Editor of *Perfect Beat: The Pacific Journal of Research into Contemporary Music and Popular Culture* and author of the book, *Open Up The Doors: Music in the Modern Church* (Equinox Publishing, London). He is Series Editor for Genre, Music and Sound and Executive Editor of *The Encyclopedia of Film Music and Sound* (Equinox Publishing) and is Head of the School of Communication at the University of Technology, Sydney.

6 Paranormal Product
The Music and Promotion of Ghostbusters

Jon Fitzgerald and Philip Hayward

Introduction

Paramount Pictures' feature *Ghostbusters* (Ivan Reitman, 1984) was a major commercial success for the company. The film topped the US box office in its year of release with an eventual domestic gross of US$238 million and international revenue of US$53 million[1] and achieved substantial success on subsequent video and DVD releases. The film also spawned a group of associated media products, including a film sequel (*Ghostbusters II*, 1989); two animated TV series (1986–91 and 1997)[2] also subsequently released on video and DVD; a continuing series of video games; a number of allied comics and novelizations; and a theme park attraction at Universal Studios in Florida. The creative property is estimated to have grossed over a billion US dollars worldwide[3] and, at the time of writing (August 2013), a third film instalment and associated products are mooted, suggesting that there is still considerable life in the franchise.

Despite this high level of commercial success, the initial film project was far from an obvious commercial prospect as a left-of-field genre meld of supernatural horror, fantasy and comedy produced on a budget of US$30 million. As this chapter will identify, music was crucial to the style, 'tone' and impact of the film and played a key role in its marketing. This chapter considers the principal elements of the film's musical score – its theme song, other pop-rock tracks and Elmer Bernstein's orchestral compositions – and how these combined to create an integrated thematic text. Additional consideration will be given to the nature and function of the promotional video for the film's theme song and the manner in which its style template facilitated subsequent unauthorized product.

Production history

Ghostbusters was conceived by Canadian comedian Dan Aykroyd in 1981. Aykroyd rose to prominence as a member of the cast of the long-running US comedy show *Saturday Night Live* (*SNL*) in 1975-79. During his period at *SNL* he teamed up with fellow cast member John Belushi to form The Blues Brothers, a rhythm and blues ensemble that they fronted (in semi-parodic roles as singers Jake and Elwood Blues) with instrumental support from such noted performers as (former Booker T and the MGs members) Steve Cropper and Donald Dunn. The band first appeared on *SNL* in 1978 and subsequently performed and recorded an album entitled *Briefcase Full of Blues* in 1978. Interest in the act led to the production of an eponymous feature film in 1980, directed by John Landis, which was one of the top 10 box office attractions of the year in North America and eventually grossed over $115 million worldwide.[4] The film combined numbers performed by the band with score for narrative sequences provided by veteran Hollywood composer Leonard Bernstein. Aykroyd originally developed *Ghostbusters* as a project intended for him and Belushi to co-star in while working with Belushi on the vexed production of the 1981 film *Neighbours* (John Avildsen) – subsequently revising the script after Belushi's death in 1982.

While *The Blues Brothers* may have given Aykroyd a blueprint for successful combinations of music and comedy (in a fictional 'band bio' format), his experience on *Neighbours* gave him an insight into the manner in which poorly conceived scoring could undermine a production. Originally conceived as an edgy, dark suburban comedy designed to showcase its star duo's dramatic and comedic skills, *Neighbours* was critically panned on release – largely due to its awkward genre mix and 'tone' – and performed poorly at the box office. As documented in Woodward (1984: 252-267), music was almost an afterthought to a film that was marred by constant clashes and creative differences between its writers, producers, the director and Belushi (who teetered on the brink of drug-induced megalomania and paranoia during much of the production).

Saxophonist/composer Tom Scott, a long-time Blues Brothers' associate, was brought into to score *Neighbours* late in the production process. After Scott hurriedly composed a score and theme song for the film in cool jazz-rock style that was something of an antithesis of the overall mood that Belushi intended, the actor attempted to replace Scott's title song with an aggressive track by the Californian punk rock band Fear. When Scott objected, Belushi suggested the whole score be performed by Fear, in order to give the film a heavy punk feel throughout. Taking a different tack, with a suggestion that infuriated Belushi, co-producer David Brown proposed ending the film with Bing Crosby's version of the song 'Love Thy Neighbor'. When preview sessions for the film featuring Scott's music received highly negative ratings the studio decided to ditch

Scott's score entirely. Bill Conti, composer on Avildsen's previous smash hit film *Rocky* (1976), was brought in at short notice to give the film a far lighter tone and the final soundtrack also included sequences from The Doors' 'Hello, I Love You', The Bee Gees' 'Stayin' Alive' and (in its producers' only concession to a punk feel) The Dead Kennedys' 'Holiday In Cambodia'.[5] As accomplished as it was, Conti's score failed to 'save' the film by dragging its dark, intense comedy into the more mainstream attraction its producers desired and the film was a notable flop for its stars at a time of media prominence and box office success. The lessons were not lost on Aykroyd.

The original scenario for *Ghostbusters* featured a small group of time-travelling paranormal investigators but this aspect was modified, at the suggestion of director Ivan Reitman, with the film relocated to contemporary New York in a script co-authored by Aykroyd and Harold Ramis. Along with Aykroyd, the film starred Ramis and Bill Murray as ghost-hunting researchers and Sigourney Weaver as a woman whose apartment is haunted by a demonic entity. *Ghostbusters* eventually delivered a highly successful blend of elements, determined by (what was then) a 'hot' star actor/writer (Aykroyd) working with an accomplished production team. In order to retain the potency and effect of the film's genre components for a film that attempted to combine elements of classic (supernatural) horror and science fiction with a more contemporary (youth-orientated) comedy style; the film's soundtrack combined orchestral score sequences, composed by Elmer Bernstein, with pop/rock/soul tracks (both pre-recorded and re-recorded for the film). Bernstein was employed as composer on the strength of his previous work with Reitman and Aykroyd and his success in providing music for high-performing films.

Bernstein began composing for film in 1952, scoring David Miller's acclaimed thriller *Sudden Fear* (starring Joan Crawford) before working on two low-budget 3-D science fiction films in 1953, *Robot Monster* (Phil Tucker) and *Cat-Women of the Moon* (Arthur Hilton). By the mid-late 1950s he had progressed to bigger budget productions such as *The Ten Commandments* (Cecil B. DeMille 1956) and *Sweet Smell of Success* (Alexander Mackendrick, 1957) and subsequently became one of the most prolific American screen composers of the late twentieth century. In the late 1970s, in a period when he was working mainly in television, his work achieved fresh prominence when he began collaborating with the iconoclastic young comedians associated with *SNL* as a result of a personal connection with John Landis, director of the breakout youth comedy *National Lampoon's Animal House*, in 1978. Bernstein went on to score Reitman's directorial debut *Meatballs* (1979) and his subsequent hit *Stripes* (1981).

Reflecting a division of responsibilities that became increasingly entrenched in the industry as the decade progressed, Bernstein was not involved in the choice of popular music tracks used in *Ghostbusters*. These, including its iconic theme song, were chosen and/or commissioned by Aykroyd, in consultation with Reitman and other key creative personnel. As the following sections outline, the effective combination of orchestral music and popular music makes a substantial contribution to the overall impact and appeal of the film and enhances its hybrid quality – part comedy, part supernatural science fiction and part action movie.

The score

a. Scene setting – the opening

The two distinct musical elements of the film – orchestral score and pop-rock music – feature in an introductory sequence that neatly encapsulates the dynamic of the production. These musical elements effectively complement each other, with orchestral scoring used to create and underscore suspense and drama and popular music used to lighten the mood and underline the comic aspects of the movie.

Example 1 Horror-style motif

The opening scene is supported by a suitably 'scary' orchestral score. The movie begins with a bubbling synthesizer sound, followed by the eerie, glissando-infused sound of the ondes Martenot (discussed below) hinting at the ghostly events to come. Major seventh and semitone intervals are used to create a typical horror-style melodic motif (see Example 1). A minimal, transparent orchestral texture is augmented by the sound of flapping bird wings before the main dramatic orchestral motif of the movie is heard as the camera settles on a stone statue of a lion at the top of the library steps. This motif features loud dissonant brass chords with whole tone steps in contrary motion between the upper and lower parts. As the camera follows a lone librarian into the haunted library corridors, various sounds of short duration (such as glockenspiel and harp) assist in creating suspense, while also providing an effective contrast to the sustained sounds of the ondes Martenot. When library card draws open spontaneously, scattering cards everywhere, the dramatic brass motif reappears – with the tone idea now extended into a whole-tone note series on low brass. The whole-tone idea is also used in the string melody at this point. The frightened librarian runs away, accompanied by a dramatic underscore with a driving bass rhythm supported by timpani and a high string melody. The scene culminates in the librarian's look of horror and terrified scream.

The sudden, unexpected entry of a short sequence of (what subsequently transpires to be) the *Ghostbusters* theme song accompanying a very brief title sequence provides a striking contrast, immediately interrupting the suspenseful tone of the opening scene with an obviously light-hearted element. The song, a groove-driven number with a prominent bass line, shouted 'join-in' chorus, and tongue-in-cheek quality to the lyrics and vocal delivery, clearly signals that the movie will be a comedy (even though it may be a little 'scary' at times). In an effective ploy, the number is only allowed a brief appearance in truncated form; enough to signal the movie's light-hearted quality but not enough to overstate the comic elements or allow the repetitive aspects of the music to become annoying. The extended version of the song doesn't appear until much later in the film, at which point the full-length arrangement is ideally suited to the visual sequence it accompanies – a series of brief snapshots of activities by the (now successful) team of ghostbusters.

The opening section also signals another aspect of the sound design that ultimately becomes a notable and highly effective element within the movie; namely the use of prominent sound effects. By the time the librarian emits her terrified scream, the *Ghostbusters* audience has encountered sonically enhanced versions of elements such as flapping bird wings, footsteps on the wooden library floor and scattering cards. The opening also demonstrates the importance of silence in creating a suspenseful atmosphere[6] and the choice of a library for the location of the first ghost encounter facilitates the seamless incorporation of silence into the overall sound design. A brief moment of silence is also used to highlight the librarian's scream when she sees the ghost (the same technique is used later in the movie when Dana (Sigourney Weaver) sees the 'beast' in her refrigerator). Absence of music is also used throughout the movie to heighten the impact of dialogue, a technique that is apparent in the film's opening. After the brief title sequence, the short excerpt of the *Ghostbusters* song fades to silence as ghostbuster Peter Venkman (Bill Murray) talks to his experimental subjects in his ESP laboratory.

b. Orchestral score

Bernstein's score combines (and occasionally merges) two distinct elements: eerie/unearthly music, meant to signify the supernatural, and music scored to accentuate more comic passages. As Bernstein emphasized in an interview shortly after the film's release:

> The interesting thing about GHOSTBUSTERS, as a film, is that it walks a very fine line. I think it's basically a very original film – I don't think anyone's ever

seen anything quite like it ... Part of it is comedy, and yet you have to take the ghost business quite seriously. You have to believe, along with these guys, that the ghosts really do exist. Therefore the score also has to walk a very fine line. What I did with the guys was to get a kind of "antic" theme - it's kind of cute without being really way out ... The other element was the last part of the film, all the stuff with the possession and climax on top of the building. I treated that in an awesome and mystical way. (quoted in Larson, 1985: 10)

The first element, the eerie, draws on established scoring traditions and utilizes Yamaha DX-7 synthesizers (the first popular commercially distributed digital synthesizers) and the ondes Martenot. The synthesizers are deployed to various ends. For example, synthesizer sounds provide a quietly spooky backdrop when Venkman takes a sample of ectoplasmic residue from the library ghost, and when eggs spontaneously break and fry in Dana's apartment. Dramatic synthesizer sounds at high volume are heard when the ghostbusters use their weapons, and when ghosts escape from the ghost trap (after it is shut off by an environmental protection officer). Synthesizer sounds are also regularly employed as low bass sounds and to reinforce low orchestral parts.

The ondes Martenot (named after its inventor, the French cellist Maurice Martenot), heard prominently in the film's introduction, is an early analogue synthesizer that uses a keyboard interface and produces tones with a distinct vibrato. The instrument was most notably pioneered in western art music by French composer Olivier Messiaen in works such as his *Turangalîla Symphony* (1948) and the instrument later featured in concert pieces by Edgard Varèse, Arthur Honegger and Darius Milhaud. Its first use in film scoring was in the music added to Berthold Bartosch's short animated film *The Idea* (1930) four years after its premiere. The instrument also featured prominently in Brian Easdale's (Academy Award-winning) ballet music sequence for *The Red Shoes* (Michael Powell and Emeric Pressburger, 1948) and was frequently used in horror and science fiction movies and television, notably in the 1950s. Maurice Jarre's score for *Lawrence of Arabia* (David Lean, 1962) also makes use of it for exoticist purposes, to emphasize the Arabianness of the film's narrative. After working with other synthesizers on his 1950s science fiction films, Bernstein incorporated the instrument into his score for films such as *Heavy Metal* (Gerald Potterton, 1981).

Bernstein's choice of the ondes Martenot reflects the instrument's ability to glide between notes and quickly move from low to high pitches (and vice versa), providing an eerie, otherworldly character ideally suited to evoking a ghostly atmosphere. As already noted, ondes Martenot motifs and melodies also often use the sort of 'dissonant' interval movements (such as major sevenths, semitones, tritones) typically associated with horror movies. Ondes Martenot motifs typically occur in eerie, suspenseful situations - such as when books float off the library shelves and when Venkman slowly looks through Dana's apartment for supernatural elements.

The orchestral score includes a number of recurring thematic ideas. Two prominent brass themes regularly evoke a sense of awe at the ominous (or potentially ominous) power of the ghosts and ghostly occurrences. The first involves a melody that leaps before descending by a semitone, highlighting the tritone interval (the so-called 'Devil's interval'). The second motif involves loud dissonant brass chords with whole-tone melodic movement on top of the chords (and sometimes on the bottom in contrary motion). The two-note whole-tone sequence is often extended into a three-note (or longer) sequence. A list of some of the scenes (in order) that are supported by either or both of these brass themes and their variants provides a sense of how these elements are utilized within the film:

- Opening scene: a view of stone lion statues [00:00:34]
- The ghostbusters encounter ectoplasmic residue in the library [00:08:54]
- Library cards scatter spontaneously [00:01:53]
- View of haunted apartment building and animal statues [00:16:05]
- Overhead shot of apartment building [00:16:10]
- A dark night, lightning flashes above apartment building [00:46:41]
- Dana levitates [00:56:04]
- Dana wakes; ghosts explode out of apartment [01:07:17] with explosion at [01:07:39]
- Looking up at apartment building [01:16:45]
- Dana and Louis appear on the damaged apartment building roof [01:19:08]
- The giant marshmallow man is destroyed [01:30:11]

Another prominent recurring theme is used as a type of ghostbusters group theme. It is typically associated with lighthearted and/or humorous moments involving the team, as opposed to tense scenes or action scenes. The theme is characterized by a simple, on-beat bass line (typically a tuba part, as in many march-style brass band arrangements) together with a rising line that represents a 'classical' version of a standard minor blues accompaniment riff. The theme evolves in a gradual and subtle way. It is first heard with just a hint of the blues riff idea when the ghostbusters arrive at the library and is subsequently presented in various tempos and as either a major or a minor blues idea – depending on the nature of the particular scene. A list of scenes (below) that use this theme and its variants show how this musical element supports another side of the movie.

- The ghostbusters arrive at the library [00:06:24]
- The ghostbusters re-group after first ghost encounter [00:11:55]
- The ghostbusters come out of the bank with a business loan [00:14:37]
- The ghostbusters decide to rent a dilapidated apartment for use as headquarters [00:15:54]
- The ghostbusters' van arrives at headquarters [00:19:40]
- Dana agrees to go back to apartment with ghostbuster Peter Venkman [00:22:57]
- Venkman goes to check fridge where Dana had seen the 'beast'[7] [00:25:01]
- The ghostbusters patrol corridors looking for green ghost [00:31:01]
- The new ghostbuster recruit is handed a ghost trap [00:40:44]
- Police and crowds gather outside the apartment building after the monster chases Louis [00:52:50]
- Ghostbusters climb the steps of damaged apartment [01:18:43]

Lush, 'romantic' orchestral themes also appear several times in the movie to underscore actual or potential romance between lead characters. For example, Venkman's interest in Dana is musically foreshadowed by a sweet, cello melody (supported by gentle rhythmic backing on woodwinds) that is heard when Dana appears in the movie for the first time (getting out of a taxi). Romantic music is also used later in the film when Dana comes out of a rehearsal and sees Venkman in the street. Romantic music is also used when Dana and Louis (both now 'possessed') meet on top of the damaged apartment building. The use of the romance theme at this point represents a subtle piece of musical irony (in 'normal' life Dana has been constantly rejecting Louis' clumsy romantic overtures) and heightens the comic nature of the new romantic liaison. Romantic orchestral music near the end of the movie hints that a real romance might eventuate between Venkman and Dana.

Bernstein further demonstrates his skill and subtlety as a film composer by integrating several of the themes detailed above on a number of occasions. For example, when Dana hesitantly enters the ghostbusters' headquarters, we hear a number of the orchestral ideas that have been used to this point, presented in the following order: spooky low strings, the romantic cello theme, the comic bluesy theme, more spooky music, more romantic cello. This subtle piece of underscoring provides a brief yet effective aural précis of some of the moods that have been used to this point – suspense, romance, lighthearted humour. It also signals Dana's dual role in the film (a major character within the ghost narrative and reluctant participant in the 'romance' with Venkman) by cleverly superimposing the romantic cello theme over spooky string sounds.

At the end of the movie (after an orchestral 'tour de force' by Bernstein during the final action scenes), a number of themes are subtly integrated and modified. Ondes Martenot glissandi are followed by romantic music for Venkman and Dana, before the rising three-note whole-tone motif transforms into notes 1 2 3 4 of the major scale as Dana escapes from the monster shell. The melody then morphs into a major key romance theme, with a little bit of the bluesy theme added (in the major) before the *Ghostbusters* theme song is reprised.

c. Songs and popular music sequences

While Bernstein's score was commissioned and developed early in the production, the production of a theme song was a less orderly and, indeed, vexatious process. The final choice of Ray Parker Junior's submission – which went on to become a crucial signature and marketing hook for the film (see below) – arose late in the production after a substantial number of compositions had been considered. In 1984 Parker was an accomplished and commercially 'hot' performer who had achieved singles and album chart success with his late 1970s/early 1980s band Raydio. Parker emerged as a guitarist in the late 1960s working as a session musician for Holland-Dozier-Holland productions before working with Stevie Wonder, on his albums *Talking Book* (1972) and *Innervisions* (1973), and with Barry White's Love Unlimited Orchestra in the mid-1970s. His work as a songwriter, musician and producer combined Tamla Motown and rock-pop sensibilities with a strong funk underpinning.

Parker has recalled that he produced the song in 48 hours when Aykroyd was desperate to complete the film's score. Due to time pressures Parker produced the track at his home studio, playing almost all the instruments and using his girlfriend and her friends to provide the song's distinct shouted chorus. Citing the awkward nature of "Ghost-busters" as a sung refrain as a problem for previous songwriters (*WGN Morning News* – 9 October 2008),[8] he settled on the shouted chorus as a solution to the problem after seeing the *Ghostbusters* TV ad featured in the film and conceiving the song as a similarly functional promotional piece.

Bearing the hallmarks of its short gestation, 'Ghostbusters' is simple, repetitive and spontaneous-sounding. It has an infectious, joyous, minimally arranged quality. The song opens with an up-tempo, driving bass riff (set very high in the mix) associated with a relentless, Motown-style, pop-gospel chord pattern (I ♭VII IV). As has been widely noted, its main riff bears a striking resemblance to the repeated riff underpinning the song 'I Want a New Drug' by Huey Lewis and the News (1984); and Parker also uses a brief, rapid bass glissando at the beginning of his song in an almost identical manner to the way Lewis uses a guitar glissando. During 1984–85 Lewis brought a plagiarism suit against Parker, with the parties eventually reaching an out-of-court settlement.

Parker's vocals have an appealing, irreverent, tongue-in-cheek quality that sets the perfect tone for the film – resonating with the cheeky, subtle humour that pervades the movie. (Indeed, it's possible to imagine that if the irreverent, comically sleazy Peter Venkman character was a singer he might articulate a song in this manner.) The shouted vocal hook ("Ghostbusters!") is the ultimate 'join-in' idea. Fitzgerald (2007: 110) notes the presence of short chorus hooks consisting of "few memorable catchwords" in Motown's 1960s gospel-based pop songs, and Parker seems to have learned the Motown lessons well. One doesn't need to be able to sing to participate in the "Ghostbusters" hook, and Parker goes so far as to divide his memorable catchwords into a question-answer format that only requires a one-word response (Q: "Who ya gonna call?" A: "Ghostbusters").

Other black pop influences include the repeated I ♭VII IV gospel-style chord progression, as well as blues-influenced vocals and keyboard/synthesizer riffs. The first of these keyboard/synthesizer riffs highlights the major third, while the second highlights the minor or flattened third (the latter riff also articulates a catchy cross-rhythmic, 'three-against-four' hook idea). The song arrangement emphasizes the appealing hybrid nature of the musical arrangement, with 1980s-style production elements (such as synth bass and keyboards, 'fat' drum machine sounds, a highly processed lead guitar) allied to a heavy Motown-style gospel-pop groove (with some funky elements) built around a repeated chord vamp. The prominent synthetic sounds in the song also provide an effective aural connection with the synthesizer sounds used throughout the orchestral underscore.

Buoyed by its lively and humorous promotional video (discussed below) the song achieved high radio rotation and reached the Number 1 position in the *Billboard* singles charts during 1984 and also scored high chart positions in the UK, France, Canada and Netherlands. Recognition of its success – both within the film text and, externally, as a promotional vehicle – resulted in its nomination for an Academy Award for Best Original Song (which was eventually awarded to Stevie Wonder for 'I Just Called to Say I Love You' from another hit comedy, Gene Wilder's *The Woman in Red* (also 1984)).

d. Other pop rock songs

A number of other pop songs and instrumentals are used in the score. The first of these, 'Cleanin' Up the Town' (Bus Boys 1983, written by Brian O'Neal), is a 1950s-style rock'n'roll song. The song's instrumental groove is heard as the ghostbusters attempt to capture the library ghost, only to have it transform into a bestial creature that chases them out of the library building. The music is a loud, fast, 12-bar blues shuffle with heavy bass and drums and a prominent acoustic piano riff, and this frenzied groove provides a perfect accompaniment to the (supposedly 'heroic') ghostbusters' comical flight from danger. The sudden appearance of this music parallels the earlier unexpected emergence of the *Ghostbusters* theme song. In both instances, popular music provides effective, lighthearted relief from the serious orchestral score, and is used to draw attention to the comic nature of the movie.

'Cleanin' Up the Town' reappears later in the film, again in association with frenzied activity by the ghostbusters. On this occasion, they spring into action after their secretary announces the first paying client by shouting "We got one!" The song now includes vocals and the lyric theme has obvious resonance with the ghostbusters' line of work. The music continues as a low-volume instrumental as the ghostbusters enter the hotel building where the ghostly activity has been reported. It is still present under the initial dialogue with the hotel manager, but fades to silence to leave the ongoing dialogue exposed.

1980s 'synth pop' is also used at times to lighten the mood and/or act as (1980s-style) aural backdrop (rather than as an action-enhancing or narrative-enhancing element). For example, when the ghostbusters arrive back at their headquarters and toast their first paying customer, a brief section of the 1980s UK pop song 'In the Name of Love' (Thompson Twins 1982, written by Tom Bailey) is heard. When the ghostbusters are shown driving after a discussion about the idea of Judgment Day, they choose synth pop on the car radio to lighten their mood.

In the latter part of the movie, 1980s-style pop/rock music also plays an important role in underscoring action scenes. Accompanying images of explosions and escaping ghosts is the sound of loud, studio-enhanced rock drums and bass, plus distorted vocals singing "I believe it's magic" from the song 'Magic' (Mick Smiley 1984). The drums and bass groove continues as ghosts appear around the city, with dissonant melodies and chords added to heighten the dramatic intensity. When the ghostbusters arrive at the mayor's office we hear the instrumental groove from the song 'Savin' the Day' (Alessi Brothers 1984, written by Bobby Alessi). The rising three-tone chord progression used in this song (written for the movie) appears to be intentionally integrated with the rising three-note orchestral theme discussed earlier in this chapter. The instrumental groove, featuring heavy bass and drum machine sounds and a repeated, syncopated rhythmic riff, is heard as the army mobilizes and the ghostbusters travel around the city, cheered on by adoring crowds. This funky, synth-pop funk song incorporates brief interjections of the lyrics "danger signs" – another example of lyrics with an obvious connection to the surrounding action. The syncopated rhythmic idea makes a re-appearance as the ghostbusters emerge from post-earthquake rubble.

Ghostbusters: the music video

Along with its function within the score, the theme song was a major marketing element for the film in its own right. Its international success in singles charts and associated radio airplay promoted the *Ghostbusters* title and product image in the media and the single and film were also cross-promoted by the high rotation afforded to its music video. At the time of the film's release (1984), music video was enjoying a major expansion as a television form, particularly with the rise of the MTV channel in the United States. Launched in August 1981, MTV rapidly gained an audience for a schedule of wall-to-wall music videos and inspired HBO to launch a short programme of music videos – entitled *Video Jukebox* – in the same year, with NBC launching its music video showcase, *Friday Night Videos*, in 1983.

While programming was initially constrained by the limited number of video clips produced by recording companies, the popularity of the services with the music industry's target audience – youth – encouraged both a proliferation of material and a competition for impact, reflected in increased experimentation in style and an escalation of production budgets. A number of artists were so successfully promoted through the medium that they achieved a distinct market edge as 'music video artists' – Adam Ant, The Cars and Duran Duran being three leading examples.[9] Music video also allowed African-American artists such as Michael Jackson the opportunity to break into mainstream pop/rock markets through 'breakout' videos such as 'Billie Jean' (1983) and, most significantly for Jackson, MTV and music video in general, by John Landis's 14 minute-long music video 'featurette' for Michael Jackson's single 'Thriller'. While 'Thriller' has been extensively discussed elsewhere,[10] the most pertinent aspects of the video for this chapter are its combination of horror elements (principally, zombies), comedy and dance music. Indeed, the music video pre-dated and to some extent anticipated the style and feel of *Ghostbusters* (the film and video); its success identifying a similar niche for Aykroyd and Reitman's product, and a similar context for the film's own central rock-funk track.[11]

The advantage for Reitman in producing the *Ghostbusters* music video was that, unlike Landis's production (which was touted in contemporary publicity as costing US$1 million to produce but actually cost closer to US$500,000),[12] a substantial proportion of its production costs (and activity) was absorbed into the overall film budget. Likewise, a significant proportion of its visual sequences were directly sourced from the film. Similarly to the 'Thriller' video, which used the device of the Jackson character scaring his sweetheart (model Ola Ray), the *Ghostbusters* video opens with a young women (actress Cindy Harrell) being spooked by a ghostly Ray Parker Junior in a haunted house; and, in a further echo, the video concludes with a sequence of Parker and key cast members (in role) dancing in Manhattan.

The video combines various elements:

- sequences from the film
- alternative footage from the film
- sequences of the cast of the film dancing to the theme song
- sequences of the performer (Parker) miming to the theme song
- sequences of the cast and Parker together dancing to the theme song
- insert shots of celebrities not associated with the film miming the shouted word 'Ghostbusters' from its chorus line

The latter aspect merits comment. The high-profile friends co-opted by Aykroyd and Reitman included comedians associated with *Saturday Night Live* (Chevy Chase, John Candy and Danny DeVito), actresses Teri Garr and Melissa Gilbert and singer Carly Simon. Their presence effectively provided a sustained celebrity endorsement of the film that associated it with the hit TV show (an aspect reinforced by various *Ghostbusters*-linked sketches and allusions on the show in 1984). The video's varied and effectively edited footage resulted in it attaining Number 1 music video status on MTV in mid-1984 and has led to its regular inclusion in 1980s and/or 'classic' music video programming slots. The video thereby served as both a promotion for Parker's single and for the film itself, functioning as a free three and a half minute advert for the film amidst the main sequences of music video show programming, blurring the lines between the two.

The relationship between these specific components can be summarized as follows

Core commodity: the film

- - -

Derivative commodity: the theme song (released as a single and as a track on the soundtrack album)

[*Function*: promotes the film, Ray Parker Junior's career and the soundtrack album]

- - -

Promotional artefact: the music video

[*Function:* promotes the film, the single, Ray Parker Junior's career and the soundtrack album][13]

This type of textual and functional relationship has clear antecedence in commercial cinema (and, before that, theatre), in that sheet music product was often marketed in association with films during the pre-synch-sound era, with cover artwork identifying the 'tie-in'. During premiere runs at large metropolitan theatre audiences were often encouraged to purchase and sing along to the sheet music for songs by devices such as their lyrics being projected on a blank screen accompanied by organ (or other instrumental) accompaniment. Indeed, short film sequences were specifically shot to enhance the mood of such pre-screening sing-alongs in the 1920s, providing a direct forerunner of the music video form that emerged in the mid-1970s.

In terms of promotional pop song tie-ins to movie releases, one of the most successful (and enduring) has been the series of title songs to James Bond films performed by popular music artists from the early 1960s to present. In some instances, these have provided key career moments for artists (such as Shirley Bassey, performer of *Goldfinger*'s theme in 1964) and in general have resulted in cross-promotional boosts for established performers (such as Paul McCartney, who wrote and performed the *Live and Let Die* theme in 1973). The early-mid-1980s saw a further development of the association between film, theme song and artist that drew on the rise of MTV as a medium and the cross-promotional possibilities offered. While *Ghostbusters* remains the most commercially successful film/single/music video 'package' of the period, a number of other 1984 film releases featured hit songs promoted by videos that included sequences from their feature films, such as the Pointer Sisters' 'Neutron Dance' from the soundtrack of *Beverly Hills Cop* (Martin Brest, 1984) and the title track to Steve Barron's film *Electric Dreams*, written by disco producer Giorgio Moroder and sung by Human League vocalist Phil Oakey. Demonstrating an even greater integration of core and promotional texts, Prince's film *Purple Rain* proved the 9th most successful film at the US box office in 1984, with the *Ghostbusters* theme displacing its hit single 'When Doves Cry' from the Number 1 slot in the *Billboard* charts in August 1984.

Signature blend and parody

As discussed above, the film's distinctive and effective mix of musical modes sonically emphasizes and sustains its disparate elements and is now an innate signature element of the *Ghostbusters* commodity that the public has been familiarized with through sustained exposure. Indeed, so strong is this musical chain of attractions that the film's iconography and narrative can readily bear significant re-inflection, at least when anchored by close replication of its key sonic elements. One notable recent 're-vision' and re-inflection of the property is *Nut Busters* (2003, Cash Markman).[14] The film is what is often referred to as a 'porn parody', in which elements of the characterization, setting and iconography of the original are utilized as the frame for a series of sexual interactions between a cast (loosely) in role as the original characters. Like any other film productions, these vary in budget, ambition and competence of execution. The *Ghostbusters* porn parody emanates from a 'high-end' porn production company entitled Muffia[15] and the company website summarizes the film's plot as follows:

> *Gizz Clortho aka Keymaster of Goozer in a possessed state finds his way to the rooftop where Zuul the Gate Keeper is waiting for him. She lifts up her dress and bends over, he rips her clothes off and begins to follow through with his destiny. The Nut Busters then walk onto the roof and fire their beams at Goozer who attempts to fight them off. Eventually Egoo and Wankman jump on top of Goozer, tearing him apart with their raw sexuality.*[16]

Aside from the significant substitution of the male ghostbusters with a trio of young women, and their use of 'raw sexuality' to quell 'Goozer' when the energy beam technology that proves more effective in the original fails, the film retains several key design aspects from the earlier film. The latter include key musical motifs and the production of an audio-visual promo set to the film's reworking of the original theme song. In clear violation of copyright, the music sticks close to the original.

The *Nut Busters* theme is a modified version of Ray Parker Junior's original and mimics many of its prominent elements. Unsurprisingly, given the title of the porn parody, the shouted vocal hook is now "Nut Busters!" (rather than "Ghostbusters!"). The trailer begins with a short, sustained synth melody that resembles the introduction to the original song.[17] As in the original movie, sound design elements are highlighted (beginning with ominous storm sounds) before a drum machine pattern leads to the famous 'Ghostbusters' bass+chords riff. The copy version places the bass line less prominently in the mix, thereby losing some of the distinctiveness of the original sound, and synth brass riffs from the original song are also used in the copy.[18] Sound design elements continue to be prominent as the clip unfolds – for example, 'beastly' noises now function as both ghostly growls and sexual grunts – and, as in the original score, silence is used in the trailer to effectively highlight dialogue. Mimicking the scene in the original when a giant Stay Puft Marshmallow Man rampages through the city, before being blown to smithereens and spraying the team with liquid marshmallow, *Nut Busters* renders this scene as a final 'explosion' (representing the sexual climax). At this point sonic atmos and underscore drop out to ensure that the audience doesn't miss one of the film's key comic punch-lines, when one the three female 'busters remarks, "Jeez, somebody must've jacked off a fucking geyser." The prominence of highly imitative music in the porn-parody emphasizes the centrality of the original film's theme song as a dynamic expression and condensation of its comedy-action format and focus. This aspect allowed easy parodies and extensions of its thematics into other genre areas, such as a series of 1980s TV adverts,[19] a continuing series of video parodies[20] and the humorous tribute scene in Michael Gondry's *Be Kind Rewind* (2008).

Conclusion

Ghostbusters' mixture of supernatural thriller scoring, provided by Bernstein's orchestrations, and up-tempo soul/rock tracks, including its highly promoted title track, plays an important role in setting the genre 'tone' (or, rather, juxtaposed genre 'tones') for the film's particular blend of action, comedy and supernatural science fiction. *Ghostbusters* deftly interlinks and alternates musical elements appropriate to its particular narrative progression and its alternations between comedy, suspense and drama; and it is a measure of the success of the film's soundtrack that the blend of musical elements is so effective that it does not appear incongruous. The significant commercial success of *Ghostbusters* and its ancillary musical and music video product reflect the film's distinctive blended musical score, and the effectiveness of parody texts such as *Nut Busters* relies on the original movie's 'pre-designed' textual subtlety. However, despite its commercial achievements, *Ghostbusters'* model of careful and integrated thematic design and cohesion were largely ignored by subsequent producers – and, indeed, by the *Ghostbusters* team themselves on the film's lacklustre sequel, *Ghostbusters II* (1989).[21] The aural strength of *Ghostbusters* (1984) resides in its successful exploitation and combination of classic Hollywood scoring and accomplished popular music composition and performance (without compromising either element). In this regard, the film's combination of musical styles and sensibilities provides a richer aural palette than the more highly integrated digital orchestral scoring, popular music and sound design elements that have come to dominate contemporary cinema in the years since its release.

Notes

1. Source: http://www.boxofficemojo.com/movies/?id=ghostbusters.htm, accessed August 2009.
2. *The Real Ghostbusters* (re-titled *Slimer! and the Real Ghostbusters* in 1988) and *Extreme Ghostbusters* (1997).
3. Figures provided at http://www.zimbio.com/Ghostbusters/articles/15/Bill+Murray+Dan+Aykroyd+Star+Ghost+Busters, accessed August 2009.

4. The band continued sporadically after Belushi's death in 1982, with a second feature film, *Blues Brothers 2000*, also directed by Landis, being produced in 1998.
5. Both Scott's and Conti's scores were included on a soundtrack CD issued by Varese Sarabande Club in 2007.
6. See Chion (1998) for various discussions of the use of silence in the soundtrack for dramatic effect.
7. This is a clever and subtle use of the theme. The lighthearted theme, rather than the dramatic scary theme, hints that the beast won't be there this time – which proves to be the case.
8. Archived online at http://blog.ghostbusters.net/2008/10/video-ray-parker-jr-talks-ghostbusters-on-the-wgn-morning-news/, accessed August 2009.
9. See Hayward (1991) for a discussion of music video production in this period.
10. See, for instance, Mercer (1986).
11. Jackson's and Parker's musical styles were also similar, as made manifest by the popular 'mash-up' of the *Ghostbusters* theme and Jackson's 'Bad' track – available online at https://www.youtube.com/watch?v=QZ7XOpBHyoI, accessed August 2009.
12. Celizic (2008: online).
13. N.B. The music video was produced as an audio-visual sequence freely provided to broadcasters; later commercial exploitation of the promo on video and (later) DVD compilations was a by-product of its principal function.
14. A distinct single film product not related to the series of eponymous compilation porn films.
15. Also responsible for titles such as *Star Trix: The Next Penetration* (2005).
16. Accessed August 2009.
17. Although the copy version opens with a minor third (rather than minor sixth) leap before moving in semitones.
18. But for some reason the second riff in the copy version uses a major third rather than minor third interval.
19. See http://trailertrasher.com/2009/03/30/the-7-worst-ghostbusters-commercial-parodies/, accessed June 2010.
20. See http://www.funnyordie.com/topic/ghostbusters-parody, accessed June 2010.
21. Scored by Randy Edelman and featuring popular music tracks by Bobby Brown, Run DMC and Glen Frey.

References

Celizic, M. (2008). Director: Funds for 'Thriller' were Tough to Raise. *Todayshow.com*, 29 April 2008, http://www.today.com/id/24314870, accessed October 2009.

Chion, M. (1998). *Audio-Vision: Sound on Screen*. New York: Columbia University Press.

Fitzgerald, J. (2007). 'Black Pop Songwriting 1963–1966: An Analysis of U.S. Top Forty Hits by Cooke, Mayfield, Stevenson, Robinson, and Holland-Dozier-Holland'. *Black Music Research Journal*, 27(2), 97–140.

Hayward, P. (1991). Industrial Light and Magic: Style, Technology and Special Effects in the Music Video and Music Television. In P. Hayward (Ed.), *Culture, Technology and Creativity* (pp. 125-147). London: John Libbey and Co/Arts Council of Great Britain.

Larson, R. (1985). 'Music for Ghostbusters: A Conversation with Elmer Bernstein'. *CinemaScore*, 13(14), 9-11.

Mercer, K. (1986). 'Monster Metaphors: Notes on Michael Jackson's 'Thriller''. *Screen*, 27(1), 26-43. http://dx.doi.org/10.1093/screen/27.1.26

Woodward, B. (1984). *Wired: The Short Life and Fast Times of John Belushi*. London: Faber and Faber.

Jon Fitzgerald is Adjunct Associate Professor in the contemporary music programme at Southern Cross University. He is an experienced performer, composer, recording artist and music academic, and his research interests focus on the musical analysis of popular music.

Philip Hayward is research advisor in Music and Media Arts in the School of Communication at the University of Technology, Sydney. He has written extensively about screen soundtracks and also researches the music cultures of the Amami and Okinawa archipelagoes of southern Japan and is also a member of audio-visual ensemble The Moviolas.

7 Red in Tooth and Lipstick
Music and Sound Design in Lesbian Vampire Killers

Clarice Butkus and Jon Fitzgerald

Introduction

Lesbian Vampire Killers (henceforth *LVK*) combines elements of comedy, horror and action cinema, graphic novel traditions and music video style. Most predominantly, it intertwines two prominent strands of post-war British low-budget populist cinema: gothic horror and comic parody. In particular, *LVK*'s horror directly derives from the work of Hammer Film Productions, which produced a series of low-budget horror films featuring a variety of monstrous entities and enjoyed sustained box office success between the 1950s and 1970s (see Meikle, 2009). *LVK*'s comedy reaches back to the crude thematic satires of the 'Carry On' film series (produced by Peter Rogers and directed by Gerald Thomas), responsible for a number of domestic box office successes (and subsequent TV staples) between 1958 and 1978, including their Hammer Horror parody *Carry On Screaming* (1966). The series' mantle was taken up, albeit with greater subtlety, by the Comic Strip, a team of British comedians[1] which produced several TV series and feature films between 1982 and 2005 parodying various film and TV drama genres (including the horror spoof *Demonella* (1993)). Twinning the two traditions and giving them a contemporary currency through the casting of rising TV comedy duo James Corden and Matthew Home (playing the 'vampire hunters' of the title), enabled the film to both access a familiar UK cinema tradition and appear novel and distinct (in a similar manner to the British comic re-inflection of the zombie movie in Edgar Wright's *Shaun of the Dead* (2004)).

The film's title (and the visual marketing angles it suggested) gave the product an instant promotional edge. As Clayton has emphasized:

> I think it's been the most enjoyable film ever to market. When you've got a title like that, all the marketing people just get hold of it. [Evil Dead director] Sam Raimi was speaking to Rob Lewis at MTV in an interview, and he was talking

about Lesbian Vampire Killers. *He said that if you can't sell that film, you've got no business in the film business ...* (quoted in Anderson, 2009: online)

The marketing angles identified by Raimi were those designed to tap the extensively documented male heterosexual interest in the (mis-)representation of nubile young females engaged in on-screen sexual caresses and congress. As theorists such as Inness (1996) and Williams (2005) have discussed, this interest is predicated on the presentation of 'lesbian spectacle' in carefully coded and promoted ways to appeal to the ostensible sexual tastes and expectations of male viewers. This form of "hetero-lesbianism", as Williams (2005: 206) terms it, has become a staple of the erotic thriller, for example, in popular films from *The Hunger* (Tony Scott, 1983) to *Basic Instinct* (Paul Verhoeven, 1992) and *Wild Things* (John McNaughton, 1998). Beyond representation within the films themselves, the attendant promotion of these aspects often dominates pre-publicity and post-film commentary. Williams remarks, for example, that *Wild Things'* online promotional banter "positively salivates" in its "enthusiasm for prominent key lesbian scenes" (2005: 205).

The enthusiasm for *LVK*'s marketability based on title alone transparently participates in this phenomenon. In fact, the film's promotional vehicles draw upon a key aspect of 'hetero-lesbianism' – the cultural coding of 'lesbian' characters, cuing them as heterosexual actors playing out male fantasy. As Inness notes in reference to popular magazine imagery:

> *Viewers are given a fantasy image of lesbians which is as unrealistic as the image that all lesbians are ugly. Also, using models who look stereotypically heterosexual pretending to be lesbians provides titillation without threat as there is an implicit understanding that these are not 'real' lesbians* (1996: 66).

LVK's DVD artwork and promotional trailer prominently feature the scantily clad figures of the lesbian vampires in highly stereotypical hypersexualized poses most contemporarily associated with softcore pornography and also frequently used in mainstream music videos. The male heterosexual viewers' "titillation without threat" is further underscored by the girls' infantilizing/submissive stances in which they are variously attired in pink gingham dresses and 'schoolgirl' skirts while arching their backs and flaunting childish pouts, pigtails and lollypops. Simultaneously, the contextualization of "hetero-lesbianism" within a vampire story introduces a second thread to these representations, one premised specifically on *intensified* threat and therefore *heightened* sexuality. The depiction of vampiric "female murderousness" (Williams, 2005: 206) adds a predatory carnality, offering blood, conquest and oblivion in addition to the more usual couplings. In addition, the apparently indiscriminating nature of the vampiric females' bloodlust allows for the delirious prospect of male submission to erotic violence, rendered most graphically in

Frances Ford Coppola's rendition of *Dracula* (1992). In a key fantasy sequence, Jonathan Harker (Keanu Reeves) floats in water and is suddenly overwhelmed by Dracula's brides, three bare-breasted vampires who rear up and drag him under to a bloody oblivion.

LVK's clearest antecedence in this regard is the series of lesbian-themed vampire movies produced by Hammer in 1970–72 (*The Vampire Lovers* (Roy Ward Baker, 1970), *Lust for a Vampire* (Jimmy Sangster, 1971) and *Twins of Evil* (John Hough, 1972)), which were scored by regular Hammer house composer Harry Robinson (see Hannan, 2009 for discussion). The dangerous buxom temptresses of these films were a key element of their marketing appeal, with tantalizing production stills displayed in cinema preview windows to raise audience expectations. Working in the early twenty-first century, the marketers of *LVK* updated this approach by linking up with the online and print magazine entity *Total Film* for an extended photo and short interview feature entitled 'Meet the Lesbian Vampires' (Ashurst, 2009), which comprised a series of shots of Silvia Colloca (playing lead vampire Carmilla), Ashley Mulheron (Trudi) and Emer Kenny (Rebecca) posed in skimpy attire on the set of the production. The interview snippets emphasized the 'flirtatious' and 'fun' aspects of shooting the movie and its overall frivolity and also the actresses' familiarity with the genre. Colloca, in particular, demonstrated an interest in vampire fiction that extended to cautioning readers not to confuse her persona and the film's narrative with those offered in Sheridan le Fanu's 1872 novel *Carmilla* (quoted in Ashurst, 2009: online).

The sexualized, and particularly hetero-lesbian, themes of Hammer features and a number of subsequent vampire films have also inspired several other overtly sexual films, such as Seduction Cinema's cycle of films including *Vampire's Seduction* (John Bacchus, 1998), *My Vampire Lover* (George Freeway, 2002) and *Vampire Vixens* (John Bacchus, 2003). One of the more salient features of this material is its low-budget aesthetic, with the vampire theme principally expressed via the use of plastic vampire fangs and fake blood in otherwise more straightforward erotic scenarios. Harder-core renditions of sexualized vampiric interaction include films such *Dark Angels 1* and *2* (Nick Andrews, 2000, 2005) and dedicated websites such as xxxvampiresex.com.

The conventions discussed above fit neatly within stereotypical uses and modes of male heterosexual desire. *LVK*'s comedic trajectory, however, also significantly parodies aspects of traditional masculinity. In narrative terms, the primary male characters are variously presented as incapable of keeping their wives' attentions (as with the Baron), unable to consummate their physical desire (in the case of Fletch) or failing to demonstrate physical bravado (as in Jimmy's attempts to break down doors). The spoof element of *LVK* extends to prop gags including the vampire-vanquishing sabre shaped as a phallus.

Figure 1 Promotional still for film release showing ensemble of lesbian vampires

When the 'sacred' sword is first revealed to Fletch, he is consumed by a burst of laughter so extensive that it reads like commentary on the spoofed sexual representations buttressing the film. Similarly, when the lesbian vampires are killed, semen-like liquid erupts from their bodies in what becomes the ultimate 'anti-climax' to traditional gore. Several shots showcase Fletch covered in the white goo, again in a semi-parody of classic porn convention of the 'cum' shot and inversion of the stereotypical female receiver. Finally, upon Carmilla's vanquishing, the narrative twists the standard convention that frequently casts lesbianism as synonymously vampiric, by revealing that the vampires of Carmilla's tribe remain lesbians once transformed back to non-vampires.

LVK's various comedic elements consist of its frivolous send-up of horror film conventions, the comic byplay between the cast and a series of slapstick gags and visual effects. As discussed below, the score and sound design strongly underpins and extends this humour by giving the film's horror elements a thematic weight and subtlety that the visual elements lack, and by emphasizing the nuances of its comedy.

Score, music and sound

In addition to the clearly discernible British traditions discussed above, Claydon has also cited *Ghostbusters* (Ivan Reitman, 1984) as a significant influence (quoted in Anderson, 2009: online). *Ghostbusters* was part of a burgeoning Hollywood horror-comedy tradition that became prevalent in the 1980s and 1990s. As Carroll notes:

> *the subgenre of the horror-comedy has gained increasing prominence. Movies such as Beetlejuice, a triumph of this tendency, are predicated on getting us to laugh where we might ordinarily scream, or to scream where we might typically laugh, or to alternate between laughing and screaming throughout the duration of the film.* (1999: 145)

Carroll points out that this particular genre blend significantly relies on contextual 'positioning' to signal comedic or horrific intent. In the case of Hollywood horror-comedy of this era, musical cues have frequently been used in novel and prominent ways to negotiate and modulate the audiences' affective responses to variously comical or suspenseful/gory scenarios. *Beetlejuice* (Tim Burton, 1988) features the memorable scene of dinner guests levitating above the table to the sound of Harry Belafonte's 1956 version of 'The Banana Boat Song'. *The Witches of Eastwick* (George Miller, 1987), meanwhile, deployed John Williams' score to amplify a dark carnivalesque atmosphere. In *LVK*, the use of traditional scoring, popular music and hyperstylized sound effects combine to produce a soundscape that most closely mirrors that of *Ghostbusters*.

As discussed by Fitzgerald and Hayward in Chapter 6, *Ghostbusters*' genre mix was substantially enhanced by the employment of veteran Hollywood modernist composer Elmer Bernstein to provide the orchestral scoring. Similarly – and surprisingly for a much lower budgeted production – *LVK* employs the talents of noted British composer Debbie Wiseman to provide its orchestral sequences. Wiseman's prior works include scores for the films *Tom & Viv* (Brian Gilbert, 1994), *Haunted* (Lewis Gilbert, 1995), *Wilde* (Brian Gilbert, 1997) and *Adventures of Arsène Lupin* (Jean-Paul Salome, 2004). In 2009, Wiseman was nominated by the International Film Music Critics Association (IFMCA) for Best Original Score For a Comedy Film for *LVK*. As a low-budget comedy spoof, *LVK* presented quite a different challenge to Wiseman's previous productions. Many critics have commented on the influence of Wiseman's background in the creation of a larger orchestral/choral sound than is usually associated with this type of film. As one reviewer commented:

> *Wiseman's score elevates the proceedings to the level of a gothic epic, with huge music that gives the story a pervasive Hammer-ific power as well as a muted eloquence through Hayley Westenra's intricate, wordless vocalisms.* (Larsen, 2009: online)

As the following paragraphs detail, Wiseman's score includes several key motifs and variations that variously convey fear, suspense and mystery/innocence counter-posed to the comedic sounds and functions of the film.

'Vampire' theme

LVK's score conveys its "Hammerific power" through a key 'vampire' motif that combines elements of horror film sound and the grandeur of an epic fantasy feature. The principal recurring 'vampire' theme of Wiseman's score first appears at the opening title and continues during the introductory back story (about Carmilla the Vampire Queen) that contextualizes the ensuing movie narrative. Throughout the film's underscore, this theme is used as a leitmotif for Queen Carmilla and the lesbian vampires. The vampire music is briefly introduced on glockenspiel (supported by high-strings), before a solo soprano voice becomes predominant in the melody. The pure, high-set, vibrato-free vocal timbre simultaneously conveys a sense of mystery and innocence, while the descending, minor key melody (see Example 1) features prominent semitone movements between the fifth/flat fifth, minor third/major second, and tonic/major seventh. The use of the flat fifth scale degree also imbues the theme with the sound of the tritone (between root and flat fifth) – the so-called 'devil's interval' typical of the horror film genre. As the music unfolds during the opening scene, several new sounds are introduced (including female choir, dramatic French horns and richly-scored orchestral strings) to create more dramatic manifestations of the theme.

Example 1 Main vampire melody

Wiseman's vampire theme is developed extensively throughout the film. In the early phases of the movie the motif is used suggestively, hinting at forthcoming encounters with the lesbian vampires. For example, it reappears [17:20] in the mysterious high soprano voice when the Vicar spots Jimmy in the pub and becomes aware of his association with Carmilla's curse. It is heard again [23:22] on glockenspiel when the boys and girls arrive at the cabin in the forest where they will ultimately encounter the lesbian vampires, and the theme is then presented in extended and modified forms – a technique used increasingly as the story develops. When Jimmy peers at a painting of Carmilla on the wall of the cabin, the loud diegetic dance music on the CD player fades into the background, to be replaced by the vampire theme on strings with modulations and extensions, accompanied by low growling and wind sounds. The vampire theme appears in female voices and strings when Trudy goes missing [31:50] and it continues as the others search for her. As the tension increases, the theme is presented in new variations – for example, accompanied by the first three notes of the minor scale played in an ascending pattern. When the vampires are seen for the first time, feeding on flesh, the theme is played on strings and moves through several key changes.

From this point, Wiseman uses the vampire theme extensively as the vampires make increasingly frequent appearances. She also uses smaller components of the theme to create new recurring motifs. For example, variations of the semitone idea within the vampire melody are used as recurring elements within the underscore. Semitone melodic movement is prominent when the one of the vampires is trapped by the vicar in the shower [40:45]; when Fletch goes into the grave [55:20]; when the vampires are seen after the Vicar's daughter (now a vampire herself) is killed [1:00:03]; and when Jimmy and Lotte's blood mixes after they are trapped by the vampires. Wiseman also cleverly modifies the minor key vampire theme to deviate towards the relative major key when she wishes to create a musical metaphor for victory over the vampires – the 'triumph of good over evil'. For example, the theme morphs into the relative major key when the Vicar and Fletch go into battle against the vampires [1:02:46]; when the vampires see the sword that is ultimately used to destroy them [1:13:55]; and when the vampires are finally vanquished [1:15:03].

The vampire theme is also used as the basis of other musical motifs, such as the 6/8 clarinet theme that appears soon after Jimmy and Fletch arrive in the countryside [11:10]. This theme features both the semitone and tritone idea (see Example 2). When Judi attempts to seduce Jimmy [41:02] after she has been turned into a vampire, the accompanying clarinet theme also incorporates melodic variations of the main vampire theme.

Example 2 New motif based on vampire melody

The 'forces of good and evil'

Wiseman's score is nuanced by musical aspects associated with confrontations between the lesbian vampires and the film's 'avengers'. Minor tonality, ascending minor scale fragments and semitone ideas form the basis of much of the dramatic music that underscores the many chase and fight scenes. As already noted, fragments of the ascending minor scale are used as accompaniment to the vampire theme as the movie begins to develop more tension. For example, after Trudi's scream is heard and she disappears from the cabin, the full orchestra plays a dramatic rhythmic version of the ascending minor scale sequence (see Example 3). When the lesbian vampires attack Fletch, dramatic rising minor ideas are heard on brass. Chase scenes (e.g. 37:10, 1:04:58, 1:09:02) are typically set in a minor key and underscored by elements such as dramatic brass rhythms, French horn swells, rapid string lines, with semitone ideas and rising minor scales providing melodic material.

Example 3 Ascending minor scale motif

A number of musical ideas are connected to the battle between the 'good' forces and the lesbian vampires. When the Vicar first encounters Jimmy in the pub we hear a dramatic crescendo on a dominant seventh flat 9th chord (which contains the sound of the diminished 7th chord in the upper voices). The notes of the chord rise in pitch [17:20], culminating in a dramatic, expectant emphasis on the strongest tension note in the chord (the leading tone). This idea is used again when the Vicar assists Fletch when he fights the lesbian vampire in the shower [45:55]. Staccato chords sung by female choir appear at various times when there is palpable tension in the battle between good and evil – especially in association with appearances of the Vicar (e.g. 52:13). The sudden appearance of 'Amazing Grace' [1.00:56] as the Vicar is preparing for the final battle with the vampires provides a symbolic premonition of the triumph of the anti-vampire forces.

Incongruous and quirky music to support comedy

Incongruous and/or quirky music is used effectively on a number of occasions to accentuate the film's comedy. For example, an uptempo shuffle melody plays on kazoo as the wife of Judi's boyfriend drags her husband inside their house [8:52] when Judi's visit has revealed his adulterous ways. This music continues as the scene shifts to the pub, where Jimmy and Fletch discuss their hiking plan – with kazoo, ukelele and banjo joining in a comical two-beat country groove [9:06]. As Jimmy and Fletch nervously survey the yokels in the country pub, a quirky, organ-grinder-style waltz theme plays softly in the background.

After Judi has been turned into a lesbian vampire and attacks Jimmy in the cabin [41:45], Fletch saves the day by hitting Judi in the head with an axe, before Jimmy finishes the job by splitting her completely in two. This somewhat gruesome scene is considerably lightened through the use of the famous 'can-can' theme (the Galop from Offenbach's *Orpheus in the Underworld*). Similar use of incongruous music (this time a gentle staccato theme) occurs during the scene when Fletch accidentally skewers the (now vampiric) Vicar's daughter [59:21]. When Jimmy and Lotte are tied up awaiting their horrific fate at the hands (teeth!) of the vampires [54:20], the gentle melody that has previously symbolized their romantic connection appears as a comically incongruous counterpoint to their perilous situation.

Using music to contrast with visuals rather than to complement them (as per the more usual approach) is well documented within the literature surrounding screen studies. Tagg (2001: 328) uses the terms "affective disparity" to describe this type of approach, while Kindem and Musburger (2005: 89) use the term "counterpoint" to describe sounds and images that "are aesthetically separate and often contrast with one another."[2]

Romance theme

A gentle major key theme on flute and strings underscores the first hint of a romance between Jimmy and Lotte and recurs in various modified forms as the movie's love theme. For example, it appears again when Jimmy and Lotte are tied up close together by the vampires, and when Jimmy and Lotte kiss after the curse is lifted [1:16:04].

Rock/pop songs

After the atmospheric opening to the movie (with its lush vocal and orchestral underscore) and the two ensuing dialogue scenes without music (Jimmy and Judi's relationship discussion, Fletch's sacking from his clown job), there is a sudden shift to an up-tempo, 1950s-style rock song ('I'm Crying Blood') with an obvious metaphorical connection to the movie's vampire theme. The rock song underscores the appearance of the opening credits, written in old-fashioned fonts and colours. The stark contrast between orchestral-choral film music and early rock music parallels the contrast that worked so successfully in *Ghostbusters*. As in *Ghostbusters*, other rock and pop songs are interspersed throughout *Lesbian Vampire Killers*, providing 'antidotes' to the more traditional film scoring. Like the opening song, 'I'm Crying Blood', the other rock songs have clear literal or metaphorical connections with the movie narrative. Examples include 'Woman' (played loudly when Lotte, Heidi and Anke are first seen by a 'gobsmacked' Jimmy and Fletch) and 'I Like You So Much Better When You're Naked' (playing diegetically on the car radio as the girls sing along on their way to the cabin). 'Feelin' Hot' plays on the CD player as the girls do some sexy dancing in the cabin [24:03], while Showaddywaddy's (1976) cover of Curtis Lee's (1961) hit 'Under the Moon Above' plays as the final movie credits begin to roll [1:17:56]. As numerous authors (e.g. Rodman, 2006; Donnelly, 2005; Coyle, 2005; Tagg and Clarida, 2003) have noted, popular music genres have pervaded contemporary TV and film soundtracks, and the inclusion of rock and pop tracks in *LVK* can also be seen to appeal to what

Donnelly (2005: 135) has described as the 'pop literate' baby-boomer generation – providing the audience with some comfortable, familiar musical associations.

Elements of sound design

As might be expected from a film rooted in the horror genre, wind, thunder, and low growling sounds feature prominently in the sound mix. Their deployment is often 'knowing', acknowledging the audience's familiarity with them in scenes such as the one in which a loud, ominous thunderclap sounds as the visuals pan to a dart throw that will decide the location of Jimmy and Fletch's hiking trip [9:32]. Other elements of sound design derive from different genre contexts. The first occurrence is in the opening scene, when a swishing sound and a metallic clanking complements the sudden appearance of the *Book of Nekros* (in a similar fashion to the teleportation of objects in the opening scene of Roger Vadim's *Barbarella* (1968) (see Hayward, 2010: 109)). Other sound design elements derive from animation traditions. In the scene in which Judi and Jimmy talk about their relationship problems, for instance, Judi makes a number of unexpected, rapid, 'kung fu'-style arm movements, accompanied by sound effects such as short swishes and whip-cracks. This technique becomes a notable visual-sound 'hook' as the movie unfolds, with a variety of characters making fast, unexpected movements accompanied by 'matching' sounds.

Further comic effects are produced when the narrative undercuts expectations that have been cued by sound. One example of the latter occurs when Lotte, Heidi and Anke are first seen casually parading their attractive, scantily-clad bodies, accompanied by the raunchy rock song 'Woman' very high in the sound mix. Suddenly, the song stops to briefly expose the young women's voices very faintly in the mix, before the sound of a swinging pub sign and door slam emphasizes the next situational 'punchline' (Jimmy and Fletch expecting more beautiful girls in the pub but instead finding a group of older, male 'yokels'). The second scene in which Jimmy and Judi discuss their relationship problems deploys another technique, using diegetic sound for disjunctive comic effect. On this occasion, we hear the sound of a couple upstairs making love as Judi and Jimmy attempt to have a serious relationship discussion. The sound of the love-making becomes increasingly louder over time, to the point that it seems comically inappropriate for Jimmy and Judi to continue to ignore it. The happy and enthusiastic love-making is also incongruous, given the obvious tension between Jimmy and Judi.

Conclusion

LVK was conceived as a transparently commercial vehicle that would attract viewership with the promise of delivering hetero-lesbian pleasures and spoofed gore. Although the film was critically panned for its weak narrative and unsubtle comedy, it presents a particularly strong example of how effective music scoring and sound design can elevate and enhance the comedic and dramatic aspects of film narrative. LVK primarily produces its comic effects through the parody and subversion of its main genre reference, Hammer Horror. In order to generate sufficient comic 'traction' on this, the film has to both produce a credible rendition of horror cinema and play off its audio-visual conventions in a manner that audiences will interpret *as* comic. LVK's score delivers efficiently on the first aspect, with a finely crafted orchestral score that deploys many of the musical modernisms inherent to the source genre. The film's comic elements either offset its dramatic horror score with comic on-screen action or else use different musical styles to puncture the Gothic ambience of its narrative and locale. In this, image, narrative, music and sound effects switch audiences in and out of particular genre expectations and moods in a transparent manner. Audiences are invited to go along with the thematic 'ride' of the film's trans-genre 'romp' and its softcore hetero-lesbian eroticism and to recognize and respond to audio-visual jokes that utilize their genre knowledge. On these levels the film delivers admirably and, in doing so, emphasizes that musical craft and invention are no less effective in lightweight genre fare than they are in more overtly serious contexts.

Acknowledgment

Thanks to Philip Hayward for his comments on earlier drafts of this chapter.

Notes

1. Centred on actors Adrian Edmondson, Rick Mayall, Dawn French, Jennifer Saunders, Nigel Planer and Peter Richardson.
2. Tagg and Clarida (2003: 419), for instance, note the effectiveness of the incongruous *Monty Python* theme – which uses a "double anachronism (marching-band music from 1893 for a TV series in 1969 plus the semantic mish-mash of fun and war)."

References

Anderson, M. (2009). Interview: Lesbian Vampire Killers director Phil Claydon. Online at http://www.denofgeek.com/movies/14152/interview-lesbian-vampire-killers-director-phil-claydon, accessed July 2010.

Ashurst, S. (2009). Meet The Lesbian Vampires. *Total Film*, http://www.totalfilm.com/features/meet-the-lesbian-vampires-carmilla, accessed July 2010.

Carroll, N. (1999, Spring). 'Horror and Humor'. *Journal of Aesthetics and Art Criticism*, 57(2), 145–160. http://dx.doi.org/10.2307/432309

Coyle, R. (Ed.) (2005). *Reel Tracks: Australian Feature Film Music and Cultural Identities*. Eastleigh: John Libbey.

Donnelly, K.J. (2005). *The Spectre of Sound: Music in Film and Television*. London: BFI.

Inness, S. (1996). *The Lesbian Menace: Ideology, Identity, and the Representation of Lesbian Life*. Amherst, MA: University of Massachusetts Press.

Kindem, G.A., & Musburger, R. (2005). *Introduction to Media Production: The Path to Digital Media Production*. Boston, MA: Focal Press.

Hannan, M. (2009). Sound and Music in Hammer's Vampire Films. In P. Hayward (Ed.), *Terror Tracks: Music, Sound and Horror Cinema* (pp. 60–74). London: Equinox Press.

Larson, R.D. (2009). New Soundtrax in Review. Soundtrax website, http://www.buysoundtrax.com/larsons_soundtrax-2_25_09.html, accessed 15 May 2015.

Meikle, D. (2009). *A History of Horrors: The Rise and Fall of the House of Hammer*. Lanham, MD: Scarecrow Press.

Rodman, R. (2006). Popular Song as Leitmotiv in 1990s Film. In P. Powrie & R. Stilwell (Eds.), *Changing Tunes: The Use of Pre-existing Music in Film* (pp. 119–136). Aldershot: Ashgate.

Tagg, P. (2001). *Kojak: 50 Seconds of Television Music: Towards the Analysis of Mass Media Music*. New York: Scholars' Press.

Tagg, P., & Clarida, B. (2003). *Ten Little Tunes: Towards a Musicology of the Mass Media*. New York, Montreal: The Mass Media Scholars' Press.

Williams, L.R. (2005). *The Erotic Thriller in Contemporary Cinema*. Bloomington, IN: Indiana University Press.

Jon Fitzgerald is Adjunct Associate Professor in the contemporary music programme at Southern Cross University. He is an experienced performer, composer, recording artist and music academic, and his research interests focus on the musical analysis of popular music.

Clarice Butkus recently completed her Masters Degree in Humanities and Social Thought at New York University. Her research interests include gender studies, media, film and sound and her articles have been published in international refereed journals such as *Media International Australia*, *Science Fiction Film and Television* and *Shima: The International Journal of Research into Island Cultures*.

8 'Be a Clown' and 'Make 'Em Laugh'
Comic Timing, Rhythm, and Donald O'Connor's Face

Jonas Westover

Introduction[1]

On November 21, 2009, the featured guest star on the television show, *Saturday Night Live (SNL)*, was Joseph Gordon-Levitt.[2] The actor, known for his comedic role in the TV series *Third Rock from the Sun* (1996–2001) and, more recently, dramatic roles in such films as *(500) Days of Summer* (Marc Webb, 2009) and *Don Jon* (Gordon-Levitt, 2013), began the traditional opening monologue with a brief comment about his career before leaping into a spirited version of the song 'Make 'Em Laugh'. Citing *Singin' in the Rain* (Stanley Donen, 1952) as a personal favourite film musical, Gordon-Levitt recreated pieces of Donald O'Connor's performance from that film, including several original dance moves and physical gags. At one point, Gordon-Levitt was carried on a beam held by two stage-hands who subsequently dumped him on the ground, while at another he ran up walls before performing an aerial somersault. Of course, the actor incorporated several physical jokes, such as getting slapped when he told a member of the cast how shocked he was to be doing the number for the show. He even used a hybrid of the original and the new gags by combining the brick wall crash with another punch in the face. The monologue was all the more impressive since Gordon-Levitt was performing the song live, with the *SNL* band providing his musical accompaniment. He performed all of the physical feats and still managed to have enough breath to belt out the final lines of the song's big finish. This version of the scene was both an homage and an exciting new performance, and the young actor forever put his own stamp on the classic song.

'Make 'Em Laugh' and its musical 'fraternal twin', 'Be A Clown', have both received a number of treatments over the years in film, television, and stage performances. Just what is it about these songs that opens the door for new performers and creative teams and that allows for repeated attention? Just why are they as popular as they are? Why do they work so well as 'comic' songs, both for singers and for dancers? This chapter deals specifically with the construction of humour for these two songs in their original forms as part of the MGM film musical tradition; 'Be A Clown' is featured twice in *The Pirate* (Vincente Minnelli, 1948) and 'Make 'Em Laugh' is from *Singin' in the Rain*. Before considering the songs in context, I will analyse the songs to show exactly the textual, topical, and musical elements in which they relate to one another. Combining analyses of the filmic, musical and performance aspects of the film, this chapter hopes to extract just why the songs and their performances work as effectively as they do. Part of the reason that these scenes are so interesting is because of the different types of clowns that are used, but each of the above elements are also considered.

Song vs. song

The noted similarities between 'Be A Clown' and 'Make 'Em Laugh' are not based on new observations; according to stories told by Stanley Donen, the director of *Singin' in the Rain*, every person on the set of the 1952 musical recognized that the latter song was a direct rip-off of the original. *The Pirate* was only four years old at that point, and even though it was not a box-office smash, it was still well-known. 'Be A Clown', in particular, was engineered to be the most important song in *The Pirate* since it is heard twice, with both iterations taking place close to the end of the film. Donen's story about 'Make 'Em Laugh' is reported in numerous places, including by director Irwin Winkler in the commentary for *De-lovely* (Irving Winkler, 2004). As Donen himself describes the experience:

> We were shooting the picture and needed a number for when Donald tries to cheer Gene up. Now, Arthur [Freed] hadn't written a song in God knows how long, and Gene and I went to him and said, 'Arthur, we've been through your catalog and there's nothing that will work for this spot. Would you consider writing a new song for us?' And Arthur said, 'Herb [Brown] and I would love to write a new song together. What kind of a song do you want?' 'Well,' we said, 'there was a song that Gene did in The Pirate that would fit perfectly ... And Arthur said, 'You want a song like [that]? Herb and I will write you a song like [that].' So they certainly did that! Gene and I weren't about to say to Arthur Freed, 'Haven't you gotten a little too close?' And Cole Porter, to the day he died, never said a word to Arthur ... He just never said anything. (quoted in Silverman, 1996: 158–159)

So just how similar are the two songs? The best way to judge the degree of likeness is to juxtapose them. Traditional musical analysis considers the melodic line and the harmony, and these two components of a popular song are certainly important to determining how alike two songs might be. However, with these songs, as in the case of most popular music, the lyrics (including the syntax and meaning) need to be brought into play as well. This consideration allows for the broadest possible connections between the songs, opening up space for meaning in a variety of ways that enriches both analytic approaches.

As with most popular songs, it is difficult to point to an *urtext* version of a tune; usually a recorded (or filmed) version is substantially different from what might appear in print, especially in the sheet music that is published, and 'Be A Clown' is no exception to this. One could easily say that there is no 'definitive' version of any showtune, since these numbers were subject to revision whether they were performed on stage or on screen. However, for the sake of expediency, I will use the sheet music for the songs discussed here as a basis for consideration and will comment on the changes in the filmed versions when I discuss these.[3]

The most significant difference between the two songs can be found in the overall structure of the two tunes. Put in the most simple of terms, 'Be A Clown' includes an opening introduction and a verse, whereas 'Make 'Em Laugh' is a single extended chorus without any extraneous additions. This important difference may seem small, but in fact it has significant ramifications for the overall effectiveness of the songs when placed in a film context. Figure 1 shows the structure of 'Be A Clown' and Figure 2 shows 'Make 'Em Laugh'.

Time Signature:	'Cut' time (2/4)		
Tempo:	"Brightly (One Step)"		
Section:	Introduction	Verse	Chorus
Measures:	4	16	40
Phrase:		a b a c	A B A' C D
Key:	C Major	C Major	C Major – C Major

Figure 1 'Be A Clown' song form

Time Signature:	'Cut' time (2/4)
Tempo:	"Brightly"
Section:	Chorus
Measures:	40
Phrase:	A B A C D
Key:	F Major – F Major

Figure 2 'Make 'Em Laugh' song form

It is clear, even when looking at the basic elements, that enough features from 'Be A Clown' transfer to 'Make 'Em Laugh' for there to be a remarkable similarity between songs. The time signatures, the overall chorus lengths, and even the tempi (the uncommon marking, "brightly") find their way from the earlier song into the structure of the next. That the keys are different hardly matters; the key would have been changed to fit the performer's voice anyway, and, as later analysis demonstrates, the keys of the sheet music do not reflect the keys that are heard in the filmed versions. The important issue, at least at this level, is that there is virtually no harmonic motion from the beginning of the chorus to the end of either song – a musical stasis that allows the performer to concentrate on other things rather than on dramatic vocal acrobatics.

At a more detailed level – that of the musical phrase – the same kind of relationship prevails. In both cases, the 40 measures of the chorus are made up of five eight-bar phrases (8+8+8+8+8). The first and third phrases are in an A B A pattern, with the third phrase returning to the original material, but using a different ending. As Example 1 demonstrates, phrase 1 in both songs states the essential musical motive in the first two measures. In 'Be A Clown', the second phrase balances out the first using the same melodic motive, returning to the original idea for the final, symmetrical third section. 'Make 'Em Laugh', however, inserts new melodic material in the second phrase, but, like the previous song, it returns to the original idea for the third. The fourth phrase in each song initiates new material, acting as a bridge. It is slightly surprising that the final phrase would begin with the music that opened the previous phrase, suggesting the songs might go on for another two phrases to provide equal balance to the opening material. However, as is clear in Example 2, midway through the last section, the opening musical motive returns and repeats, looping the chorus in on itself. Thus, each song displays a similar unfolding based on relative phrase structures. The only significant difference lies in the musical material used to build the second phrase, and it is not particularly surprising that Porter's music would be more efficient in the development of less material than Brown's music exhibits.

On the level of structure, then, 'Be A Clown' and 'Make 'Em Laugh' appear to be remarkably similar. The true test of musical 'theft' in this case comes down to the melody, which is, after all, the heart of the Tin Pan Alley song. I have included the melody lines for the two songs side-by-side in Examples 1 and 2 so that they may be more easily compared.

Example 1 Both songs, phrases 1–3: melody lines[4]

Example 2 Both songs, phrases 4–5: melody lines

The melodic connections between the two songs are indeed striking, and indeed the first phrase in each number of the tune is almost identical. Kevin Kline astutely suggests in the commentary to *De-lovely* that it is the "same ratio of words to notes and the same idea; it's the same song." He is almost correct. The opening of 'Be A Clown' uses a pattern of two quarter notes ascending that leads to a 'destination' note where the melody lingers. Although 'Make 'Em Laugh' alters the rhythmic pattern only slightly, the use of a held 'destination' note is conspicuously copied from the former song.[5] Example 1 demonstrates that both songs use four destinations in the first phrase; between the two songs, three of these notes are exactly the same, including – most importantly – the first and the last held notes (E in both cases).

The ascent to the E in 'Be A Clown' is manipulated only slightly for the same effect in 'Make 'Em Laugh'. The music uses a passing tone that dips down and then returns to the E. Essentially, Brown takes the melodic idea and simply twists it slightly upside down to become something 'original'. This is the way in which Brown created something 'new' from the old song – he repeatedly took the melody and gently reshaped it, rarely deviating too far from the model provided him by Porter. In Example 2, this is how the melody in 'Be A Clown' becomes the music for 'Make 'Em Laugh'. Brown takes the melodic ingredient of a major third – used in the original between the first and last notes of the measure (see m. 45, for example) – and merely repeats the lower note. As Porter's music rises by half steps, so does Brown's, and they both end with the leap of a third to the upper note. The melodic contour between the two songs is too similar to be ignored; the result is a musical line in 'Make 'Em Laugh' that *is just similar enough* to its source material to represent a stolen musical idea. In no place is this more evident than the ending of 'Make 'Em Laugh', where the opening melodic idea returns and is rhythmically repeated three times – exactly the way 'Be A Clown' ends.

Lyrically, this powerful inheritance is maintained between the older and newer songs. At the outset, the text states the main concept of the song – the words that will become the very title of each tune – and then comments on that notion. Porter rhymes "clown" with itself in the first two lines, and Freed replicates this for 'Make 'Em Laugh.' The lyrics that follow in 'Be A Clown' are full of several inner relationships made up of alliteration (last/laugh, folks/face, doctor/dread, dentist/dead) and inner rhymes (hand/stand), all the while making use of a standard couplet rhyme scheme. Freed's rhyme scheme in 'Make 'Em Laugh' is similar, but his lyrics lack the subtle touch of Porter (although "honkytonk monkeyshines" stands out as especially creative). The third and fourth phrases expand the original idea in each song, while the fifth, much like it does musically, ends with the opening words. The texts for the opening choruses of the two songs demonstrate this pattern:

'Be A Clown' Chorus 1

1st phrase:	*Be a clown, be a clown*
	All the world loves a clown,
2nd phrase:	*Act the fool, play the calf,*
	And you'll always have the last laugh.
3rd phrase:	*Wear the cap and the bells,*
	And you'll rate with all the great swells.

4th phrase:	*If you become a doctor folks will face you with dread,*
	If you become a dentist they'll be glad when you're dead,
5th phrase:	*You'll get a bigger hand if you can stand on your head,*
	Be a clown, be a clown, be a clown.

'Make 'Em Laugh' Chorus 1

1st phrase:	*Make 'em laugh, make 'em laugh*
	Don't you know ev'ryone wants to laugh
2nd phrase:	*My dad said, "Be an actor, my son,*
	But be a comical one!"
3rd phrase:	*They'll be standing in lines*
	For those old honkytonk monkeyshines.
4th phrase:	*Oh, you could study Shakespeare and be quite elite*
	And you could charm the critics and have nothing to eat.
5th phrase:	*Just slip on a banana peel, the world's at your feet.*
	Make 'em laugh, make 'em laugh, make 'em laugh!

While there are some important differences between the two songs, both textually and musically, this analysis shows that there is no doubt that the two songs are intimately related. Just how Freed and Brown felt they could get away with taking a famous song and slightly twisting the melodic contour is certainly a mystery that will have to remain with the two of them. As Donen's comments above suggests, it was readily apparent then and it remains so today that Porter's song was the victim of musical larceny. This does not mean that the two songs are identical. The music in the second phrase of 'Make 'Em Laugh' and the melody in the fourth provides some new material that does alter the song, but not in a substantial way. After all, mimicking an older tune by copying the overall form in perfect detail does not suggest Freed and Brown were interested in developing something that was unique.

What seems so surprising, in the context of *Singin' in the Rain*, is why they did not simply use the older song in the first place. It is true that the rest of the songs in the film were by Freed and Brown, and it may simply be that to use a Porter tune may have broken the continuity of this general musical layout. However, the solution seen here was certainly not the best the songwriting team could have accomplished. While we may not know the answer to 'why', it is certainly fortunate that Donald O'Connor was on hand to perform the 'new' number – it was in his hands that the song gained its own voice and character and became immortalized as one of the most memorable performances in *Singin' in the Rain*.

'Be A Clown' in *The Pirate*

Cole Porter's interest in clowns began when he was a child in his hometown of Peru, Indiana. His boyhood friend, Tommy Hendricks, writes about their shared interest in the goings-on of the performers, including their practice routines.[6] Porter may also been aware of some of the clowns of the past, especially from the *commedia dell'arte* traditions. Since Porter lived in Venice for many years, it is likely that he gained at least a passing visual familiarity with the famous masks of the *commedia* players, and there is a strong probability that he knew the characters in more detail.[7]

Although each figure from this tradition was present in the culture of Porter's time, one of the most popular was Pierrot the clown. Appearing in many stage musicals of the 1910s – especially revues, such as *The Passing Show of 1914* – Pierrot was a prominent part of the theatrical milieu of early musical theatre, a world of which Porter also was a part.[8] Figure 3 shows a set of men all dressed for a 'Pierrot Party', each wearing a traditional outfit for the persona.

Even though there are several variations on the character's appearance over time, the 'dotted' hat, pants and sleeves are common elements of this costume, as are the spots on the cheeks. Usually a simple, loose-fitting white tunic and pants are also included, though these are not always present. Known for his 'dopey', wide-eyed personality, Pierrot is a clown that is not particularly comic, but rather an innocent caught up in the schemes of others. It is, in fact, Pierrot who is the model for Gene Kelly in the first performance of 'Be A Clown' in *The Pirate*. Figure 4 demonstrates this as Kelly poses with the Nicholas brothers, his partners for the dance. We shall return to the importance of these costumes shortly.

Recording of the Cole Porter songs for *The Pirate* began in late 1946 and filming commenced on 17 February 1947.[11] It was not released until 1948, and throughout the preparations for the movie there were a number of problems with the script and with the creative team. For example, the director, Vincente Minnelli, was just beginning to enter into a difficult period with his wife, Judy Garland, one of the stars of the film. The commentary by John Fricke on the recent DVD release and the short 'making-of' featurette on the same disc clearly document the problems with the film's creation, which are more complicated than can be discussed here.[12] However, in the shuffle of changes that the picture went through, it is important that Kelly himself requested a light, happy song while Porter was creating the score.[13] Patricia Ward Kelly, Gene's widow, says that Kelly had lunch with Porter and described what he was looking for to the composer; the next day, apparently, Porter called up with the completed song.[14] The result, 'Be A Clown', was so popular with the creative team after they filmed the first version (with the Nicholas brothers) that, based on a suggestion by Roger Edens, they decided to reprise the song

Figure 3 Generic Pierrot costumes[9]

at the end, this time featuring the film's two leads. The two versions of the song are significantly different from each other, but this was not by accident. A careful analysis of 'Be A Clown' in both its forms demonstrates that these two performances achieve radically different goals, resulting in the depiction of two separate types of clowns.

The first iteration of 'Be A Clown' comes near the climax of the film, when Kelly's character Serafin has been condemned to die for being the dread pirate, Macoco. Of course, he is truly a strolling performer and is not guilty of the pirate's deeds, but he knows who the real culprit is (the mayor) and wants to reveal him. To this end, Serafin uses 'Be A Clown' as a means to delay his own death and to allow him to create a trap for the real Macoco, which he does. Once the villain is identified, Serafin is then able to connect with the beautiful Manuela, whom he has courted throughout the movie. Jane Feuer astutely points out that the final version of 'Be A Clown', where the two stars pair up in performance, is akin to the weddings that complete so many other musicals. She suggests that this new union between Kelly and Garland is:

Figure 4 Kelly and the Nicholas Brothers as clowns[10]

> the ultimate celebration of illusionism. Now the resolution of the plot had demonstrated the triumph of the theatrical imagination released in Manuela by Serafin over the antiquated social system of the town. The 'fantasy' kingdom of the town in which Manuela dreams of the pirate Macoco becomes the 'reality' from which Manuela is liberated, first by journeying to the port city where she encounters Serafin; second by the unleashing of the performer within herself under hypnosis; finally, by the onstage revelation of the real Macoco ... Forms of illusionism which can only lead to frustration – Manuela's unrequited longing for Macoco ... are replaced by theatrical illusionism. The theatre too is a phantom form, but one which is unifying, binding and achievable, and which liberates the dreamer from the constraints of day-dreaming.[15]

Serafin's actions are all about liberation, for himself and for his love interest. He must somehow escape his own hanging, and he does so first by making fun of the noose itself, and then by performing his way out of his troubles. For Manuela, he offers a new universe of experience, totally apart from the world she had known before, as Feuer mentions. For Rick Altman, these "make-believe" elements are enough to place it in the category of the "fairy-tale" musical, where illusion is prized above all else.[16] However, I suggest both forms of 'Be A Clown' are not concerned with illusion as much as they are with alternate reality – one where the truth can be depicted, even obliquely. After all, the number is the double finale of the musical wherein truth is finally embraced by both the characters of the plot and the audience watching the film; the song itself represents an end to the charade Serafin and Manuela have maintained throughout – the former is set free from his death sentence and the latter from a life of cruelty at the hands of the *real* Macoco. This freedom allows each of these characters to become the performers they truly are. The issue becomes vastly more complicated when one considers that the second appearance of 'Be A Clown' is tied directly to the vaudeville roots that Garland and Kelly shared in 'real' life, thus blurring the lines between the characters on screen and the performers themselves.[17] As seen in Figure 4, the make-up used to turn the actors into clowns at the end of the picture does not obscure either person's face, but rather allows the audience to easily make the connection, knowing that the finale shows us who Kelly and Garland are in truth – that is to say, that they are actors.[18]

Figure 5 Kelly and Garland as clowns[19]

Kelly, however, has the opportunity to show himself as two very *different* actors. The first, as stated above, is Pierrot. This version of the number unfolds in a way that allows for a short build-up of dramatic tension with an extended release – for example, the dance that follows the song. Table 1 shows the flow of the number, including each statement of the song as it appears in the dances. The lyrics set up the tune, and then the dance becomes a visual feast of acrobatic dancing – impressive and breathtaking for the performers and audience alike.

Table 1: 'Be A Clown' version 1: Kelly and Nicholas brothers.

Section	1: Verse 1	2: Chorus 1	3: Transition	4: Dance 1	5: Dance 2	6: Dance 3
Features	Spoken, sung	Sung	Instrumental	Instrumental	Instrumental	Instrumental
Key	B♭ Major	B♭ Major	B♭ Major	E♭ Major	D♭ Major	D major
Comments			Extends length of chorus for dance	Extends length of chorus for dance	Woodwind extension for dance	Heavy brass, 'big finish' extension for dance

The music begins abruptly, without the traditional instrumental introduction that would set up a song, either on stage or screen. As the camera hovers far above Kelly's head, it follows him as he leaves the gallows (with a bit of humour) and breaks into the tune, using his hands in a similar way to a conductor to initiate the performance. He is dressed all in black, an outfit befitting his imminent demise, and slowly makes his way to the stage. The verse is delivered in a vocal style somewhere between speech and song not unlike recitative; this choice is appropriate given that the function of the verse in the movie is to place the character on the stage for the focus of the song (i.e. the aria). As Kelly moves, he uses his hands to punctuate the lyrics, and this connection between his upper body movements and the music becomes the fundamental foundation for the delivery of the first chorus. Kelly manages to take the stage just before the ending of the verse, and it is worth noting that once he is squarely placed on his destination, he can begin to sing. This scalar passage, albeit brief, acts as an excellent transition for the performance of the chorus.

The first edit coincides with the beginning of the chorus, and the new camera position places Kelly in the centre of the frame. It is clear from the outset that the actor had an excellent sense of how a body can fill space, and this is probably a combined effort between Kelly's choreographic instincts and Harry Stradling's photography. It is here that Kelly begins to 'play' with the song and with his upper body, using large sweeping motions as well as clever manipulations of his face to become the clown he sings about. During this section, he manages to act out the lyrics – which he does in great detail – without ever once moving his feet, remaining as stationary as the camera. The acting is a little exaggerated, with horns for a "calf" and a wide embrace for the world "loving" the clown, but this section, while important to the song itself, is really just the preamble of what is to come.

As Kelly completes the first chorus, the curtain behind him rises to reveal his group of players dressed in ridiculous outfits around a changing panel. This instrumental iteration of the chorus is really a transitional section, allowing for the changing of costume for Serafin and for the arrival of the other two dancers. Part of the comedy here is that Kelly is able to change so quickly – surely a trick created by the camera to delight the audience once he appears as Pierrot. Musically, we hear a repeat of the chorus, but there is a short trumpet fanfare that extends the section and allows for the three players to arrange themselves in a human pyramid and sing the final bars of the chorus. Before leaving this moment, it is important to mention that the costumes we see – designed by Irene and Tom Keogh – are striking. I feel they are meant to invoke Pierrot, but in a new and vibrant way. The white coat is replaced by an explosion of lime green and yellow, obliterating the plain tunic and replacing it with a tight-fitting, dance-friendly cut. The result is a Technicolour Pierrot, complete with hat and dots, both on the faces of the actors and on the costumes themselves. The costume is meant to be *impressive* (as opposed to *funny*), and this term is probably the best choice of words to describe the performance as a whole.

Another fanfare leads to the main dance sequence, which is constructed from three complete versions of the chorus, although there are extensions in each section to allow for dance steps here and there. An interesting twist for this dance routine is that the music, which had been harmonically static for the opening sections, goes through several keys, repeatedly shifting to give aural colour to match the difficult moves of the entertainers. Kelly and his partners, the Nicholas brothers, worked hard on the routine, which is full of as many kicks, jumps, leaps and acrobatic tricks as one might hope to see. However, through it all, it remains a dance, where the connection between the music and bodily motion is key to understanding what the performers are doing. Patricia Ward Kelly explains that "when he choreographed it, Gene put in every flash step ... Many of the things are things that Gene did in high school when he and his brother were performing at these amateur nights."[20] Kelly is credited as the sole choreographer of the routine, but Fayard Nicholas mentioned that some of the moves were suggested by them.[21] Whatever the exact genesis of each step, this version of 'Be A Clown' is a full-tilt whirlwind of movement, requiring great skill and endurance for all three performers.

The initiation of the dance itself is an excellent depiction of how music and movement are combined. As the vocal part ("Be a clown, etc.") concludes at the end of the transition, the players arrange themselves symmetrically and, within a span of four measures during the second trumpet fanfare, leap off the stage. Although this takes place very quickly, each movement is precisely connected to the musical rhythm, emphasizing specific beats with particular motions – the core of somatic movement itself. The use of the arms is particularly important for the cohort as they move forward and back on beats 3 and 1 of the first two measures and then cartwheel off the stage during the next eight beats. They land perfectly in time and officially begin the next full dance section.

An extended sequence follows wherein the performer's bodies are manipulated in both traditional and unexpected ways, but taken together, the emphasis is on the performer's ability itself – the ability to do the moves, the ability to keep going, and the ability to work together. As I said before, it is impressive rather than amusing, and it is meant to be. This does not mean there are not funny moments or silly moves, but they always happen in passing rather than lingering as the focus of the shot. For example, in the first dance sequence, the players jump back up on the stage for only a moment, concluding a sashay-like movement across the full space given to them. As they leap backwards, they land on their behinds and – within the space of a measure – put their right legs up in the air and bring them back down. This, in itself, would not be particularly amusing, but the music provides the first significant moment of 'Mickey Mousing' with the slide upwards and down in the brass, and therefore creates a comic effect. The audience does not have time to consider the experience, however, because of the fast pace of the number, and that might be one of the reasons it feels so impressive – the music (and most of the dance) never stops until the final chord. There are other instances where the dancers provide a visual cue to the amusing qualities of the routine, such as showing their rears to the audience or falling down in a pile. But, for the most part, it is the music and the music's recollection of the song's lyrics that remind us we are watching something funny; we have been told that "all the world loves a clown" and it continues to be suggested through the musical repetition of the chorus, even if most of the words themselves are not heard.

Musical cues for humour are everywhere throughout the sequence, and this is partially because the musical style is borrowed from animated cartoons of the day, especially the highly physical *Tom and Jerry* series (MGM, 1940–1957).[22] Other than outlining the main song, the music provides space for dancers to rearrange themselves in the frame in between the three sections. The first one of these extensions is heard in the woodwinds and, as it coincides with a new shot and a new section, it opens up the song spatially. The music is reminiscent of that which would be heard in cartoons; it is lively, snappy and brisk. A brass interlude follows, with the notes again sliding upwards in a glissando, followed by an accented final note that is capped off by a trill in the flutes. Again, the music is 'Mickey Mousing' the dancers' flights in the air, and feels as though we should laugh at the moment. It is entirely appropriate to do so, partially because of the joy on the performer's faces and also because this four-measure transition leads directly back to the next chorus (albeit instrumental) of the song. Another comedic instance comes when the three dance up to the gallows and mime a response to the noose. Here, the trumpets use a flutter-tongue technique to create something that sounds like cartoon-style dread, and the actors lightly bounce back down the stairs. This 'interruption' in the flow of the song connects with the motions by the performers to create the effect.

But sometimes these musical interpolations appear to have been overlaid into the sonic fabric after the number was recorded and on camera, and the result is the creation of comedy through the enhancement of what is already happening. The use of the slide whistle during the initial arrangement of the three men is a perfect example of this. The instrument's sound is part of the humour, but so is the physical connection between the characters. The addition of the cymbal when the three jump off the stage for the last time is another of these musical add-ons, where it sounds very much like the taps of the dancers' feet were dubbed in after the rest was completed.

This version of 'Be A Clown' is fast-paced and enjoyable, but the emphasis is on effort rather than on humour. All three of the Technicolour Pierrots are incredible dancers and are silly, performing weird leaps and jumps, but their emphasis is not on humour. The cartoon-like quality of the sequence is enhanced by the music and also by the physical agility involved in the number and the bright colours on the screen. It is a tour de force of Gene Kelly's acrobatic moves, and remains one of the most beloved and discussed moments in the movie, for all the reasons discussed above, from the physical to the musical.

The second time we experience 'Be A Clown', though, it is entirely another matter. The 'clowning' here is radically different, and so is the context by which it is meant to be understood. Garland and Kelly perform the number as Manuela's debut on the stage, and, of course, she shows herself to be a consummate comedienne. This time, the dancing is not so much about what the performers *can* do but about what they *are* doing. The dance moves are rather easy, but they amount to a very different comedic style: that of the vaudeville routine. Table 2 demonstrates the way the song unfolds, including the fact that the verse has been eliminated.

Table 2: 'Be A Clown' version 2: Kelly and Garland

Section	1: Intro	2: Chorus A	3: Break	4: Chorus 2	5: Break	6: Chorus 3	7: Extended End	8: Finale
Features	Instrumental	Vocals both together and traded	Instrumental	Vocals both together and traded	Instrumental	Vocals both together and traded		Instrumental
Measures	8	40 + 8 (end)	4	40 + 8 (end)	4	40 + more	End music repeated + last 4 m. of chorus	
Key	G Major	G Major	G Major	G Major	G Major	G Major	G Major	G Major
Comments		Not in sheet music; m. 28–30 new, then chorus 2	Allows for post-pin blocking	With new 2nd half	Allows for post-pin blocking		New music for new twist on pin joke	Brass 'big finish'

As stated earlier, for this act, Kelly and Garland pull out many of the tried-and-true actions they learned while part of the vaudeville circuit, including the 'pin' bit and the flopping around in the "large baggy pants".[23] The focus remains on the characters throughout, and this is achieved through two major forces that impose a certain amount of stasis on the number. The first of these is the relative steadiness of the camera. One of the only times it changes its position – at least in a significant way – is to focus in on the 'wiggling ear' trick. Otherwise, it remains settled in a position where it reminds us that we are indeed in an audience watching a stage performance (the audience-within-the movie). The second major element of stasis is musical. As Table 2 shows, there is no large-scale harmonic motion whatsoever, and the vigorous key changes that happen in the first version of the song are absent here. The two 'buffoons' go through the song, but they stick to the chorus without fail, issuing three complete iterations before finishing. These two major factors of stasis allow them to be the centre of attention, without worrying about vocal or physical acrobatics.

With more of the text heard in this version, the song's lyrics become more prominent. The most important gag delivered here is that being a clown brings the highest quality life possible – it's a topsy-turvy joke. Porter wrote five refrains for the song.[24] Each of these choruses touches on the results of becoming a clown – especially the good life that it affords. You will "rate with all the great swells" and "only stop with top folks," winning "millions" of dollars and travelling "first class". The life of the wealthy, which Porter was intimately familiar with, was certainly not one that most people who were "silly asses" aspired to, so part of the humour comes from suggesting that this is the most sure way to achieving an aristocratic lifestyle. The other treasure obtained by showing "tricks", according to the song, is that it leads to marriage and true love. In the narrative world of *The Pirate*, this happens to be true, but clearly this is not usually the way to someone else's heart, especially not in the format mentioned in the second chorus:

> *Be a crazy buffoon/*
> *and the 'demoiselles'll all swoon,/*
> *dress in huge, baggy pants/*
> *and you'll ride the road to romance./*
> *A butcher or a baker, ladies never embrace,/*
> *A barber for a beau would be a social disgrace/*
> *They'll all come to call if you can fall on your face.*

The dopey antics suggested in the song are not typical when one is wooing a woman, and that itself is a major part of the joke. What this does suggest, though, is that Feuer's reading of this version of 'Be A Clown' is accurate: we are seeing the result of being a joker in a romantic light, a variation on what Manuela has wanted since the beginning of the film, though not in the way she was expecting it.

Physical humour is present here, too, but unlike the first iteration, the dance is meant to convey the meaning of the motions (which happens primarily through mime) rather than become the focus of awe in and of itself. One way that this happens is by highlighting the outrageous clown costumes that are worn. For example, near the beginning of the first chorus, the couple symmetrically sway back and forth with their arms and legs, spotlighting the relationship of their body to the oversized costumes. Later, when on the ground, Kelly raises his foot in the air (see Figure 4) and is matched by Garland. Even though the move they make is nonsensical (flopping feet), it allows for the clearest look so far at the giant shoes each dancer is wearing. During the third chorus, Garland sings about travelling "first class" while hiking up her long coat and wiggling her rear, obviously making fun of the "hoity-toity-ness" of the comment.

In some cases, the dance moves themselves are funny. The most prominent one of these comes in the form of the recurring joke involving the pin. As the two characters get into position towards the back of the stage, they each do a waddle that is particularly amusing. After the last time through they mime a fighter's stance after they have both been hit on the head by the pins, creating another funny moment, although the appearance of the multitude of pins that follows directly after that move helps to drive the joke to a crescendo. In the beginning of the second refrain, Kelly dances on his knees for a moment and tries to get Garland to do the same. When he has to physically pull her down with him, she imitates him like an ape with a short shuffle. And, throughout it all, the exaggerated expressions on the faces of the two dancers serve to underline the physical comedy of their bodies and in their song. These jokes are not prolonged, but fleeting; the joy of the number comes in part from so many of these funny pieces piled on top of one another at a speed that culminates in the final pin joke.

This time, the music does not play a significant role, but is instead a sonic backdrop for the two players to perform. One first notices that, once the singing begins, the music is very far down in the mix of sound. It only becomes louder when performing a transitional function, such as during the pin bit or in between the choruses. Its primary function is that of punctuation rather than a contributor to the comedy itself. It facilitates the delivery of the lyrics and a continual rhythmic beat by which the pace is kept moving forward. The tempo is not so frantic that it seems to push the characters out of a comfort zone of movement, but rather it matches the stasis of the key areas and of the camera itself. The purpose of this is to keep the two characters and their antics in the centre of the frame and as prominent as possible.

The two versions of 'Be A Clown' demonstrate two decidedly different types of clowns: an acrobatic, Technicolour Pierrot and a silly vaudevillian. It is clear from the re-use of the song that the producers were hoping to forge a hit, but what they did not seem to consider in great detail is how, exactly, the song connects to the plot. Although this is a topic for an altogether different study, neither of the 'Be A Clown' presentations seem to 'fit' well into the overall narrative. The second performance, especially, makes use of a comedic tradition that has nothing to do with the time period of the film, and leaves the audience with clear questions at the movie's finale. However, both performances are successful in their respective ways in spotlighting the song and, although the two sequences reach for different goals, they each portray the clown as a joyous character, full of life and mirth.

'Make 'Em Laugh' in *Singin' in the Rain*

Few of the moments in this movie are as well-remembered and loved by critics and audiences as Donald O'Connor's performance in 'Make 'Em Laugh'. As a result, there are several accounts written about the number, especially concerning the pilfering of the song and about the things that inspired various parts of the choreography.[25] For example, the story behind why the dummy was used, who proposed it, and the event in O'Connor's past that suggested it has been widely circulated. This is true for many of the features of the song and its performance. However, the component that seems to be lacking is the final one – the analysis of the number from both a musical and physical standpoint.

Probably the most important comment to make is that, in truth, this is not really a dance, but instead a comic routine. This point is made especially clear in Earl J. Hess and Pratibha A. Dabholkar's excellent book, *Singin' in the Rain: The Making of an American Masterpiece*. They contend that "it was a unique number, not really a dance per se but comic shtick mixed with acrobatics set to music, more akin to vaudeville than an MGM musical."[26] While vaudeville numbers of a sort were a part of the MGM catalogue (see 'Fit As a Fiddle' from *Singin' in the Rain*, 'I Got Rhythm' from *An American In Paris* (1951) and 'Under the Bamboo Tree' from *Meet Me In St. Louis* (1944) – both the latter directed by Vincente Minnelli), it is true that this particular song is frequently described as a dance when "there is very little dancing in it". So, if this isn't a dance, what aspects highlight the vaudeville nature of the performance and what, specifically, makes it work so well?

Many of the aspects of 'Be A Clown' discussed above come into play here, but they work in different ways. First of all, the type of clown for 'Make 'Em Laugh' is not hard to identify; this is the vaudevillian again, but this time in a more filmic style. The static quality of Garland and Kelly's staging is not applicable for most of the performance. In fact, Hess and Dobholkar call it a "travelling" number – one that moves from place to place in order to allow for an array of gags.[27] Cosmo begins the song while at the piano and, although today's audiences might not recognize this type of delivery, this spoken opening was very common in vaudeville as part of what was known as the 'pianologue'. It involved a quirky performance given at the piano with a twist of some sort, whether it was playing two instruments at once (as Sol Violinsky did) or singing a tune with an outrageous dialect (as did, for example, the comedians Van and Schenk). O'Connor does not so much perform a song here, preferring to bang on the keys and leap on the piano itself, but it is the opening of a common type of variety show act. The pianologue perfectly sets up what is to come. The loose rhythmical aspect of this opening section allows for the comedian to emphasize several elements that will become central during the 'real' song: his hat is already pulled down awkwardly, he uses his body in unexpected ways – pounding on the piano with his foot, his arm, and standing on it – and he deploys some silly facial expressions. Of course, part of the joke comes in the form of the text – he can't complete the rhyme after "things". When he jumps off the piano, this move is a cue for the nondiegetic music, and the song begins.

The new section starts with a trill and a descending scale in the violins that is the first of many instances of 'Mickey Mousing' in the number. As the scale slides downward, O'Connor leaps down from the piano. Since most of the music was recorded beforehand, Kelly and O'Connor, who share credit for choreographing the piece, pinpointed areas where the physical comedy could interact nicely with the musical accompaniment. Once O'Connor starts to sing, the music (but not the voice) falls far back into the overall mix of sound, just as it did in the second version of 'Be A Clown'. This was to facilitate a clear delivery of the lyrics and to spotlight O'Connor's voice, a common enough sound choice in film musicals. And, like the other songs reviewed here, its form was such that the repeated chorus could be used as a musical backdrop, and, as Table 3 demonstrates, this is exactly how the song functions.

The aspect that sets this number apart from others in the movie is not the voice and its relationship to the music, but O'Connor's body and his movements and their connection to the rhythmic patterns in the music. It is not hard to see why many people have mistaken this for a dance – it is primarily because O'Connor's body moves in and out of synch with its accompaniment so gracefully that, even when he is merely being carted from one space to another on a beam, it seems as though he dances. In this last instance, he first kicks his feet to the beat, then takes a position that mimics swimming – this time moving his hands to the rhythm – and then, even at the point where he merely lies on his side, swaying his hand to link this pose to the background musical fabric, weaving together a section of 'Make 'Em Laugh' that *feels* like it has been danced. His feet have not even touched the ground, but because of an extreme sensitivity to the music, O'Connor's motions transform the shtick into something far more than mere hoofer's gyrations. Kelly noted that this was one of the reasons that so much work was put into 'Make 'Em Laugh': "To get the beats where he slaps his head on the musical counts was the most difficult."[28] While it may have been challenging, there is no question that this element of the song's performance is what truly sets it apart.

From the start, O'Connor's body keeps time with the music. He taps with his feet for the first two measures, then hits Gene Kelly with his hat for an equal two measures, keeping both of these gestures strictly in line with the strong beats. His jumping and exclaiming on the eighth beat is perfectly in time, and though it doesn't take up more than a beat, it prepares the next phrase. Using another single beat to pull his hat down, he reserves the following seven beats for a side-to-side jig on his knees, relying on the incorrect placement of his body on the floor and its unusual appearance in this move for yuks.

The next section sees him taking the same motion forward, eventually moving to a series of hops, each of which occupy two beats. Here the actor discusses Shakespeare, during which the only part of his body that keeps

142 Sounding Funny

Table 3: 'Make 'Em Laugh'

Section	1: Intro	2: Chorus 1	3: Chorus 2	4: Chorus 1	5: Chorus music	6: Chorus music	7: Chorus
Features	Spoken and sung	Fully sung	Fully sung	Spoken and sung	Instrumental	Instrumental	Spoken and sung
Measures	n.a.	40	40	40	40	40	40
Key	n.a.	E♭ Major	E♭ Major	E♭ Major	A♭ Major	A♭ Major	F Major
Comments	Pianologue			Partial lyrics			

time is his feet. When O'Connor throws his hat upwards (another action funny because of its speed and its reversal of the expected direction of the hat), more of his body quickly moves into play; he uses the facial expressions from the introduction in time with the music. This section culminates with the actor singing about a banana peel, falling while in line with the beat, and shaking his head on "world's at your feet", simply in order to keep rhythm at the heart of the experience.

Despite being raucously funny on its own account, the physical elements of time-keeping are not the only ones at play in the song. The scansion of the text also follows differing beat patterns, sometimes falling directly on the beat, and at others making use of the triplet in the music:

```
Text:  "BUT   BE   A    COM - I - CAL      ONE!"
Beats:  1  -  2 -  1 -   2  -  1      - 2 -  1 -  2
```

During this spoken playfulness with the text, the orchestra also toys with the beats. The violins at first match the spoken declamation, but then they can only be heard on the off-beats, sounding only a fraction of a beat after O'Connor sings the notes. This interplay between the text, its setting and the orchestral overlay all complicate the joke, allowing for a rhythmic structure that constantly sets up expectations only to break them down by presenting quirky variations. Dropping the text completely, which O'Connor does after being picked up by the board and when he smacks up against the brick wall, is also an effective manipulation of text rhythms.

Amidst the overt comedy of the dummy dance-partner, while Cosmo jumps in and around objects and falls on the floor by miming a non-functional body, the music still plays an important part in flavouring the humour. This is most clearly seen through the use of percussion sounds that were recorded and added later. A ratchet can be heard clicking through several moments, including the brick wall bit and the dummy section. The flirtation with the dummy is also made more humorous by the inclusion of clave sounds. But the percussion sounds most central to the success of the routine are the timpani rolls, the snare rolls and the cymbal crashes that are laid over the manic physical choreography during O'Connor's gyrations on the floor. Since these gestures do *not* usually fall within the regular beat structure, such additions ensure that the audience experiences an aural equivalent to the comedian's strange body twists, dislocating them in a way probably meant to mirror the height of O'Connor's exasperated insanity.[29]

The manipulation of rhythm is partially what is so important for O'Connor's humour in 'Make 'Em Laugh', but it is the complete picture that makes the difference. The props frequently present a bodily challenge of some sort that needs to be overcome (e.g. the moving couch) or explored (the door to be opened). Intensifying all of this interplay with his physical surroundings, O'Connor's relationship with the camera is equally important. For the most part, his body is fully in the frame, comfortable with medium shots that allow spectators to watch his full body twist and dance. While he spins on the floor (on his arm), the camera takes a cue from Busby Berkeley and is raised above the performer, reducing his silliness to a geometric form. This shot does not last very long, and once he has gotten up, the camera returns to its original framing position. One of the tricks with the camera, according to O'Connor, was trying to find a point where the camera could do a close-up of his face to allow for the post-brick-wall bit. The resulting shot, although it is different from what had come before, seems perfectly natural, and its resolution is also seamless, bringing the audience back to the previous frame without difficulty. Even though Cosmo's body and the frame of the camera do not comprise the most important relationship in the number, the way the camera moves with him is certainly part of the act.

The truth of the matter is that 'Make 'Em Laugh' ties together the best elements of both versions of 'Be A Clown' from the earlier movie. Not only is it athletic, but it is also full of comedic schtick that plays the audience for laughs. O'Connor manages to employ a wide variety of gags and infuse them with an 'impressiveness' that causes an audience to repeatedly be in awe of his abilities as a performer, if not as a dancer. The vaudeville elements are apparent in this performance, not only from the physical jokes that are used, but also in the static quality of the music heard during the delivery of the text. The song is straightforward and does not modulate until the instrumental sections begin (see Table 3). Therefore, both versions of 'Be A Clown' are used as models for the song. From the acrobatic leg work of the opening of the song to the close-up facial machinations, O'Connor and Kelly (as co-choreographers) present a stunning combination of comedic elements that keeps the audience laughing, forging the two clown types in 'Be A Clown' into one and – additionally – blending this performance seamlessly into the overall narrative.

As a final note on these songs and their appearances in these two movies, it is important to mention that Gene Kelly was intimately involved with both performances. His vivacious and energized dancing is perhaps the central reason that all three of these versions are so memorable. Without Kelly's hard work and extensive planning, none of these sequences would have worked as well as they did – this is particularly evident when counting the small number of edits that occur. It is a testament to his choreographic skills that in each case, the other entertainers involved were able to produce numbers that made the best of their own abilities. The results are three very exciting and interesting musical performances that showcase the best of what the MGM musical had to offer.

Later versions

Both 'Be A Clown' and 'Make 'Em Laugh' have been performed repeatedly since their first appearances in these big-budget musicals. O'Connor himself performed a modified version of the routine for a Gene Kelly television special on 16 October 1960. The song used is called 'Smile, Darn You, Smile', and is structured in a similar manner as the two previous songs. Judy Garland also reprised her role *sans* Kelly with the song 'Be A Clown' on her own television programme on 8 March 1964. In both cases, the actors were put in costumes that were reminiscent of the original garb. Each of these performances was taped live and thus have a very different feel from the polished, lip-synched versions from the two respective movies.

Kevin Kline offers an interesting version of 'Be A Clown' in *De-lovely*, a modern telling of Cole Porter's life. Here, Porter and Louis B. Mayer, alongside a large chorus of dancers and singers, perform the number as part of a nondiegetic moment in the movie. Although Porter seems to be the centre of attention, the camera continuously cuts to other cast members, allowing for a shared spotlight that diffuses the entire number. Rather than allow for dancing, this 'Be A Clown' becomes a catalogue of Hollywood jokes, from Harpo Marx's held-leg gag to O'Connor's upside-down hat trick. The frenetic quality of the editing makes the number feel hurried, but perhaps this is what the filmmakers were trying to achieve. According to the commentary, they were trying to show Porter's cynical reaction to Mayer's comment that he should write songs that were not 'clever funny' but 'funny funny'. This number falls flat in trying to be funny, and only comes across as a forced version of what funny is supposed to be. And, whatever the movie's creators were attempting to depict, the joy and energy apparent in the previous versions is missing here, putting *De-lovely* out of synch with the MGM classics.[30]

Conclusion

As this chapter demonstrates, the relationship between 'Be A Clown' and 'Make 'Em Laugh' is as close as detractors usually claim. A close look at the phrasing shows similarities, but 'Make 'Em Laugh' does have some unique elements. Freed and Brown's song hovers as close to musical theft as might be allowed, and one can only speculate what the result of any copyright dispute may have been. The appearances of each song in the two MGM films discussed, *The Pirate* and *Singin' in the Rain*, show that the creative teams behind the movies were able to build different meanings with similar material – even with the same song. The two clowns represented in 'Be A Clown' are not the same; Gene Kelly's Technicolour Pierrot is athletic and agile, while Judy Garland and Kelly's vaudevillians use humour to keep the audience laughing. Donald O'Connor's presentation of 'Make 'Em Laugh' combines physical comedy and music to forge something new. As stated, *Singin' in the Rain*'s version is a synthesis of the previous movie's separate takes, hence the effusive praise for the routine. As with Joseph Gordon-Levitt's performance on *Saturday Night Live*, it is clear that both of these songs have continued to be featured in different contexts, from episodes of the Muppets to live, stage versions. Both have become iconic songs attached to important routines that have impacted popular culture, funny faces or not.

Notes

1. I want to thank my "Analysis of American Popular Song" graduate seminar students at Brooklyn College, CUNY, from the fall of 2009 for their helpful comments while developing this article.
2. Thanks to Amy Rae Weaver for bringing this version to my attention.
3. It is all too common for scholars to confuse the different versions of songs in their work on musical theatre, with stage songs frequently conflated with their filmed adaptations. Authors such as Gerald Mast (1987) avoid this simplification, but it remains a problematic issue for others. I have tried to remain aware of separating recorded versions, film versions and excerpted versions of songs for this chapter.
4. 'Make 'Em Laugh' has been transposed from the key of the sheet music version for the sake of comparison.
5. In both performances of 'Be A Clown', the rhythm is altered so that the two quarter notes in between the 'destination' notes sound like dotted quarter notes. In 'Make 'Em Laugh', this aspect of the original song appears as a half note and

quarter note pattern (see m. 1 in both songs). Therefore, it is the performance of the first song that influenced the writing of the latter.

6. See McBrien (1998: 12–14).
7. *Ibid*, 86–117.
8. For more information on Pierrot, see Green and Swan (1993). There is a side of the character that is based on tragic love, but that is not a factor in this particular performance.
9. See http://graphicsfairy.blogspot.com/2008/06/old-photo-pierrot-clown-costume-party.html for image.
10. See http://www.freewebs.com/geneius/nbPDVD_1177.JPG for image.
11. See Levy (2009: 161).
12. *The Pirate* (1948). Warner Brothers Home Video, 2007. DVD 79522.
13. Fricke's commentary reveals that even though the 'legend' of the song suggests that it was written well into shooting, 'Be A Clown' was, in fact, submitted in 1946 before shooting began.
14. See 'The Pirate: A Musical Treasure Chest' featurette on the DVD.
15. Feuer (1993: 83–84).
16. Altman (1987: 190–193).
17. The issue of performer vs. character is especially prominent in Porter's *Kiss Me Kate* in both the stage and film versions. The movie from 1953 goes so far as to use Howard Keel's photograph with Kathryn Grayson (the two are portraying lovers who have split after years of matrimony) from the film *Show Boat* (Gerald Sidney, 1951) as a prop. Porter is even portrayed by an actor in the movie. The line between fantasy and reality in musical theatre is particularly important to Porter during this era, and could make for a very interesting study.
18. Fricke suggests that this method of portraying stems comes from *The Wizard of Oz* DVD commentary.
19. See http://www.thejudyroom.com/filmography/images/pirate4-lg.jpg, accessed 20 December 2010 for image.
20. See 'The Pirate: A Musical Treasure Chest' featurette on the DVD.
21. *Ibid*.
22. See Daniel Goldmark (2005) for an excellent discussion of this topic.
23. The complicated relationship between Garland, Minnelli, and Kelly in this movie is discussed in more detail in Levy (2009: 160–171).
24. For the complete lyrics, see Gill (1971: 208). See also Kimball (1983).
25. See Wollen (1992) for several viewpoints on this story.
26. Hess and Dabholkar (2010: 94–5). The discussion of what does and does not constitute dance is too extensive to examine here, but the idea is useful and will be used for the purposes of discussion.
27. *Ibid*, 95.
28. *Ibid*, 96.
29. Though it is not stated anywhere, it is probable that the sounds used in 'Make 'Em Laugh' were probably dubbed in, as well as the percussion instruments that seem to 'Mickey Mouse' several of O'Connor's actions.

30. Of all the modern versions, probably the most controversial is entitled 'Peterotica' (Season 4, Episode 14) of the animated series, *Family Guy*. A section of the show references O'Connor's routine, and I will leave it to the reader to discover this 'special' version for themselves.

References

Altman, R. (1987). *The American Film Musical*. Bloomington, IN: Indiana University Press.
Feuer, J. (1993). *The Hollywood Musical* (2nd ed.). Bloomington, IN: Indiana University Press.
Gill, B., & Kimball, R. (Ed.) (1971). *Cole: A Biographical Essay*. New York: Delta.
Goldmark, D. (2005). *Tunes for 'Toons: Music and the Hollywood Cartoon*. Berkeley & Los Angeles, CA, London: University of California Press. http://dx.doi.org/10.1525/california/9780520236172.001.0001
Green, M., & Swan, J. (1993). *The Triumph of Pierrot: The commedia dell'arte and the Modern Imagination*. University Park, PA: Pennsylvania State University Press.
Hess, E.J., & Dabholkar, P.A. (2010). *Singin' in the Rain, The Making of a Hollywood Masterpiece*. Lawrence, KS: University Press of Kansas.
Kimball, R. (Ed.) (1983). *The Complete Lyrics of Cole Porter*. New York: Da Capo PressNotes.
Levy, E. (2009). *Vincente Minnelli: Hollywood's Dark Dreamer*. New York: St. Martin's Press.
McBrien, W. (1998). *Cole Porter: A Biography*. New York: Knopf.
Mast, G. (1987). *Can't Help Singin': The American Musical on Stage and Screen*. New York: Overlook Press.
Silverman, S.M. (1996). *Dancing on the Ceiling: Stanley Donen and his Movies*. New York: Knopf.
Wollen, P. (1992). *Singin' in the Rain*. London: British Film Institute.

Jonas Westover received his PhD from the City University of New York in 2010. His work has focused on pre-1927 Broadway musicals and revues, but he also writes on film musicals and other popular music styles. He also contributed over 400 entries to the *New Grove Dictionary of American Music*. A monograph on the 'Passing Show' series of revues is forthcoming (2016) from Oxford University Press.

9 Sound, Comedy and Cinematic Modernism
Kaasua, komisario Palmu!

Kimmo Laine and Anu Juva

The Finnish director Matti Kassila (born 1924) started his career in the late 1940s. During the next decade he directed some of the established classics of the Finnish studio era, drama films like *Sininen viikko/Blue Week* (1954) and *Elokuu/The Harvest Month* (1956), as well as comedies like *Hilmanpäivät/Hilma's Name Day* (1954). Kassila often wrote the scripts for his films himself, or participated in scriptwriting, and in the manuscripts there are plenty of notes on music and sound.[1]

Unlike many of his colleagues in Finland at the time, Kassila trusted in sound and its capability of contributing to the narration, or adding to it considerably. This aural interest is at its most notable in a series of three comedy thrillers he directed in the beginning of the 1960s, at a moment when the studio system and the major production companies were on the threshold of a final crisis, and new cinematic forms were gradually emerging, both in terms of production and film style. These three films, *Komisario Palmun erehdys/Inspector Palmu's Error* (1960), *Kaasua, komisario Palmu!/Gas, Inspector Palmu!* (1961) and *Tähdet kertovat, komisario Palmu/The Stars Will Tell, Inspector Palmu* (1962) were among the last major successes of the studio era. They were based on crime novels written by the beloved Finnish writer Mika Waltari.[2] Kassila developed the characters of the novels towards a more comical direction, and created films that have had lasting popularity in Finland, achieving cult status especially in the 1990s and 2000s. The music to all of them is composed by Osmo Lindeman, whose fruitful collaboration with Kassila produced six films altogether. Lindeman (1929–1987) started his career as a jazz pianist and continued with Latin rhythms. At the end of the 1950s, he studied composition with Carl Orff among others and became a classical composer. His approach was always fresh and he showed both interest in and understanding of filmic device. One could compare his film compositions to those of Bernard Herrmann – except that Lindeman in general was the more experimental of the two. Later in his career Lindeman was dedicated to electronic music (Juva, 2008).

In this article we concentrate on the second film of the series, *Kaasua, komisario Palmu!*, because the sound is clearly used for comical purposes throughout the film. The first film, *Komisario Palmun erehdys* is, unlike the other two, a period film set in the 1930s. It has its comic elements, as well as moments of self-conscious narration, but as a whole, it is the most serious detective film of the series with an emphasis on grotesque horror. The third film, *Tähdet kertovat, komisario Palmu*, begins with a highly self-conscious use of a voiceover narrator interrupting the course of the action repeatedly, but the latter part of the film is fairly serious in tone, consisting of a hunt for a Nazi-like murderer.

Our starting point is that comic art in its different forms originates from unexpected transgressions of either esthetical or social borders. In the words of Steve Neale and Frank Krutnik (1990):

> comedy necessarily trades upon the surprising, the improper, the unlikely, and the transgressive in order to make us laugh; it plays on deviations both from socio-cultural norms, and from the rules that govern other genres and aesthetic regimes. In the case of comedy, therefore, generic conventions demand both social and aesthetic indecorum.

All cinematic transgressions, of course, are not comic: indeed, many of the comic devices analysed here converge with those of horror or suspense. Also, as we shall attempt to demonstrate later, the borderline between some of these devices and those associated with European modernist film movements of the late 1950s and early 1960s is not always clear. Making formal definitions of comedy is notoriously difficult. Sigmund Freud (1999/1905), for example, in his classic study on the wit, realized that it was not enough to analyse the formal structures of different comic situations; neither wit, comic, nor humour would take place without a proper atmosphere. Thus it is necessary to keep in mind that it is up to the narrative whole of the film, and to the viewing situation in the last instance, whether we conceive a given sound device as comic, horrific, suspenseful, modernist or something else.

Screen theorists of the 1970s and 80s divided comedies roughly into two categories, social comedies and crazy comedies. While the former disturbed the socially institutionalized discursive hierarchies, the latter played on the codes and conventions of cinema itself (Neale, 1980). As Neale and Krutnik's consideration on comic transgressions reminds us, social and formal indecorum are not mutually exclusive possibilities; rather, they are tendencies that usually work together. The sound devices discussed here, however, tend to emphasize the formal dimensions of comic instances. This is not to say that comic uses of sound are totally devoid of social implications; the tone of Lina Lamont's voice in *Singin' in the Rain* (1952) is certainly a central means of depicting her as a "dumb blonde". Further, the different forms of verbal humour are also largely left out of discussion here. This, too, is a matter of emphasis: while the success of aural comedy is often due to the interaction between dialogue, music and sound effects, studying dialogue in itself is quite another matter. Thus, we shall concentrate more on the aesthetic surprises and transgressions in music, dialogue and sound effects, and less on what the characters are actually saying.

These aural transgressions we divide into spatial and temporal ones. Different kinds of collisions take place, when the rules and expectations of aesthetic regimes are tested or played on. The spatial comical effects that we examine are the collision of music and picture (i.e. they do not 'fit' in the sense expected in classical narration); the collisions between different musical styles; the collisions between diegetic and nondiegetic sound; unexpected connecting of different diegetic spaces through sound; and manipulating the direction, distance or volume of sound. Other possible spatial effects could be, for instance, the collision of colour or pitch of the sound with its assumed origin, or the confusion of the boundaries of speech, music and noise; these kinds of effects, however, do not come up through our material.

The temporal comical effects that emerge from this film are repetition, manipulation of duration and manipulation of rhythm. Playing with the synchrony could be still another temporal comical effect, albeit absent from the Palmu films.

In the following, we examine these comical effects in several scenes, starting with the opening scene, which both sets the tone and atmosphere for the film and introduces many of the comic devices used more systematically later in the film.

I Spatial transgressions

Collision of sound and picture

Kaasua, komisario Palmu! opens with an establishing shot of sunny Helsinki and its seaside. The camera pans to and then zooms in on an apartment house on the right. There is a cut to the caretaker and his wife carrying out their cleaning duties in front of the house. A lady comes out of the door and claims that there is a smell of gas in the corridor. A young postman arrives, greeting them cheerfully. The camera follows him inside, and shows from above how he delivers mail in the staircase and smells something odd. Back to the standard camera level, we see him delivering a letter to an apartment, sniffing through the open lid, turning to the camera and covering his mouth with his hand, terrified.

Figure 1 Postman's face

The camera quickly zooms to the postman's face and the picture freezes (Figure 1). At the same time the music starts: a dissonant chord with a honky-tonk piano that sounds like the ones in western saloons. The chord creates a stinger that strengthens the postman's reaction. The piano music continues right away, with both downwards running descant and upwards running bass. The two clash in the middle range of the piano, and after a disorderly meeting continue together downwards, ending in chaotic chords. The opening credits appear on the frozen frame right after the music starts: "ADAMS-filmi esittää/ förevisar", "KAASUA, komisario Palmu!" and "Vem mördade fru Skrof?", that is, "ADAMS-film presents", "GAS, inspector Palmu!" The Swedish title gives away that this is about a murder case with its straightforward question: "Who murdered Mrs Skrof?"

After this the music stops, the young postman is defrosted, and there is a cut to his profile in close-up in the front of the staircase in strong underlight, when he anxiously cries out: "Caretaker, there's gas in here!" The caretaker rushes up the stairs, smells the gas from the mail slot, and rings the doorbell. The postman mentions that the dog is not barking either. The caretaker says that he has no key to the safety lock, and realizes in the excitement that one should call for the police. He rushes down the stairs, and the music starts again, now with a jolly saloon music-like tune, which at times seems to get lost, as if the player was a bit drunk, but always finds its way back to the tune. The credits appear again and continue running while the picture stays on the door.

The sound of a manipulated honky-tonk piano leads our thoughts to numerous western films and their saloons, which should have nothing to do with a Helsinki apartment house in 1961, nor with any of the characters. In the very first appearance of the music it is the sound of the instrument on the one hand and the film diegesis on the other that clash, thus creating an amusing result. When the music continues after a while with a merry and rhythmic happy-go-lucky tune on the same instrument, the sense of comedy is strengthened. The mode of the music also collides with the behaviour of the characters, whose expressions show fear and alarm, even if in a somewhat exaggerated manner. Here, the film works quite differently from the first Palmu film, which begins more like a horror film with its low-key lighting and music with a deranged feel to it (Juva, 2008). The previous film also has its big comic moments, but *Kaasua, komisario Palmu!* is clearly meant to be taken more facetiously.

Figure 2 Mail slot view

When the cast list ends, the music stops and the camera moves closer to the open mail slot, and focuses right through it on a large crucifix opposite the door, inside the apartment (Figure 2). We hear the hissing sound of gas, and also running steps. As soon as the crucifix is in focus, there is a cut to the people running up the stairs: a policeman, a young boy, the postman and the caretaker. The policeman wants a crowbar and a phone, and he orders the postman to open the corridor window. They all run down, since the crowbar is in the basement and the phone in the boy's home on the ground floor. On the way the postman opens the big corridor windows facing Helsinki Cathedral in the distance. The panning movement stops and the camera stays in front of the window, letting the characters exit the frame.

Figure 3 Window scene

The music re-appears while the policeman is giving the orders, this time a harmonium playing dissonant, grave, slightly pompous music in moderate tempo. The credits also re-appear on the window scene and when they end the small crowd runs back upstairs. They can be heard approaching, and pass the camera before the window, but the camera stays put and lets them go (Figure 3). The violent opening of the door can be heard, but not seen, because the camera focuses on the scenery instead. It zooms in, focusing on the cathedral, then cuts closer to its clock tour; it is half past nine. The music stops and the bell tolls once.

The practice of having the credits appear only after the introductory scenes was something of a novelty at the time the film was made. In the 1950s it was still virtually the norm for the credits to be shown in the very beginning of the film, before the actual narration started. There had been several notable exceptions to this rule from the 1930s on, but according to the authors of *The Classical Hollywood Cinema* the pre-credits sequence started to gain some popularity during the 1950s, possibly in response to television's technique of the 'teaser' (Bordwell, Staiger and Thompson, 1985). Still, the unconventional nature of the credits scene in *Kaasua, komisario Palmu!* is quite evident, since the credits appear in three parts altogether, surrounded by action, each time starting unexpectedly and bringing about a possibility for comic surprise.

The harmonium music is the other pole of the musical expression in this film. In the first scenes, it seems to lead us into Mrs Skrof's (Henny Valjus) religious world, of which the big crucifix in her apartment is an indubitable sign. The instrument in itself has strong religious connotations, and the dissonant, pompous music that sounds a bit too 'big' for the instrument suggests that there is an amount of hypocrisy involved – an assumption that is later confirmed by the narrative once we find out about the dubious nature of the parish Mrs Skrof is associated with. In spite of this narrative motivation, the choice of harmonium as one of the two leading instruments is unconventional, and as such it creates a potentially comical collision, while at the same time mediating close-mindedness and oppressiveness.

The choice of both of the instruments is more firmly motivated later in the film. A harmonium is seen in the victim's home, and it is shown to have been in active use. Motivation for the piano and the chosen style of music played on it comes later in the film, with a flashback scene presented as a silent slapstick pastiche and accompanied with a supposedly matching tinkling piano.

The musical language heard during the credits is partly 'old-fashioned', but in a very self-conscious way: the traditional popular song tonality is broken time after time. In this self-conscious blending of popular and modern musical features it is reminiscent of many European modern films of the era, for example Michel Legrand's tinkling piano music at the opening of Jean-Luc Godard's *Bande à part* (1964), or the Charleston-type arrangement of 'Yes! We Have No Bananas' – played in turn by a band and a tinkling piano – in Ingmar Bergman's *För att inte tala om alla dessa kvinnor/All These Women* (1964).

Yet, up to a point, the *usage* of film music under the credits is in accordance with classical film. As Claudia Gorbman (1987) has pointed out, the introductory music sets the atmosphere and presents the central musical ideas in a classical film. Here, the music does just that: we hear the main instruments used in the film, as unconventional as they are, and also the main themes. Since the honky-tonk piano and the harmonium have seldom been used as main film music instruments, these instruments can be seen as an unexpected choice. In the 1950s the most common choice was still a classical orchestra, either alone or combined with a popular music group. In addition, by the early 1960s jazz, or jazz-like music, had become recognized as a respectable alternative choice for modern and urban film sound, both in Hollywood (*The Man With the Golden Arm*, 1955; *Anatomy of a Murder*, 1959) and Europe (*La notte*, 1961; *Nóz w wodzie/Knife in the Water*, 1962). In *Kaasua, komisario Palmu!* we have neither classical music nor jazz.

The ambiguous linkage of *Kaasua, komisario Palmu!* with modernist cinema is not only due to the unorthodox music, but originates also from the use of the camera, e.g. the freeze-frames, the quick zoom-ins and the "unmotivated camera" (see Branigan, 2006). Each of these devices is also closely connected with sound. The freeze-frames and the zoom-ins are accompanied with sudden and unexpected dissonant chords, and the fact that the camera stays on the window and "forgets" about the characters means that narration, in fact, is put forward by the sounds of the characters running up and down the stairs and breaking in the apartment. Further, it has to be kept in mind that the features we find at play with cinematic modernism also connect with the mode of the film, that is, the tension between comedy and suspense. The use of an unmotivated camera that refuses to follow the characters relates to classical horror and suspense as well as modernism: for example, narrative information may be suppressed or unveiled piece by piece in order to raise suspension. This is clearly one of the functions of the unmotivated camera in *Kaasua, komisario Palmu!* too. In contrast to the static long take of the window, the zooming in and the freezing of the postman's face come very quickly, as well as his face appearing in close-up after the first credits, creating surprises that have elements of both comedy and suspense.

Collision between music excerpts

Figure 4 Mrs Skrof plays

Mrs Skrof's attorney (Toivo Mäkelä) tells the police about the life of Kirsti Skrof (Elina Salo), Mrs Skrof's stepdaughter, whom she raised alone in a very austere manner. Kirsti's loveless life is shown with a series of still images combined with atonal, dissonant harmonium music, familiar to the audience from the beginning of the film. The very religious Mrs Skrof is shown playing a harmonium in the first still (Figure 4), Kirsti in a couple of others. The highly exaggerated stills show for instance Mrs Skrof with her mouth open, just about to put food into her mouth; this kind of approach gives the series of stills a bit of a comical touch, although the uppermost feeling is distress (Figure 5). The slightly pompous music also makes a comical impact at the same time as it creates a brooding atmosphere.

As Royal S. Brown (1994) points out, already in the very beginning of the sound film era, audiences got used to listening to modernist musical devices such as open-interval harmonies and dissonant chords that not many would have tolerated in a concert hall. These devices, however, were usually restricted to genres like horror films and mysteries or moments of suspense

Figure 5 Mrs Skrof

and intrigue, indicating that there was tension in the story and between the characters. According to Gabrielsson and Lindström's (2001) empirical research on the effects of music, a complicated dissonant harmony was associated with excitement, tension, hatred, sadness and obnoxiousness. Thus, dissonant music still is a strong device in film narrative and does not necessarily follow even the contemporary experiences in concert halls. In *Kaasua, komisario Palmu!* the dissonance quite obviously describes discrepancies between the characters and creates a bizarre and uncanny atmosphere – with some comical nuances.

After the stills, the attorney continues his story in the present. To her nephew, Kaarle Lankela (Saulo Haarla), Mrs Skrof gave lots of money and attention; the attorney mentions the young man to be the black sheep of the family. Lankela's way of life is then also shown in stills, in which he fights with a policeman (Figure 6) and kisses several women (Figure 7). The music is boogie-woogie on a normal piano, in obvious contrast to the preceding harmonium.

Here, the change of musical mood creates a strong sense of collision between two totally different lifestyles and two sets of moral values by introducing them through mutually distinct systems of aesthetics. To an extent, these flashback segments resemble the classic montage sequences that were relatively

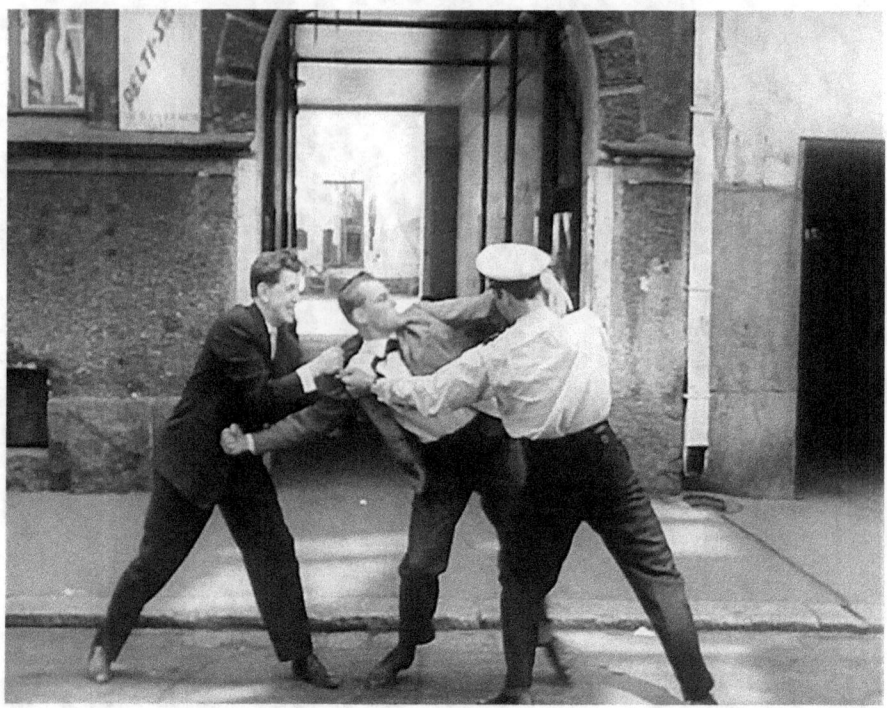

Figure 6 Lankela fights with police

common in popular filmmaking practice since the 1930s both in Hollywood and Europe. The montage sequences, usually accompanied with nondiegetic music (see Buhler, Neumeyer and Deemer, 2010), typically consist of varying kinds of shots:

> *Extreme close-ups, canted angles, silhouettes, whip pans, and other obtrusive techniques differentiate this sort of segment from the orthodox scene ... Flagrant as the montage sequence is, its rarity, its narrative function, and its narrowly conventional format assure its status as classical narration's most acceptable rhetorical flourish.* (Bordwell, Staiger, and Thompson, 1985)

Yet, as obtrusive and flagrant as the classic montage sequences are, the flashback scenes in *Kaasua, komisario Palmu!* carry the obtrusiveness even further. The fact that the flashbacks are told almost entirely in exaggerated stills and that the music changes suddenly from one unlikely style to another on the one hand verges on cinematic modernism (or perhaps reminds us of the much neglected historical common ground between cinematic modernism and classicism; see Bratu Hansen (2000)). On the other hand these flashbacks once again stretch towards comedy, this time with a hint of grotesque.

Figure 7 Lankela kisses

Collision between diegetic and nondiegetic sound

At the end of his story the attorney mentions Lankela having some sports merits, and right away a still shows Lankela in a sports car driving a rally. Suddenly there is a sound of a rally car, and at the same time the car starts moving ahead. Here, the aesthetic expectations are played on in a comical manner; after the series of still pictures it comes as a surprise that one of them suddenly starts to move and make noise. At the same time, one could say that there is also a collision between nondiegetic and diegetic sound: we expect the piano music to be nondiegetic and the attorney's voiceover to come within the diegesis but offscreen. The sound of the sports car opens up an aural space somewhere between the diegetic and nondiegetic spheres, thus creating a comic surprise.

Another variation of transgressing the borders between different diegetic spheres occurs when Inspector Palmu (Joel Rinne) and his assistant Virta (Matti Ranin) first leave the police station for the crime scene. We hear Virta

Figure 8 Virta (left) thinks Mrs Skrof has been murdered, while Palmu 'hears' his thoughts

thinking that the death of Mrs Skrof must be a murder (Figure 8). Since the scene takes place early in the film, it is for a moment somewhat unclear whether we only hear his thoughts momentarily or whether he is going to be the voiceover narrator of the film. The latter would be a good guess for those spectators who have read the original novel, in which Virta is indeed the narrator; also, it is a fairly common convention of both detective novels and films to feature a naive but adoring sidekick such as Virta as a narrator. Here, however, this turns out not to be the case. After hearing Virta's inner speculations we suddenly see and hear Palmu commenting out loud: "No, it's not a murder." Whatever the narrative source of Virta's thoughts – entering the thoughts of an on-screen character or hearing his voiceover narration – it is obviously unlikely for the other characters to hear them. There is a possibility to see a hint of social comedy involved here: the young policeman is so obvious in his eagerness to be involved in a real murder case that his senior colleague can read his mind. However, it is never explained in the film in what sense Palmu actually becomes aware of Virta's thoughts, thus leaving room for comic surprise.

Playing with the conventions of voiceover narration is developed further in the sequel *Tähdet kertovat, komisario Palmu*, with Virta acting as an actual homodiegetic narrator this time (see Kozloff, 1988) and constantly interrupting the flow of action with his bumptious comments, sometimes offscreen, sometimes straight to the camera. The first time the voiceover narration comes up he actually starts by saying: "Excuse me, but I'll have to interrupt and explain how it all began." Soon there is a cut from the action at the crime scene to him addressing the camera, and the narrative techniques that follow are as obtrusive as in the preceding film, with constant zoom-ins, freeze-frames and sound-effect-like music that in interaction lean towards comedy.

Unexpected connecting of different spaces through sound

There is a section in *Kaasua, komisario Palmu!* in which different narrative spaces, created by flashbacks, are connected by a singular, distinctive 'ping' sound of a vibraphone. This takes place while the attorney, after describing the pasts of Kirsti Skrof and Kaarle Lankela, continues to tell what had happened the day before. The story is quickly told with the help of flashbacks that give colour and strong intensity to the narration. The attorney states that Mrs Skrof had changed her will the day before the murder. While he talks, dissonant harmonium music creeps up and can be clearly heard, when he says that he will tell everything in the order it happened.

We hear the first of the singular pings with a cut to a flashback showing Mrs Skrof screaming furiously at the attorney's place that her eyes have finally opened. She tears up the old will, jumps on it and demands a new one be written at once. The harmonium music continues during the whole flashback. The attorney's voiceover is heard at the end of the scene. The picture freezes for a short moment, and as we hear a new ping, there is a cut back to the present.

Another ping sound introduces the next flashback, which begins with a freeze-frame of a testament in the attorney's hand in the staircase. Yet another ping seems to make the picture move, and the attorney is shown walking up the stairs, with no more background music. Kirsti rushes down the stairs and cries out that she will never, ever come back again. The flashback ends in a freeze-frame, and the attorney continues the story as a narrating voiceover, also during the following flashbacks. From here on the attorney's story proceeds as a series of flashbacks without the image returning to the present between them. The flashbacks are separated from each other on the one hand with freeze-frames, and on the other with ping sounds of a vibraphone. The music heard during these flashback scenes is still played by a harmonium, and the ping sounds have nothing to do with the rest of the music heard in the film either: vibraphone is not used in the musical score. Thus, the ping sounds are perceived as sound effects, not as music.

Because the pings are separated from the music, they are also unexpected. They arouse an impression of a punctuation mark of a sort, a colon, or a dash, or numbering of the scenes that took place the day before. As the attorney says, he tells the series of events in the order they happened. These singular, highly distinguishable sound effects also give special meaning to the following flashbacks, as if to underline them. All in all, the mixture of flashbacks, freeze-frames, narrative voice, harmonium music and ping sounds creates an idiosyncratic cinematic approach, once again transgressing our aesthetic expectations by combining modernist distantiation and comic surprise.

II Temporal transgressions

Manipulation of duration and rhythm

Several of the spatial comical effects discussed above also have a temporal dimension that work either together with or as a counterpoint to each other. For example, besides being an unlikely choice for this kind of film, the tinkling piano with its chaotic and extremely speedy tune is also at odds with the overall rhythm of the film. We hear the tinkling honky-tonk piano several times during the film, for instance when Palmu and Virta rush into Kaarle Lankela's penthouse apartment trying to prevent his friend Kuurna (Pentti Siimes) from committing suicide. They are called out by the phone, career to Lankela's house by police car, and look up to his window. There is a quick zoom-in to a silhouette figure of an apparently hanging man in the window (Figure 9). At exactly this moment the honky-tonk piano starts playing. The policemen charge into the staircase, and through the glass walls we see them run all the way up (Figure 10), only to find out that it is a dummy that hangs in the window.

Generic expectations would certainly bend to up-tempo or even feverish music during such a scene, but since the honky-tonk tune remains hectic all the time without nuances that would manipulate the excitement, this is far from an average musical choice for a scene that is supposed to be suspenseful. Therefore, what we get is a case of aesthetic indecorum, a discrepancy between the rhythm of the music and the supposed rhythm of the action, giving room for comic transgression. Further, the rhythm of the music is also out of tune with the grumpy and sluggish presence of Palmu; in the following film Virta, having become Palmu's superior, is constantly making remarks on his apparent inefficiency.

Also, the extensive use of still images and freeze-frames creates a disparity in temporal duration: with each freeze-frame the story time stops for a moment

Figure 9 The hanging man in the window

while the screen time goes on (see Bordwell, 1985). There is, of course, nothing inherently comic in the use of freeze-frames, as the ending of Truffaut's *Les quatre cents coups* (1959) and many other classic examples of the device remind us. In the stills and freeze-frames of *Kaasua, komisario Palmu!*, however, comic surprise is often involved. For example, some of the stills seen during the attorney's account show Mrs Skrof and Kirsti playing the harmonium. Hearing the harmonium music while seeing these immobile images that change in the dragging tempo of the music, creates such a coupling of continuity in soundtrack and discontinuity in images one would perhaps expect in a musical, but not in a detective film.

There are other forms of variation in rhythm and duration that spur comic interpretations as well. Some of the characters are themselves portrayed as comic, with a strong emphasis on the use of voice; this concerns especially the character of Kuurna. When Palmu and Virta first question Lankela and Kuurna about the murder, the two young men do not take the police seriously, until they hear that Lankela's aunt is dead. Kuurna, an upper-class bohemian modernist artist, is a chatty and witty figure, who does most of the talking. The swift rhythm of his speech while recounting his and Lankela's activities of

Figure 10 Policemen running up the stairs

the night of the murder, the expressions chosen, and sometimes also the tone of his voice, all add to the comic impression; he sometimes even punctuates his story by self-consciously raising his pitch to crow-like sounds, creating an extreme contrast to Palmu's grumpy and lowish tone of voice. At times his story is accompanied by highly exaggerated gestures. The overall effect is amusing; one does not expect anybody to give a report to the police in this manner (Figure 11). Social as well as generic expectations clash with the realization of the storytelling.

When Kuurna tells the police how he visited Mrs Skrof, the narration is full of quick flashbacks that are entered and left with a direct cut. Some of the flashbacks are told in still images, some of them start and end with a freeze-frame. There are several sound bridges to and from the flashbacks, and a few times Kuurna continues his story right from the dialogue spoken in the flashbacks, sometimes contemplating the truthfulness of or commenting on the previous dialogue. In all, the pace of the series of flashbacks is swift and rhythmic, and sudden sound cuts add to the vivaciousness of the narration. When visiting Mrs Skrof, Kuurna enters in the middle of a skirmish: the dog

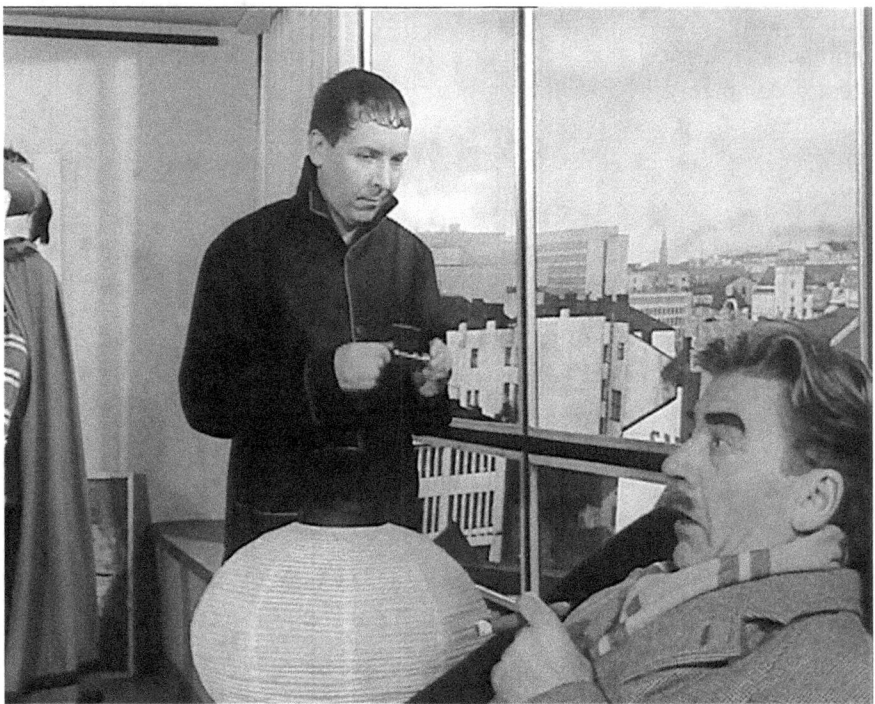

Figure 11 Kuurna talks to the police

barks, the caretaker's wife washes dishes, making a terrible noise, and Mrs Skrof is quarrelling loudly with the preacher of the dubious parish. Sudden cuts between these harsh sounds and Kuurna's narrating voice play on recurrent surprises, and in order to confirm the comicality of Kuurna's narration, he has a diegetic audience; during Kuurna's chattering Palmu and Virta try to keep a straight face, Palmu a grumpy one, Virta somewhat bemused. Palmu is obviously concentrating to make sense of all this and to put all the pieces of information in the right place in his mind.

But the most apparently comical part of Kuurna's story is still ahead. After the two had partied in a restaurant until 3 am, they thought that the national poet Runeberg deserved some attention. "That is why I said to Kalle: Listen Kalle," and the sentence is completed visually in a flashback that does not include dialogue at all, only music. Both image and sound are manipulated: the picture jumps like a worn copy of an old silent film projected a bit too fast, and the music, the already familiar jolly honky-tonk piano tune, sounds this time very narrow, like it would if it came out of a small box. The music clashes with the aesthetic expectations in one way, but at the same time it perfectly fits the visuals, since this flashback clearly takes a form of a silent film comedy presentation; in the early 1960s most Finnish viewers would be familiar with silent slapstick comedy as television compilations, which typically were accompanied by fast-moving piano.

Figure 12 In front of the poet's statue

Also, the narrative content of the flashback is a pastiche of a slapstick comedy. In front of the poet's statue the young men spot a drunken gentleman approaching. Kuurna catches his attention while Lankela steals his top hat, which he then places on the head of the relatively high statue (Figure 12). When he climbs down, the gentleman is waiting for him in the flowerbed beneath the statue. A policeman arrives, assumes that it is the drunken gentleman who put the top hat on the statue, and takes the furious gentleman away. The young men congratulate each other for a prank well done by slapping each other on the back, and the music ends in a cadence. The whole flashback is shot from a distance, as if in a 1910s slapstick comedy, and acting in this "film within a film" mimics what Roberta Pearson (1992) calls "histrionic" acting, with strictly coded and highly exaggerated gestures. Displaying a caricature of what in the 1960s was considered silent film acting, this flashback arouses comedy by contrasting the grandiose gestures of the characters with accelerated speed of action, and, at the meta-narrative level, by suddenly changing the mode of narration to a stylized and assumingly anachronistic form of comedy.

Repetition

Kuurna's story has not ended yet. After the statue episode the two comrades decide to do some sport. Kuurna tells: "First, Kalle drove, and I was standing." He does not use Kaarle Lankela's proper name, but the nickname "Kalle"; otherwise there is pretentious dignity and pathos in Kuurna's voice. He continues to mock the authorities by telling the story to the police as if he was entertaining his young friends over a beer. A direct cut to the flashback shows a small convertible sports car – extremely rare and exclusive in the early 1960s Finland, expressing the wealth of the owner – driving on a sidewalk in an empty city centre. A military drum is drumming briskly. Kuurna, standing in the moving car, grabs a hanging signboard off a shop while the car drives under it. A couple of cymbal sounds add to the assumed heroics of the young man, as well as the accentuation with a bass drum. After a cut back to the present tense, Kuurna announces with similar pompousness as before: "Then: I drove, and Kalle was standing." Thus there is an effect of repetition with a variation. The military drum keeps rolling softly while he speaks, as if waiting for the action to start again. And it does: there is a cut back to the summer night's entertainment, showing Lankela driving and Kuurna grabbing a barbershop sign. The agile drumming also continues, giving the action a mockingly heroic touch.

Given that the previous flashback featured the statue of Runeberg, the chosen music style and instrument are likely to bring to the minds of Finnish audiences the epic and heroic poems that J.L. Runeberg wrote about the war between Sweden and Russia 1808–09. Kuurna's pretentious narrative voice associates with the tradition – familiar also from several classical Finnish films – of reciting these poems with great pathos. Connected to the silliness seen in the pictures, which no doubt gives the young men merit among their social circles, the music and the narrative voice create a social collision, the goal of which is to make us laugh.

The sound of drumming also connects the different narrative spaces and, while doing it, adjusts the musical dramatics to the situation. It takes advantage of the pause in the other space, using it as a means of increasing the excitement of what is to happen next. What we get is repetition, a temporal comical effect, as well as a spatial transgression: unexpected connecting of different diegetic spaces through sound.

Conclusion

When discussing the comic aural instances in *Kaasua, komisario Palmu!* we have constantly noticed the ambiguous relation between comical, suspenseful and modernist devices. In each of these, there are elements of surprise and playing with expectations involved, arguably even more so in aural than in visual or verbal comedy. The extent to which we interpret these surprises and transgressions as comic has very much to do with the context of the reception, and, retrospectively, also with the reception history of the film.

While modernist cinematic devices often become 'domesticated' and naturalized as we get used to them – Soviet montage of the 1920s was adopted to Hollywood montage sequences in the 1930s, Godardian jump cuts later became trademarks of prime-time US television series like *Homicide* (1993–1999) etc. – we argue that the Palmu films are likely to seem more modernist now than in the early 1960s. Just like many of the early 1960s New Wave films, *Kaasua, komisario Palmu!* now easily strikes viewers as both a classic detective story and a self-conscious re-working of the genre. At the time, however, it was deeply rooted in and associated with the traditional studio production system, and thus quite distinct from the modernist film movements usually coming from outside the big studios. For present viewers the studio association is definitely still relevant – the familiar professional actors, the technical skill, the relatively high production value – but the self-conscious narrative devices are arguably more likely to catch one's eye now. No doubt, the element of comedy is still there, but the more self-conscious the narrative appears, the more liable we are to pay attention to formal instead of social aspects of comedy.

Later, the director Matti Kassila stated in an interview (1995a) that at this stage of his career he was determinedly looking for fresh cinematic approaches within the studio system. Indeed, he had also made an excursion into independent film production just before the Palmu series, with *Lasisydän/ The Glass Heart* (1959), an art cinema-influenced road movie – or a "walking film" as Kassila (1995b) also classifies it, referring to European films with protagonists drifting aimlessly from one place to another – that broke away from studio traditions, for instance by using only post-produced sound and introducing jazzy popular tunes instead of a classical soundtrack. Compared with *Lasisydän*, the Palmu-films have a stronger affiliation with studio filmmaking: in the director's own words these detective films summed up everything he had learned about filmmaking so far, while at the same leaving room for playing with musical sound effects, flashback transitions etc. (Kassila, 2004).

There is, actually, a two-way relationship between modernist and comical devices. Not only do some formal comedies in particular historical circumstances come close to cinematic modernism – as can be seen in the praise given to

Jerry Lewis by French modernist circles in the late 1960s – but also not all forms of modernist movement lack the touch of comedy. A case in point here is the early and mid-1960s Jean-Luc Godard, renowned for his experiments with film sound. Whatever is involved in, for instance, the sudden and unexpected cutting off of music over and over again in *Une femme est une femme* (1961) or the famous 'one minute' total silence in *Bande à part*, nuances of comedy cannot be overlooked. Due to narrative, generic and reception historical contexts such playing with aesthetic rules in Godard is bound to be considered experimental – exploring the limits and foregrounding the conventions of cinematic narration – rather than comic. In a popular studio film like *Kaasua, komisario Palmu!* aesthetic transgressions are more likely to serve the narrative goals of the film, to keep us in suspense and to make us laugh. Perhaps, however, an analysis of the sound in the Palmu films might remind us that at a given historical moment there was common ground well worth rethinking in the use of sound in a modernist film and a popular detective film.

Notes

1. The manuscripts can be studied at the Finnish National Audiovisual Archive.
2. The third film was actually based on an original script by Waltari, who later revised it into a novel. Yet another sequel, *Vodkaa, komisario Palmu/Vodka, Mr. Palmu* was made in 1969. No longer scripted by Waltari, this film is a political thriller dealing with Finnish–Soviet relations and differs from the original three films substantially.

References

Bordwell, D., Staiger, J., & Thompson, K. (1985). *The Classical Hollywood Cinema. Film Style & Mode of Production to 1960*. London, Melbourne & Henley: Routledge & Kegan Paul.

Bordwell, D. (1985). *Narration in the Fiction Film*. London: Methuen.

Branigan, E. (2006). *Projecting a Camera. Language-Games in Film Theory*. New York, London: Routledge.

Bratu Hansen, M. (2000). The Mass Production of the Senses: Classical Cinema as Vernacular Modernism. In C. Gledhill & L. Williams (Eds.), *Reinventing Film Studies* (pp. 332–350). London: Arnold.

Brown, R.S. (1994). *Overtones and Undertones. Reading Film Music*. Berkeley & Los Angeles, CA, London: University of California Press.

Buhler, J., Neumeyer, D., & Deemer, R. (2010). *Hearing the Movies. Music and Sound in Film History*. New York, Oxford: Oxford University Press.

Freud, S. (1999). *Wit and Its Relation to the Unconscious*. London: Routledge (orig. 1905).

Gabrielsson, A., & Lindström, E. (2001). The Influence of Musical Structure on Emotional Expression. In P. Juslin & J.A. Sloboda (Eds.), *Music and Emotion* (pp. 223–248). Oxford: Oxford University Press.

Gorbman, C. (1987). *Unheard Melodies. Narrative Film Music.* London, Bloomington, IN: BFI & Indiana UP.
Juva, A. (2008). *'Hollywood-syndromi', jazzia ja dodekafoniaa. Elokuvamusiikin funktioanalyysi neljässä 1950- ja 1960-luvun vaihteen suomalaisessa elokuvassa.* Åbo: Åbo Akademi University Press.
Kassila, M. (1995a). An interview by Anu Juva, 22 August 1995.
Kassila, M. (1995b). *Mustaa ja valkoista.* Helsinki: Otava.
Kassila, M. (2004). *Käsikirjoitus ja ohjaus: Matti Kassila.* Helsinki: WSOY.
Kozloff, S. (1988). *Invisible Storytellers. Voice-Over Narration in American Fiction Film.* Berkeley & Los Angeles, CA, London: University of California Press.
Neale, S. (1980). *Genre.* London: BFI.
Neale, S., & Krutnik, F. (1990). *Popular Film and Television Comedy.* London: Routledge.
Pearson, R.E. (1992). *Eloquent Gestures. The Transformation of Performance Style in the Griffith Biograph Films.* Berkeley, Los Angeles, New York: University of California Press.

Kimmo Laine is a collegium researcher at the Turku Institute for Advanced Studies (TIAS) and a lecturer of Film Studies at the University of Oulu. He has published two books (in Finnish) and a number of articles (in Finnish and English) on film and genre history, as well as co-editing a series of anthologies on Finnish filmmakers Valentin Vaala (2004), Hannu Leminen (2008) and Matti Kassila (2013). His ongoing research seeks ways to analyse film style with an awareness of contextual factors.

Anu Juva is a music researcher at Åbo Akademi University in Turku, Finland. She has published two books (in Finnish) and several articles on film music and cultural history of music.

10 Spanish Film Music in the 1940s
Comedy, Subversion, and Dissident Rhythms in the Films of Manuel Parada

Laura Miranda

Introduction

Post-war cinema was dominated by comedy. Researchers' dedication to particular aspects of filmmaking during the Franco regime has led to a biased vision of the reality of Spanish film of the 1940s–50s, during which comedy rose to account for 40 per cent of total production. This prominence renders it the genre *par excellence* of the period, representing an "attempt at Hollywood-esque high comedy or sophisticated comedy" which was far from the supposed ideology of the dominant class (Ortiz, 2001: 115, 124).

Despite attempts to create and elevate a national cinema, throughout these two decades it was obvious that the Spanish public had already accustomed themselves to North American productions during the pre-war years, a trend that had consolidated during the Republic, logically resulting in a preference for American imports over domestic productions. It is probable that this was the reason that the Spanish comedy of the era opted for a sophisticated path that critics stigmatized as being excessively superficial during a period of famine. In this context, the influence often ascribed to the so-called 'white telephone' comedies, imported from Mussolini's Italy, is not particularly plausible, with Hollywood films providing the principal emulated models. In fact, those same Italian productions can be regarded as essentially imitations of the North American model anyway.

Drawing on a tradition deriving from Segundo de Chomón (with his *Hotel Eléctrico* (1905), and passing through Gelabert, Buchs and Delgado, Benito Perojo used comedy in *Susana tiene un secreto* (*Susana has a secret*) (1933) and *Rumbo al Cairo* (*Bound for Cairo*) (1935) before his success in the folklore genre. In a similar vein, Harry D'Abbadie D'Arrast directed *La traviesa molinera* (*It Happened in Spain*) (1934) and then Luis Marquina and Eduardo García Maroto appeared as directors. But it was Edgar Neville, influenced by the *sainete*,[1] who gave comedies an air of modernity without losing sight of the folkloric and popular roots of the Spanish tradition, an approach that some of the most important directors of the post-war period adopted. This is certainly the case with Juan de Orduña and his *Deliciosamente Tontos* (*Deliciously Silly*, 1943) or *Tuvo la Culpa Adán* (*Adam Was Guilty*, 1944), Rafael Gil in his surrealist *Eloísa Está Debajo de un Almendro* (*Eloísa Is Under an Almond Tree*, 1943) and José Luis Sáenz de Heredia with his popular *El Destino se Disculpa* (*Destiny Apologizes*, 1945) and *Historias de la Radio* (*Radio Stories*, 1955).[2]

The relationship between the members of the so-called 'other' generation of '27[3] was prominent in filmmaking, where each member's different contributions gave the movies a graceful air of modernity. These films were far removed from the Manichean and ideologically over-determined films of the 1940s and, by extension, the 1950s. The link between the members of this group was, without a doubt, the use of humour as a catharsis for the depressing situation the country was facing at the time. The comedy produced by the group of filmmakers belonging to or related to the 'other' generation of '27 was not particularly to the taste of the regime, which tried various means to convert the initial scripts into something closer to the popular comedies of the previous decade.

Enrique Jardiel Poncela, Wenceslao Fernández Flórez and the Mihura brothers were the main architects of the genre, capturing in their literary works the implausible situations that later on were transferred to the screen. The plots of these films proposed a vision of reality usually focused on economic security. The majority of the protagonists face love relationships as a necessary catharsis at the end of the films; once the main character notices his error by attempting to fall for the wrong girl, he returns to the arms of his girlfriend despite her (generally) lower social status.[4]

The two examples that I address in detail in this chapter are *El Camino de Babel* (*The Path to Babel*, Jerónimo Mihura, 1944) and *El Destino se Disculpa* (*Destiny Apologizes*, J.L. Sáenz de Heredia, 1945), the former with a screenplay by Jerónimo Mihura (in collaboration with José Luis Sáenz de Heredia) and the later by Wenceslao Fernández Flórez. Music for both films was provided by Manuel Parada, one of Spanish cinema's principal composers of the period. The two films provide an interesting perspective on the era in question which moves away from the Manichean ideology of *cine de cruzada*, the splendour of historical drama and the sordidness of film noir (*cine negro*), presenting a discourse with a great deal of humour which was not widely popular (probably due to the films' somewhat elitist aesthetics, which allowed them to avoid undue censorship despite their highly subversive nature).

El Camino de Babel or post-war social banalities

Provincial delegates were explicit at the premiere of *El Camino de Babel*, asserting that "Films of this type should be thoroughly revised before launching to the national or international market, because they obviously lack values which ratify our cinematographic position."[5] There is an evident lack of cohesion between Mihura's vision and the censors' tastes. It is clear that the film showed a way of life, marked by excessive debauchery, parties, cabarets and, of course, the dominant position of women, that was different to that which the new regime expected for Spaniards. All of this contributed to the film being officially denounced and deemed unworthy of being labelled as a 'Spanish' product.

Written and directed by Jerónimo Mihura and produced by Chapalo Films, the film centres on César (Alfredo Mayo, the main male pin-up of the era), Marcelino (Fernando Fernán Gómez) and Arturo (Miguel del Castillo), three university classmates who have to separate after finishing their studies in Medicine. César proposes a deal whereby they return to their home towns, choose the wealthiest woman to marry and then use the fortunes of their respective wives to increase the capital of the group. Marcelino happily accepts, but Arturo has serious doubts because he doesn't believe that anyone can put their social and economic desires before their emotional interests. At the end of the film, desperate and annoyed by their own lies, Arturo, who has married a wealthy heiress, brings them back together and hands each friend 30,000 *duros* so they can start new lives.

In this film, Parada uses a series of musical cues that create specific comic atmospheres in a soundtrack full of structural cues and 'Mickey Mousing' effects. Musical episodes are clearly separated by long silent scenes, allowing the characters' dialogue to develop the action; action that, at the same time, often appears somewhat static due to the lack of musical continuity. In fact, the main criticisms of the film were directed at the actors, who were characterized as excessively theatrical, showing little mobility. Mihura appears to have been trying to produce a film where the dialogue provides the centre of attention and where the music reasserts what is presented on the screen.

The music selected by Parada in the first numbers establishes the social tastes of young university students and new graduates and the chosen pieces parody their ridiculous aspirations to social ascent. The film commences with opening credits displayed in a sophisticated manner on presentation cards. The score accompanying these is performed by an orchestra with traditional wind and string sections and a brass section (featuring trumpets, trombones, and alto and tenor saxophones), together with percussion, a harp and piano. These elements provide a clear jazz orchestration that prepares the spectator for an unpretentious Hollywood-style romantic comedy.

The principal function of the initial jazz orchestration is to distance the film from the established social mould. This is made all the more evident by the subsequent musical passage, a solemn and somewhat pompous musical cue that accompanies a scene in the main auditorium of the University, where the male protagonists are about to graduate and where the rector is reading his speech. With a *solemne* tempo, Parada indicates the seriousness of the University in G major. A ternary metre with a constant rhythm, with dotted quaver, semiquaver and two quarter-notes a bar, is emphasized by the use of tonal scale chords, which Parada's score marks as *very accentuated* and where the brass and string sections *en masse* alternate with the woodwinds. With this alternation between military and processional, the theme can be understood to mock the pomposity of the scene.

The apparent seriousness of this event is undermined when Parada introduces an intertextual Bach reference, a piece of the dance suite, 'Badinerie', performed by the first flute, clarinet and violin. The B minor passage injects an element of humour while the Vice Chancellor's pompous speech tires the students, who are eager to dance and party after finishing their studies. The graduates' party, where a jazz band with tuxedos gives its version of the song 'Olé, olé, olé, que mañana ya no hay cole' ('Tomorrow There's No School'), provide an interesting narrative counterpoint where various socio-cultural practices of the era are challenged by a new generation that wants to dispense with them, at least at this point in their lives.

In his analysis of Jerónimo Mihura's comedies, Steve Marsh comments that 'high' and 'low' culture become blurred in a cinema whose performances acquire a comic format and where binary oppositions (innovation/tradition, village/city ...) appear confused due to the centrifugal power of the secondary characters, who rise to the category of protagonists, and who either come from a low social class and/or are female. Marsh identifies that the fools in Mihura's films do not only parody others, but also themselves as a result of their desire for social and economic ascent. The cases of César and Marcelino are no exception: Marcelino supports the decisions of his friends 'hook, line and sinker', despite not having the courage to follow them through, involving himself in a series of ridiculous situations, heading for failure.

Parada presents the aforementioned binary oppositions not only between innovation and tradition, but also between village and city. The latter is evident when César returns to his birthplace in search of a wife, with two musical segments illustrating the behaviour of the villagers before the arrival of the destabilizing element, César. César's desire to marry a wealthy woman is represented in a positive manner and validates a widespread aspiration in Spain portrayed in many films in the 1940s–50s, in G minor. Parada chooses 3/8 for a *pasodoble* rhythm with the introduction of two women in mourning with shawls, one of them explaining César's situation to the other in extravagant detail. Parada chooses the oboe for a graceful melody, pizzicato with V and I chords and small feature for the flute, piano and harp, which underline the idyllic effect of the countryside, at the same time as emphasizing the absurdity of the situation.

Example 1 Pasodoble theme

The dynamism of the above passage transitions to an idyllic and pastoral mood in the subsequent segment, when César has decided on Clotide, an ugly but rich heiress who spends her hours painting the surrounding landscapes. As César approaches the (eccentrically dressed) woman during her walk towards the river, the music features the ternary subdivision (6/8) again, this time in the major (G) with a *dolce* and *vibrato* incidental theme in the flute and a pentatonic scale background, while the base organ uses only I and V chords. The naive feel of the music remains constant. César comments on the characters' similar personalities and common interests accompanied by this incidental theme of 8 bars, which is subsequently repeated by the oboes in the lower octave. Parada plays with this theme, repeating the musical segments on three occasions to frame the plans of the characters and their emotional reactions while accentuating the ridiculousness of the scene and the characters' attire, creating a mood that is broken by the seriousness and common sense that represents the appearance of César's future wife: Laura.

Common sense is represented in Mihura's comedies through the female characters. In this film Laura, the female protagonist, has a clearly subversive function. Marsh defines the female characters as "swindlers", more in touch with reality than of the rest of the male characters (crazy and dazed by their own daydreams), which allows them to take control over their destinies. But, despite assuming credible roles, such women cannot exist outside of a fictional setting, defined by the typical canons of comedy, and are required to abide by dominant socio-moral codes (Marsh, 2006: 35–36).

The incidental theme set out for César and Clotide's engagement presents the duality M/m (major/minor) in its two appearances, with a background of harp and piano: the first time (repeated) in D, illustrating Clotide's happiness, and the second time in its minor homonym, illustrating the presence of Encarna (Laura's friend) and the ensuing gossip:

Table 1 Engagement theme

Time	Theme	Instrument	Tonal Plan	Scene/Dialogue
28:04	Engagement	Concertino	D Major (I-IV)	Clotide with her friends
28:30		Violin	D Major (II-V-I), re (IV-V-I)	Lady Luisa with her friends
28:54		Flute, oboe, 1st trumpet	D minor (I-IV-V-I)	Lady Luisa praises César; receives the call from Encarna
29:15		Flute, oboe, 1st trumpet	D minor (I-IV-V-I)	The friends of Lady Luisa gossip about Laura and César

After Laura's trick at the engagement party, César leaves the house with a whip ready to make things clear. The music provides a structural element, an *agitado* passage in B minor, which generates tension from a dominant chord and develops an ascending progression of crochets, dotted quavers and semi-quavers (which is a characteristic rhythm of these comedies). The women lock César in Laura's house while on the other side of the door the milkman measures the milk in a vase and Encarna begins to play 'Ensueño de amor' ('Dream of Love') by Liszt on the piano.[6]

The depiction of young women of marrying age performing pieces on the piano in private rooms was a regular feature of various genres in the era (such as literary adaptations, which explored the role of women in the private sphere). However, in this case the scene departs from convention and mocks this socio-cultural practice with a secondary character (Encarna), who has only received basic education in the village, performing Liszt on the piano. The interesting combination of dialogue and music presents a comical situation, dominated not only by the witty and mischievous behaviour of women but also by representing a cultural background well above the average of Spanish society of the era, especially in a village where pianos appear all over the place and women dress in sophisticated style with high heels. Edgar Neville also went on to present a hilarious scene in his last film, *Mi calle* (*My Street*) (1960), where he represented a bourgeois couple who aspired for upwards social mobility by hosting celebrities in their home while the woman performed a version of the composition 'El pajarito' ('The Bird'), deafening her audience in the process.

Unlike the women in the film, the male protagonists are mocked because of their supposed seriousness and due to the audience's awareness of the manner in which the narrative is unfolding, finally requiring the help of their wives to overcome the difficulties that they have found themselves wrapped up in. Through stylized jazz rhythms, the music provides a sophisticated atmosphere and seriousness in the scenes in which the male characters plan their conquests, although this only results in absurdities that neither César, nor Marcelino, nor Arturo are aware of. An example of this occurs at the beginning of the film. After the performance of 'Olé, olé, olé', the friends go out to the terrace to speak about their future and promise each other to only marry rich heiresses. This same musical setting presents itself again when, after the protagonists have met their respective wives, César and Marcelino get together to talk business. In this case, the music does not present a rhythm marked by the brass section, like in the previous case, but rather a jazz melody equally stylized in a slower tempo with violins. This use of a slow tempo, with pronounced lyricism, presents calm and maturity for a considered and calculated plan and not a spontaneous outburst started at a party. Moreover, the change in timbre from brass instruments to the violin provides more comfort for the protagonists, who lodge in a sophisticated hotel on the coast (supposedly Santander) and which generates major doses of irony for its function as a counterpoint.

The continuation of the lies brings with it a waste of money on the part of both couples, who do not hesitate to dress in an opulent manner and even bet large sums of money at the racetrack, a situation which is represented by a musical setting in a dull and uninspiring C major. After his conversation with the crazy Brandolet (the secondary character Manolo Morán), César and Marcelino arrive at the racetrack charged with adrenaline. The change to A major emphasizes César's aspirations to become a millionaire and, similarly, his subsequent celebration in the cabaret Los Incas[7] suggests his desire for a different style of life to ordinary Spanish society.

In the case of the cabaret, it is the female lead characters who demonstrate an interest in and the taste for the fashionable rhythms and 'modern' style of life, proposing a fun night at the cabaret. By contrast, the secondary female characters opt for the national traditions of *pasodoble* or for the pastoral sophistication of the countryside (Cloti) or for the classic bourgeois concert halls (Encarna). In any case, it remains obvious in this film that the male characters are no more than puppets in the hands of the secondary characters, for example the crazy Brandolet or the women. The music presents this masculine dependence in the jazz numbers, where the women are the ones who try and get their husbands to participate in the novel cultural forms.

In the cabaret scene, orchestral jazz musical numbers are performed to an audience adorned in designer clothes and abundant fur coats. The camera emphasizes the importance of the saxophone and the trumpets in the orchestra while the four protagonists enter elegantly, with their desire to be frivolous being emphasized by their ordering four bottles of champagne. The bandleader, speaking with a clearly foreign accent (which allows for the elaboration of his speech), asks the attendees to release themselves from social obligations and show themselves "just as they are", "The bullfighter way!", reciting the following song lyrics (in translation):

> It's worth everything, it's worth everything, there is no stopping, nobody has to pretend,
> It's worth everything, don't fall silent, say everything that you need to say.
> If your friend is a bore, throw him off the balcony
> If you like the woman next to you, tell her that she is yummy
> Today there are no boyfriends nor husbands who can get angry!
> It's worth everything, it's worth everything, there is no stopping, nobody has to pretend,
> It's worth everything, don't fall silent, say everything that you need to say.

The audience dances, lets off party blowers into the air and gets drunk. It seems highly improbable that lyrics like these would have evaded official scrutiny but it seems likely that the comic genre context enabled them to get by. After consuming the four bottles of champagne, César and Marcelino rest drunkenly in the men's bathroom, wearing false moustaches, while the music changes tempo, with the piano leading a slower tempo passage. A man then enters the restroom and confuses César for a woman. Parada's use of extra-diegetic jazz music as a background during the male conversation inescapably recalls the previous discussions between the protagonists and now emphasizes the incoherency of their thinking. This manner of questioning masculine behaviour is also apparent in the analysis of the following film, where silence is used to enhance the scenes with senseless dialogue and with use of musical segments that reclaim subversive spaces.

El destino se disculpa (*Destiny Forgives You*) and the metempsychosis

This film by José Luis Sáenz de Herida exemplifies the Spanish director's capacity for adaptation. Despite the fact that his most remembered and accomplished works are more in line with the contemporary hegemony, the director also found space in his cinematic portfolio for work with a different inflection. Connected to the 'other' generation of '27 through friendship, the script of the film is based on *La fantasía occidental* (*The Occidental Fantasy*) by Wenceslao Fernández Flórez, who was responsible for the plot and dialogue (although officially the script was co-authored by Sáez de Heredia).[8]

The film concerns Ramiro Arnal (Rafael Durán), a playwright whose best friend is the actor Teófilo Dueñas (Fernando Fernán Gómez). After enormous success in his home town with a work written by the former and performed by the latter, they move to Madrid. However, the protagonists' hopes to triumph are cut short. Teófilo has an accident and dies, only to go on to appear to

Ramiro as a spirit, materializing himself to Ramiro in various forms (as a coat hanger, a statue, a dog etc.) In spite of Teófilo's advice, Ramiro invests a recently acquired fortune in scientific studies which end up being a fiasco. When this transpires, Elena (Mary Lamar), Ramiro's fiancée, who was only after his fortune, walks out on him. The protagonist realizes his mistake and that he is in love with Valentina (Mª Esperanza Navarro), a woman from his village who teaches him how to run a grocery business that she has bought with her sister Benita.

The main problem as regards censorship lay in the appearance of Teófilo. In fact, the initial report of the script stated that it "offers serious objections to the natural moral doctrine", a characterization that relates to the complaints resulting from the premiere of the American film *El difunto protesta* (*Here Comes Mr. Jordan*, Alexander Hall, 1941). The report indicated that these issues demanded "a doctrinal sanitation of the script", which had to be modified as an obligatory requirement for its approval. A final passage of dialogue was required that would explain that the ghost was actually just Ramiro's conscience. However, this passage never eventuated and all of these issues seem to have been forgotten by 30 January 1945 when the film was put forward for authorization.[9]

With all of this in mind, Parada presents a very interesting soundtrack for the mid-1940s, which, in addition to its regular orchestral formation, again includes a jazz band in a couple of numbers. In spite of the lack of density of comedy soundtracks, the maestro included two leitmotifs (associated with the spirit of Teófilo and with death) and various main themes that, balanced with long scenes in silence, support potentially subversive inflections. Parada dedicates a musical theme or rather a leitmotif to each character or fundamental element of the work, starting with Destiny which, as an innovative and uncommon element in Spanish cinema, Parada links with the film's opening sequence. Steven Marsh comments that this "character", humanized through his functional and amusing role, presents an open argument by intertwining destiny and common sense. In fact, he adds, this film utilizes mythological elements (the supernatural, mystical and heroic) and includes them in the realm of the mundane (Marsh, 2001: 102).

Example 2 Destiny theme

Parada does not dedicate a specific theme to Teófilo's character while he is alive, but after his death he receives a leitmotif characteristic of five notes which play when his spirit appears on-screen. Steve Marsh speaks of the "hybridization of Ramiro" after the death of Teófilo due to the spirit of the latter acting as his conscience. Even accepting this, it seems quite obvious that the spirit of Teófilo was something more than Ramiro Arnal's conscience. Before the first appearance of this leitmotif, Parada presents a cell of six notes, associated with Teófilo's death, in violins and violas with a pentatonic scale in C. The premonition of the death reinforces the metatextual nature of a large part of the film's music and prepares the audience for the second stage with Teófilo transformed into a ghost.

Example 3 Death cell

Example 4 Leitmotif of Teófilo's spirit

The music contributes to the gestation of the new emotional state, no longer the protagonist's, but the audience's. When Ramiro holds several conversations about his past mistakes with Teófilo, in the guise of a dog, the leitmotif appears in a constant form before it changes from A♭ major via a type of centripetal feedback. Parada chooses a final tonality of F minor to present the leitmotif on the piano for a desperate Ramiro, before final passages in G major, A♭ major and D major, concluding in F minor with a mischievous cadence that coincides with the final appearance of Destiny. The following chart demonstrates the appearances of the leitmotif in detail and makes evident the referenced 'hybridization' of Ramiro:

Table 2 Appearance of Ramiro and Teófilo leitmotifs

Time	Instrument	Character (on screen)	Tonality	Dialogue/Scene
1:17:44	Flute	Ramiro	G	Teófilo dissuades Ramiro from committing suicide and says goodbye because his time as Ramiro's conscience is up
1:17:50	Flute	Ramiro		
1:17:52	Clarinet	Ramiro		
1:17:56	Flute	Dog		
1:17:59	Clarinet	Ramiro		

Spanish Film Music in the 1940s 181

Time	Instrument	Character (on screen)	Tonality	Dialogue/Scene
1:18:03	Oboe	Both	A♭	Teófilo tells Ramiro that there was not a lot he could do for Ramiro
1:18:15	Violoncello	Both, Ramiro, dog	A♭/D♭	Teófilo tells him again that he should talk himself out of his madness
1:18:25	2nd violin	Ramiro	D♭	
1:18:28	Clarinet and viola	Ramiro	D	T: "man's enemy is not Destiny, but man himself"
1:18:38	Bassoon, horn and French horns	Ramiro, dog		
1:18:42	Flute	Ramiro	G	Ramiro recognizes that Teófilo was right about everything
1:18:45	Clarinet	Ramiro, dog		
1:18:50	Flute	Ramiro		
1:18:53	Clarinet	Ramiro		
1:18:57	Oboe	Ramiro, dog, Ramiro	A♭	Ramiro insists that he is a failure
1:19:10	Piano	Dog, Ramiro's legs	F minor	Ramiro believes he can't change the situation
1:19:25	Violoncello	Both, Ramiro	A♭/D♭	Teófilo asks him to pay attention to him and enters through a door
1:19:33	2nd Violin	Ramiro, dog	D♭	
1:19:36	Clarinet and viola	Dog, Ramiro	D	Teófilo insists and Ramiro enters. Destiny interrupts

Parada presents the first theme in the village that Ramiro and Teófilo visit because Ramiro has to cover the opening of a fountain designed by the engineer, Ramiro Quintana (Manolo Morán again), in a live radio broadcast. There he meets Elena, who is the patron of the event. In this scene he demonstrates a lack of common sense that Parada reinforces through a number performed by the village band, which plays continuously. Initially, the music stays in the background while Ramiro covers the event, with the music stopping to allow for interviews of the mayor and professor. The absurdity of the situation transforms Parada's silence into a key piece of this carnivalization: "On ridiculing them (the civil powers), it situates itself in a context of the carnivalesque to the open-air dance of the village and the multitudes of potential threats to the 'natural' order of things" (Marsh, 2001: 104). The repetitive brass and percussion music, which employs tenor chords and a dominant ostinato, accentuates the ridiculousness of the general situation and, on a more specific level, Ramiro's own situation. While he feigns to be a serious writer he is reduced to the level of local announcer.

Parada presents a rupture with the absurdity of the situation of the village and presents a more sophisticated number when Ramiro flirts with Elena. Ramiro's attempts at sophistication, presented during the film in part due to Parada's music, continue to manifest themselves in absurd situations. Parada illustrates this with an *Allegro* ternary subdivision in E, with base chords that summarize the nonsensical position of Ramiro with piccolo, flute and clarinets. The tonal base and dominant approach of the music establishes the ridiculousness of the scene and suggests Ramiro's absurdity and, by extension, that of all of the village, personified by the band.

Ramiro is a person hungry for social ascent. His work on the radio, which at first he craves, is no longer to his liking after a few months of employment, and particularly after the episode in the village. When Teófilo finds out that his friend is a millionaire, he runs to find him at the radio station, where he finds Ramiro broadcasting with Kety del Rey, a popular Spanish announcer from the era. Del Rey is a 'modern' woman equally tired of her work situation, as revealed by her facial expression when announcing 'Clotide girdles', in the beginning of the following dialogue sequence (in translation):

> Ramiro: *Almacenes Feromundo are the best in the world*
> Kety: *Ladies, hide your imperfections with Clotilde girdles*
> R: *¡Cock-a-doodle-doo! There are always special chicken legs for sick people in the Asian Chicken Shop (...)*
> K: *At eleven...*
> R: *Cañí*
> K: *At one...*
> R: *La Cañí*
> K: *At 2...*
> R: *Cañí*
> K: *At five...*
> R: *Cañí! Every hour is good to drink La Cañi from the cellars of Jerez.*

Ramiro's character has, according to Marsh, a populist tinge: "the role that Ramiro is given to perform helps to ridicule the assumed 'prominent' figures of the community" (Marsh, 2001: 104). The music articulates a sense of the ridiculous through a jazz number that is a recording, instead of a piece performed by the band in the background to accompany the advertisements in the studio. However, only the background of the recording is apparent; the music can be heard at the same level as the advertisements. What is more, between advertisements, the volume rises and acquires a focal scale. Parada writes a jazz number for this sequence for clarinet, trumpets, bass drum, piano and double bass, which is repeated due to its brevity. A busy, syncopated and dotted/staccato theme in clarinet and piano is presented, whose harmonic base in I and V is provided by trumpets and double bass.

Example 5 Jazz theme on the radio

The jazz segment indicates a specific moment in Spanish society, when 'intoxicating' rhythms were allowed into film and radio to be used for quotidian and irrelevant matters like radio advertisements. But, above all, the use of North American rhythms, accepted by the audience of the era as a symptom of a relaxed and 'modern' society, presents an interesting space for subversion; especially when the only segment of the film that references regional folklore is heard in a mocking context, in the scene of the inauguration of the fountain. This is not the first example of such a usage: recalling that at the inauguration of the fountain, the popular rhythms change character before the conversation between Elena and Ramiro, making room for a more realistic view of women (one of the few inclusions of the xylophone with offbeat rhythms). As Ortiz points out, "[the women] smoke, drink, drive cars and travel alone. Certainly, they do not seem to go to church, but they do go to cabarets and parties" (Ortiz, 2001: 121-122).

When Ramiro and Elena go to the golf club, where Ramiro meets an engineer while she flirts with an old boyfriend, the music that accompanies the scene is a foxtrot number written for clarinets, alto saxophone, trumpets, trombone, percussion, strings and piano.[10] The tonality chosen, G major, projects an idea of relaxation which is imbued in the golf club. Parada maintains the first part of the musical segment (which again is repeated) while the pair walk through the building, where groups of friends and couples of their age are enjoying themselves, smoking and practising elite sports.

Example 6 Golf course theme

The use of part of the number in G to present the couple in society – as if recalling the adventures in the village with the inauguration of the fountain – gives the scene a pronounced comic feel, enhanced by the nature of the dance rhythm. The music attempts to transfer the ideals of North American romantic comedy to Spanish life without achieving it. What is more, it is accomplished in a mocking tone, allowing the adventure of the golf club to become a farce in which Ramiro is the main character. Nothing in the scene is actually realistic (neither the couple, nor Ramiro's social ascent, nor the engineer), but instead is rendered absurd by the humorous touch of Parada's foxtrot.

Love is, of course, one of the main themes in this type of comedy and composers usually dedicate long themes to express it that, in general, avoid jazz rhythms and what they connote. The love theme in this case is related to Valentina, eternally in love with Ramiro. It is the only one with continuity (if we don't take into account the leitmotifs for Teófilo and his relationship with the afterlife). Valentina fulfils the moral expectations of a 'good' woman: working in the grocery business, being quiet and, above all, being in love with her husband and dedicated in body and soul to looking after him. Valentina waits patiently for Ramiro to pay attention to her and waits equally patiently for his plans to marry Elena to be ruined.

The melodic nature of the love theme (which appears in five musical segments), the fact that Parada gives solo versions of this theme to the leader of the orchestra and the ample numbers of bars which span over each of its appearances, allow the audience to identify it and to identify themselves with it. What is more, he allows the female audience to identify with Valentina's character and, contrary to what occurs with Laura in the previous film, suggests the continuity of traditional moulds through the lyricism of this love theme in the face of the intoxicating invasion of cheerful and relaxed rhythms that relate to the 'flirt' Elena.

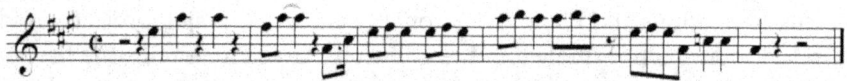

Example 7 Theme of love

The tonal construction of the theme while Benita speaks about her brother in front of Valentina is interesting:

Table 3 Changes in tonality during Benita's conversation

Minute	Tonality	Dialogue/Scene
32:32	C	Benita and Valentina speak about the grocery store
33:01	A♭ (IV-V-I)	Benita comments on how different her brother's personality is
33:15	C (I-IV-I-II-V-I)	B: He doesn't have any practical/pragmatic spirit [...] V: He's admirable! B: Yes, deep down, I'm very proud of him. He deserves one who loves him a lot, like we love him.

The changes in camera shot are also interesting. When the theme begins in C, a mid-shot captures Benita moving through the kitchen and talking with Valentina. The camera then presents a mid-shot fixed on the two women conversing about Benita's interests before the change to A♭, with the women then starting to move again through the kitchen while speaking as the theme adjusts to A♭. The return to C comes defined by another mid-shot which frames the women, but in this case in switched positions, in a way that centres the attention on Valentina and her captivation with an image of Ramiro, which becomes palpable to Benita.

Ramiro and Valentina's love theme is not heard again until the end of the film, when Ramiro, desperate, enters the store and finds Valentina. The musical number includes the love theme in an *Andante cantabile* played by the strings, and subsequently joined by the harp and, in the conclusion, the full orchestra. With this appearance of the theme, the issue of social ascent returns with the interference of the family in the couple's private sphere. Ramiro and Valentina's love situation is not only of concern to them but also to Benita, who has bought the grocery stores, allowing them to form an ideal family.

The importance of women in the patriarchal system of the era is a recurring theme in the cinema of the 1940s, which reflects the dominant social circumstance of the times. Benita's character rises to the status of a key protagonist as the film progresses, and her importance as a housewife destined to care for her brother and nephews changes radically when she makes the courageous step of buying the grocery stores. Parada uses F major to illustrate the future of the lovers who have overcome many obstacles before coming together. The selection of D minor for Valentina's explanation of Benita's purchase acts to diminish the importance of Ramiro's sister in the plot (although he permits a four bar solo concertino part that signals Benita's new status), with this suddenly changing to C major to provide a neutral ground on which to await Benita's explanation.

Conclusions

The freedom that Parada presents in the films discussed above reflects his relaxed and confident creative persona and his knowledge of how to use cinematic music as a mode of articulating certain attitudes that deviate from hegemonic ideology. The music in these films communicates these attitudes through offsetting the strict Catholic-national morality of the time and generates subversive situations that were of interest, in the end, not only to elite intellectuals. The scenes of silence in the films reaffirm the libertinism of romantic comedy films influenced by North American cinema, particularly evident in the use of diegetic and extra-diegetic jazz numbers that provide an escape route from moral rectitude and dominant music. Foxtrots, waltz rhythms and boogie-woogies contribute a note of colour to the cold framework of post-war Spanish music, allowing young people to come into contact with a modernity not only prevailing in Europe, but also in the USA.

Notes

1. A humorous dramatic piece in one act, Carlos Arniches (1866–1943) was a prolific author of *sainetes* and comedies and was a big influence on Neville. See Burguera Nadal, 1994, 1999; Ríos Carratalá, 2000; Gómez Tarín, 2001.
2. For a historiographical reference on comedy in the Spanish cinema, not only within the period of my study, see Rubio Lucia, 1986.
3. The *Generación del 27* (Generation of '27) was made up of a number of Spanish poets (Jorge Guillén, Pedro Salinas, Rafael Alberti, Federico García Lorca or Vicente Aleixandre, among others) who became known in the cultural landscape around the year 1927, starting with the homage to Luis de Gongora. The *'otra' generación del 27* ('other' generation of '27) emerged in parallel with the *Generation of '27* and centred on José López Rubio, Jardiel Poncela, Edgar Neville, the Mihura brothers, K-HITO or *Tono* to renovate Spanish humour. See, among others, Burguera and Fortuño Llorens, 1998.
4. Julio Arce has also approached the study of music in postwar Spanish comedies by director Ignacio Farrés Iquino. See Arce, J. (2013). "Castanets and White Telephones: (Musical) Comedies During the Early Years of the Franco Regime". In G. Pérez Zalduondo and G. Gan Quesada (Eds.), *Music and Francoism*. Washington: Brepols. 253–264.
5. Provincial Delegate of Orense. General Archive of the Administration AGA (36/04665).
6. In the composer's original manuscripts, the first 7 bars of 'Ensueño de amor' are in an orchestral version with complete wind, woodwind, harp and piano. In the final version, only the piano version appears, which Encarna plays.
7. *Los Servios* Cabaret, according to censorship records, which demanded the modification of the scene. Document 64-44, 24 of April of 1944. AGA (36/04665).

8. While the budget for the film was not excessive, it is interesting that Manolo Morán's wage as a secondary character, already pigeonholed in these types of 'Spanish-style' comic roles, earned him the far from insignificant amount of 25,000 pesetas, revealing the undisputable awakening interest in comedy in post-war times.
9. AGA (36/04671).
10. This jazz theme (and the previous ones) were conceived by Parada as appendices to the film.

References

Burguera, Mª.L. (1994). *Edgar Neville: entre el humorismo y la poesía*. Málaga: Diputación Provincial.

Burguera, Mª.L., & Fortuño Llorens, S. (1998). *Vanguardia y humorismo. La otra Generación del 27*. Castellón: Universidad Jaime I.

Burguera, Mª.L. (1999). *Edgar Neville: entre el humor y la nostalgia*. Valencia: Institución Alfonso el Magnánimo.

Gómez Tarín, F.J. (2001). Edgar Neville: sainete, intertextualidad y anclaje temporal. In L. Fernandéz Colorado & P. Couto Cantero (Eds.), *La herida de las sombras. El cine español en los años cuarenta* (VII Congreso de la AEHC) (pp. 219-235). Madrid: AACCE y AEHC.

Gubern, R. (2006). La guerra civil vista por el cine del franquismo. In S. Juliá (Ed.), *Memoria de la guerra y del franquismo* (pp. 163-196). Madrid: Taurus.

Marsh, S. (2001). Negociando la nación: tácticas y prácticas del subalterno en la comedia cinematográfica de los años cuarenta. In L. Fernandéz Colorado & P. Couto Cantero (Eds.), *La herida de las sombras. El cine español en los años cuarenta* (VII Congreso de la AEHC) (pp. 99-113). Madrid: AACCE y AEHC.

Marsh, S. (2006). *Popular Spanish Film under Franco: Comedy and the Weakening of the State*. Houndmills: Palgrave Macmillan.

Miranda, L. (2007). 'El compositor Manuel Parada y el cine patriótico de autarquía: de *Raza* a *Los últimos de Filipinas*'. *Cuadernos de Música Iberoamericana*, 14, 195-227.

Miranda, L. (2009). 'La música en el cine policíaco de Edgar Neville: del cosmopolitismo hollywoodiense al casticismo de posguerra. Propuesta de análisis audiovisual'. *Revista de Musicología*, XXXII(2), 685-700.

Miranda, L. (2011). Cine de cruzada en España: creación musical cinematográfica para un Imperio. In C. Alonso (Ed.), *Creación musical, cultura popular y construcción nacional en la España contemporánea* (pp. 143-167). Madrid: ICCMU.

Ortiz, A. (2001). La comedia española de los años cuarenta: una producción diferenciada. In L. Fernandéz Colorado & P. Couto Cantero (Eds.), *La herida de las sombras. El cine español en los años cuarenta* (VII Congreso de la AEHC) (pp. 115-125). Madrid: AACCE y AEHC.

Ríos Carratalá, J.A. (2000). *El humor en España. Carlos Arniches y Edgar Neville*. Online at http://www.cervantesvirtual.com/nd/ark:/59851/bmcxg9k9, accessed 15 May 2015.

Rubio Lucia, J.L. (1986). *La comedia en el cine español*. Madrid: Dicrefilm.

Laura Miranda received her PhD in December 2011 for her dissertation, *Manuel Parada and Spanish film music during the Franco regime: analytical study*. She has published in the journals *Cuadernos de Música Iberoamericana*, *Revista de Musicología* and *MSMI*, and has collaborated on the book *Cine de cruzada en España: creación musical cinematográfica para un imperio* (IICMU, 2011). At present Dr Miranda's area of research focuses on the audio-visual analysis of Spanish culture and society. She is currently writing a book entitled *Canciones en el cine español de autarquía* for publication by Shangrilá Textos Aparte.

11 An Okinawan Romance
Lyrical Dialogue, Comedy and Music in Nabbie's Love[1]

Philip Hayward

Introduction

The Ryukyu islands (often referred to as Okinawa, after their main island) form the southerly part of a chain that stretches from Taiwan in the south through the Amami and Tokara islands up to Kyushu, the southernmost main island of Japan. Until 1609, when Japanese forces occupied and annexed it, the area was an autonomous kingdom, with a distinct local language, song and dance culture (and pronounced regional variants on outlying islands). Subjugation by Japan removed the region's self-government and chances of socio-economic progress (as their economy was subservient to the needs of its colonial power) but allowed local cultural forms to persist, and indeed, prosper as a point of local identification. After the new Meiji era regime ended Japan's 'closed border' policies in the 1880s, the socio-economic stress on the islands resulted in a marked mobility in Okinawans, many of whom either moved to other areas of Japan (or, later, areas of Japanese-controlled Micronesia) to work or else migrated overseas (to destinations such as Hawai'i and South America). Japanese hegemony over Okinawa was interrupted in 1945 when US forces invaded and subsequently separated Okinawa from Japan as a US zone of influence, a status it retained until 1972, when it reverted to Japan (although some 20 per cent of its central island's landmass remains under US military control).

Separated from Japan for 27 years, with restricted travel between the two areas, Okinawa was a significant cultural (and climatic) 'other' for main island Japan following its reversion. Its distinct culture and rich natural environment has attracted tourists and creative artists indulging in what Toru Mitsui (1998) has termed a form of "domestic exoticism". Culture, and particularly music, dance, alcohol and cuisine, has been emphasized in this vision, and the region has been regularly depicted as a site of constant festivity, with an easy-come/easy-go population comfortable in a balmy, sub-tropical climate.

Such exoticist tendencies are particularly apparent in the field of popular music. As Mitsui has discussed (*ibid*), the 1980s and 1990s saw a major vogue for Okinawan music in main island Japan, with Okinawan acts such as Nenes and Shoukichi Kina purveying forms of "domestic exoticism" to metropolitan consumers. In addition to music (and music videos), popular Japanese cinema has also produced a number of exoticist representations of Okinawa. Mika Ko (2006) has identified Yuji Nakae's *Nabbie's Love* and his later film *Hotel Hibiscus* (2002) as prime examples of the exoticist tendency in main island Japanese media that neglects Okinawa's social and political circumstances in favour of a bland celebration of the islands' exotic difference. In particular, Ko contrasts Nakae's work to that of Okinawan director Takamine Go, whom she identifies as pioneering a new form of radical local cinema (*ibid*). Yet while Nakae is not ethnically Okinawan, his work is more closely associated with and attentive to Okinawan culture than this binary opposition suggests. Nakae was born and raised in Kyoto but re-located to the Okinawan capital of Naha in the late 1970s to study at Ryukyu University. He continued to reside in Okinawa during the 1980s and worked on a series of short films before collaborating with two other directors on a compendium film about contemporary Okinawan life entitled *Painappuru Tsuaazu* (*Pineapple Tours*, 1992). His transition into what Ko describes as exoticism occurred with his first feature film, *Paipatiroma* (1994), which featured a female character from main island Japan on a quest for a mythical southerly Japanese island paradise, who lingers on Hateruma Island and finds peace and tranquillity there instead.

Nabbie's Love also includes travellers from main island Japan visiting an unidentified and isolated southern isle[2] but goes beyond surface exoticism by engaging with elements of Okinawan tradition as the base for a filmic 're-boot' of those traditions. Okinawan vernacular music includes a variety of topical songs (referring to love, society and/or historical events) known collectively as *shima uta* and usually accompanied by the *sanshin* (the three string, banjo-like instrument iconic to Okinawa). The term can be translated literally as 'island songs', but the Okinawan notion of *shima* (and hence of *shima uta*) is more complex than can be captured in this simple description, since the term conveys a pronounced identification with locality and of local traditions, spiritualities and mythologies (see Suwa, 2007). One practice associated with performance of *shima uta* in social contexts is that of *uta gake*, an interactive form in which singers alternate lines of lyrics, often with embellishments or variations on a 'core' lyrical text. Both *shima uta* (in general) and *uta gake* (in particular) were prominent in the *mo-ashibi* events that were popular in Okinawa until the mid-twentieth century (when first wartime austerity and then the US occupation interrupted enactment of the custom). *Mo-ashibi* were evening (and often all-night) festive occasions focused on drinking, music-making, dancing and courtship. In this context of loosened inhibition, *uta gake* served a means of stylized interaction, allowing for humorous commentary on characters and/or flirtatious interactions between duettists. This context for *shima uta* performance was markedly different from that of the present. Despite the prominence of *shima uta* in contemporary Okinawa, where it is commonly recognized as an important local heritage form that constitutes a significant attraction for tourists,[3] it is now increasingly an ossified form in which particular aspects and moments in *shima uta* repertoire have become fixed as canonical versions that are performed with little (if any) variation in successive performances and/ or by different performers. The fictional social space represented in *Nabbie's Love* is one in which older senses of *uta gake* and *mo-ashibi* are alive and well and, indeed, define island life and infuse all aspects of social relations. At the same time, the film's representation of its tiny Okinawan outlier island does not attempt to romanticize it as a pristine cultural isolate but rather as a place where traditional cultural practices persist at a time of increased mobility and access to metropolitan and international influences.

Narrative

In a manner that invites comparisons to Shakespearean comedies such as *Love's Labour's Lost* and *A Midsummer's Nights Dream*,[4] *Nabbie's Love* intertwines the vicissitudes of individuals who are seeking romance with others. The central pairs are the septuagenarians Nabbie (Tomi Taira) and Sanrâ (Susumu Taira) and the twenty-somethings Nanako (Naomi Nishida) and Fukunosuke (Jun Murakami). In contrast to these two couples, whose romances are fraught and uncertain until the end of the film, two other couples seen almost exclusively in musical performance mode provide stable and harmonious examples of romantic interaction: opera-singing shop-owner Reiko (Reiko Kaneshima) and the fiddle-playing O'Connor (Ashley McIsaac) and *shima uta* duettists Rinshō Kadekaru and Misako Ôshiro, in their roles as the island patriarch and his wife.

Set in the late 1990s, the film opens with the arrival of two of its central protagonists, Nanako and Sanrâ, who are returning to the island on the same small ferry to visit Nabbie, grandmother to Nanako and former youthful lover of Sanrâ. As a flashback sequence (presented as a scratchy extract from an old black and white film) later reveals, Sanrâ had been banished from the island in the early 1940s by the local *yuta* (female shaman)[5] after she had divined that he was an unsuitable partner for Nabbie. Left alone, Nabbie miscarried his child and pined for him ever after, inspired only by his promise to return one day to reclaim her. While the flashback sequence discussed above functions primarily to provide the back story of Nabbie and Sanrâ's previously thwarted romance, it also serves a more subtle and complex purpose, locating the film within previous Japanese representations of remote (southern) islandness. The short (three and a half minute) sequence doesn't simply use monochrome to convey the earlier historical period of the lovers' interaction but also provides an intertextual element that reflects earlier moments of Japanese cinema and, in particular, of main island directors' engagements with romance and islands. Entitled "An Okinawan Love Story: The Spring when she was 19" in its introductory caption, the sequence explicitly invites comparison to the work of Tokyo-born director Heinosuke Gosho, who directed a (now lost) feature entitled *Jūku no haru* (*The Spring of a 19-year-old*) in 1933.[6]

Gosho began directing films in the 1920s and worked through to the 1960s (see Nolletti, 2005). He is best known for his work in the *shomin-geki* genre, often infusing his films with a lightly humorous touch. His work between the 1920s and 1950s included a number of films that addressed island themes, such as *Nantô no haru* (*Spring on a Southern Island*, 1925), *Shima to ratai jiken* (*The Island of Naked Scandal*, 1931), *Izu no odoriko* (*The Dancing Girl from Izu*, 1933) and *Izu no musumetachi* (*Girls of Izu*, 1945). The latter films were set in the Izu islands, off the Izu peninsula, south of Tokyo, which offered an accessible island escape to metropolitan dwellers. Aside from the general allusions to the themes and styles of Gosho's films, there are also more obvious links. Both *Nanto no haru* and *Izu no odoriko* have direct points of similarity to *Nabbie's Love* in that they feature love affairs between island girls and male students on vacation from the mainland. *Izu no odoriko* also has a close affinity to the audio-visual style of *Nabbie's Love*'s monochrome period sequence in that it made sparing use of sound and retains many stylistic elements of pre synch-sound era cinema.

The 'film within a film' (another device similar to aspects of Shakespearean drama) directly cross-associates its sequences with the film's main audio-visual text, beginning with the young Nabbie and Sanrâ at Sanrâ's family memorial, the same location at which the couple reunite some 60 years later. Narrated by Nabbie's husband Keitatsu, recollecting the strength of Nabbie and Sanrâ's passion, the sequence relates how she became pregnant to Sanrâ, how the *yuta* divined the couple's unsuitability and how the villagers subsequently exiled Sanrâ. The opening of this sequence is accompanied by a tango version of the song 'Jūku no Haru' (discussed further below). While this musical style may seem somewhat anomalous to contemporary audiences, the choice of music serves to reinforce the period setting and feel of the sequence since tango music enjoyed a vogue in Japan in the 1930s in the form of imported recordings and local productions.

The monochrome sequence also reveals that Keitatsu's 'courtship' of Nabbie comprised his eliciting a commitment from Nabbie that she would marry him in return for his untying her from the post she has been bound to during Sanrâ's expulsion from the island. Once untied she runs to the shore and calls out to Sanrâ as he is rowed away, begging him to take her with him, to which he replies "I promise to come back for you." She responds that she will wait for that day. A flute melody then enters, introducing a line of a song that the actress lip-synchs to, "I believed we would be together forever." Off-screen, his voice responds (as if from a physical point far closer to her than he actually is), singing "I shall never forget our parting today." She replies with a final line "as long as my life lasts."

Cued by the black and white sequence, Nabbie's Love documents the elderly couple's initially tentative reacquaintance, the resigned acceptance of their reunion by Nabbie's husband Keitatsu and the couple's eventual elopement by boat. In a parallel narrative, Nanako's gradual acceptance of Fukunosuke (a traveller from main island Japan) as a suitor also has a complicating element in the form of local male Kenjii, whose unsophisticated island ways contrast to her metropolitan Japanese identity. Like her grandmother, Nanako's love also bears a prohibition in that the *yuta* also instructs her to marry Kenji. Unlike her grandmother – and illustrating the changes in social patterns and expectations in the modern era – she chooses the Japanese boy (and, implicitly, an inclusive Japanese-Okinawan identity) over the *yuta*'s instructions. As the Introduction to this chapter outlined, the interactions and key events in the film are premised on and reflected by musical interactions detailed below.

Musical sequences and communications

Nabbie's Love opens with a sequence that directly alludes to Gosho's *Izu no odoriko*.[7] The latter commences with a scene where the main female protagonist, played by (then) rising young *enka*[8] singer Hibari Misora, punts a small boat carrying passengers across a channel. As she punts, she sings an *enka* song, her melodic lines sounding clear in the mix (as in a studio rather than location recording). As she crosses, her punt is passed by a faster, motor-powered ferry, emphasizing the changes occurring in Japanese life as old island ways are replaced by modernity. *Nabbie's Love* opens with an update of the latter image, showing a small ferry boat ploughing through open sea towards a small island. Japanese pop music sounds from an onboard sound system, accompanying variably pitched vocals singing lyrics that foreground the film's island theme from the outset. Shortly after, the song is revealed as a karaoke-style performance by the ship's pilot, Kenji, singing from the roof of the cabin to entertain his guests in transit. The choice of this music, sung by an islander to a group of (mainly) off-islanders, is significant for a film otherwise so steeped in *shima uta*. As the film develops, it can be understood, in retrospect, to characterize a strange in-betweenness to Kenji's role. While he is indisputably *of* the island, he is also outside the central *shima uta* culture that links the main characters.

Attracted to Nanako, he lacks sufficient cultural capital in either domain to secure her affections – an outcome foreshadowed by Nanako's sudden, tetchy interruption of his song as she climbs up alongside him on the cabin roof.

Positioned as a prelude, the interaction described above precedes the film's title sequence, which begins with the image of Sanrâ standing on the prow of the boat, staring out at the approaching island. This image, and a subsequent cut to the first view of the island itself, is accompanied by a plaintive minor-key piano theme (entitled 'Rafuti' on the soundtrack CD) written by British composer Michael Nyman (best known for his collaborations with British director Peter Greenaway in the 1980s and 1990s and for his score for Jane Campion's *The Piano* (1993)). Nyman's motif creates a sense of mystery to the narrative and, as the film's title comes on screen, colours the audience's anticipation of *Nabbie's Love* with the melancholy reflective nature of the music.[9]

Once ashore, *shima uta* permeates the soundscape and narrative space. As soon as Sanrâ steps off the ferry a *sanshin* riff enters the mix over the noise of the ferry docking. Low in volume, as if played by a radio within the diegesis, two vocalists begin to duet faintly, foreshadowing the film's major use of the distinctive island music. The first visually represented performance of *shima uta* begins when Nanako arrives back at her grandmother's house. Seated cross-legged on the front platform, her grandfather, Keitatsu, begins to sing slowly, elongating the syllables and using pronounced vibrato:

To blossoms comes a storm
Blowing from the mountains
To moonlight comes fog

As he sings, Nabbie goes out to gather bougainvillea blossoms, reinforcing the suggestive lyrics that serve as a forewarning of disruption to come. His rendition is cut short as Nanako wakes from an afternoon sleep and joins him, commenting on how beautiful the flowers are.

Keitatsu's musicality, symbolized by his carrying the *sanshin* everywhere with him, is core to the film's musicalized drama. The role is invested with authenticity by virtue of being performed by veteran *sanshin* player and singer, Seijin Noborikawa. Born in Hyōgo prefecture (on Honshu) in 1932, he moved to Okinawa as a child and began performing on *sanshin* in the late 1930s. He retained his interest in *shima uta* through the US occupation years, accompanying theatrical troupes and becoming one of the founder members of the Ryukyu Min'yo Kyokai association that led the post-war revival of Okinawan song culture. Although he never achieved significant success as a solo recording artist, only releasing a handful of cassette albums in the 1960s–1980s, his central involvement in local music traditions both informs his performance in the film and gives it a particular gravitas for local audiences. Keitatsu's musicality

Figure 1 Promotional still for *Nabbie's Love*, featuring (left to right) Naomi Nishida (as Nanako), Seijin Noborikawa (as Keitatsu) and Jun Murakami (as Fukunosuke)

(cross-associated with Noborikawa's early life experiences) also provides the film with its only allusion to Okinawa's post-war period of US occupation. While the locale represented in the film is something of an island 'out of time', where heritage and community appear predominantly pre-modern, Keitatsu's habit of routinely picking out the melody from 'The Star Spangled Banner' on the *sanshin* as he leaves for work each day serves as a subtle sonic reminder of the occupation years (and continuing US presence in main island Okinawa) which is otherwise absent from the film.

Further grounded reference to local tradition, and particularly that of *mo-ashibi*, is provided by the presence of Rinshō Kadekaru and his female duettist Misako Ôshiro, playing the island patriarch and his wife. Immediately recognizable to an audience with any degree of familiarity with Okinawan traditional culture, the performers further ground the film's fiction in a recognizable roots tradition. Like Noborikawa, Kadekaru also began performing in the 1930s and was particularly renown as a *mo-ashibi* performer. After a period in Micronesia in the late 1930s and early 1940s, Kadekaru returned to Okinawa and established a career as the most consistently successful *shima uta* singer during the 1950s–1990s, recording a series of popular albums and performing regularly around Okinawa and in main island Japan. He began an association with Ôshiro in the 1980s and worked with her as his favourite *uta gake* duettist in concert and on a number of recordings. Their duets in the film typify the wry vocal interactions of their live performances and provide a ready-made warmth to their characters' onstage interactions.

Kadekaru and Ôshiro's first appearance in performing mode occurs on Nanako's first night back on the island, when she visits the village patriarch and his wife with her grandparents. After prayers and consumption of food and *awamori* (a strong Okinawan liquor), Kadekaru's character introduces a version of the song 'Jūku no Haru' (also known as 'Jurigua Kouta'). Performed in several different versions throughout the film, 'Jūku no Haru' is central to *Nabbie's Love*. The song has a complex history. Far from being a local song whose origins fade into historical obscurity, it is a more recent composition born out of the experiences of Okinawan migrants. While elements of its melody and/or lyrical themes may have traces back to earlier *shima uta*, performances of 'Jūku no Haru' date back to the early twentieth century, when it began to be sung by coal miners from Yoron island (in the north of the Okinawan archipelago) working in the Miike coalmine in Fukuoka (on Kyushu island). After various lyrical and musical modifications it became popular back on Yoron island and in Okinawa more generally. The modern version originated in 1972 (the year of Okinawa's reversion to Japan) when Yusuke Hontake, a singer from Yonaguni island (in the far southwest of Okinawa), wrote new lyrics for the melody and recorded it.[10] The song became widely popular in Okinawa and has continued as a staple of local repertoire. The film's various versions of the song are thus entirely congruent with its flexibility as an element of lived culture (rather than as a canonized essential text). Nakae's selection of the song as a recurrent motif in the film reflects the similarity of its lyrical theme to that of his narrative. 'Jūku no Haru' is a poignant ballad of unrequited love. Its vocal protagonist is a mature woman who declares her continuing love for a boy she met back when she was 19. Despite the boy's marriage to another woman, the protagonist retains her desire for him and her hope that they may be together as lovers in the future and – if not – wishes that she could revert to being 19 again in order to pursue her life differently. As will be apparent, the song's topic is apposite for the film. Similarly, the song's reference to blooming flowers as a sign of continuing love resembles Nabbie's cherished bougainvilleas, grown from a single cutting sent by Sanrâ soon after he was exiled.

In its first performance in the film, Ôshiro and Kadekaru alternate the first and second verses, constructing the song as a duet between two estranged lovers. Their *sanshin* riffs continue as the image cuts to Nabbie, Nanako and Keitatsu walking off down a dark lane. Nanako then picks up the melody (with far less vocal accomplishment and more than a little tipsiness), singing the third verse, to which she adds the line, "I'm no longer an innocent girl." In combination with the verse's reference to an unrequited love for a married man, the ad lib suggests the reason for her return to Aguni. Music continues to inform the narrative the morning after. Walking down a shady laneway Nabbie and Nanako encounter the island's busker, played by veteran Ishigaki island singer Yamazato Yukichi,[11] who emerges from the shadows wearing a facemask and strikes up a lively festive riff on his *sanshin*. Walking ahead, he sings the highly suggestive lyrics from the song 'Roko-cho bushi':

You and I are like water in an ink slab
The more the ink stick grinds
The thicker our love becomes

Once I make the first move
My legs lock the woman in
She's under my spell
She can never say no to me

Nabbie and Nanako follow, amused, Nabbie waving her hands in festive dance style and Nanako patting her thighs in time with the rhythm. The lyrics, and the women's casual amused enjoyment of their performance, mark Aguni out as a place of significant difference from the 'polite society' of metropolitan Japan, which Nanako has just left. In the film's fictionalized island space, sexuality is far from taboo and its discussion is frequently the cause of mirth and amusement.

In addition to its bawdiness, the musical world of Aguni (as represented in the film) is nothing if not diverse. Rounding a corner, Nabbie and Nanako encounter an incongruous kilt-wearing *gaijin* (westerner) holding a fiddle outside the village shop. The fiddler then strikes up a spirited rendition of the Scottish reel 'Craignish Hills', accompanied by a drummer, keyboard player and saxophonist. Delighted, Nanako and passers-by begin to dance. The fiddler turns out to be 'O'Connor', the lover of Nanako's aunt, the shopkeeper Reiko. After a brief conversation Nabbie asks Reiko to sing her favourite song. Accompanied by O'Connor, Reiko then launches into its first line "I believed we would be together forever," singing the Okinawan pentatonic melody in (accomplished) operatic style. The image then cuts to the Nanako and Nabbie walking away as the verse continues to declare "I'll never forget our parting today/as long as my life lasts," prompting Nabbie to start to cry (with the melody receding in the mix).

While the presence of a Celtic fiddler on the island is less easily explained than that of the stalwarts of *shima uta* discussed above, he can be seen to represent an embodiment of the Okinawan tradition of incorporating diverse ingredients into a distinctive cultural 'stew'. Charmingly characterized by Nabbie as a fiddler from somewhere called "I-love-land" (a mishearing of 'Ireland'), the fiddler concerned is one who is just as recognizable in his home culture as Rinshō Kadekaru is in Okinawa. Far from being Irish, the fiddler, Ashley McIsaac, hails from Cape Breton, in Canada's northeastern province of Nova Scotia, where he has managed to juggle the somewhat unlikely roles of being a spirited exponent of a Scottish-derived fiddle tradition and a hell-raising homosexual *bon vivant*.[12] While McIsaac's biography (2003) suggests that he was employed by Nakae somewhat opportunistically during a tour of Japan (and that he had little idea of what the film was about), his own conscious attempts to extend and develop Cape Breton music into various modern contexts render him an apposite choice for the role.

Opera singer Reiko Kaneshima's principal number, delivered as a music video-like sequence at a pivotal moment in the narrative, is a rendition of the 'Habanera', the love theme from Bizet's opera *Carmen* (1875). While seemingly out of place in the film and Aguni Island (dominated as it is by *shima uta* performance), the musical style of the 'Habanera' is linked to (and 'localized' by) its rhythmic similarity to the music accompanying the film's monochrome flashback sequence. While the composition of the 'Habanera' pre-dated the development of the tango as a form, its distinctive rhythm was one that was directly adopted by early tango ensembles. In addition to its musical affinities with the monochrome sequence, the piece's lyrics (and their heartfelt rendition by Kaneshima) are strongly integrated into the film's narrative and thematics. Based around a descending chromatic phrase with lyrics that refer to love as a "rebellious" and "untameable" bird and characterize it to be as wild and unpredictable as a "Gypsy's child", the 'Habanera' is singularly appropriate to the film's themes and complements the commentaries on love, life and courtship offered by the film's *shima uta* and its *uta gake* interactions.

Less prosaic meditations on love and lust inform the scenes in which Fukunosuke is inducted into island life by Keitatsu. Encountering him while taking a break from work in the fields, Keitatsu engages Fukunosuke in conversation. After confiding that "there's nothing on this island," he plucks idly at his *sanshin* before shifting the conversation to a more specific focus, informing the visitor that "if you're after girls with big tits, go to the next island." When Fukunosuke intimates that such a quest wasn't a significant motivation for his visit, Keitatsu responds "you're weird" and – foreshadowing the reasons for the subsequent break-up of his own marriage to Nabbie – suggests to Fukunosuke that "you should get in early with women, women never forget their first man." After recalling how Nabbie was once "the belle of the island," and reminiscing about her ample breasts, he tells Fukunosuke that "girls with small tits aren't bad either," to which Fukunosuke nods his affirmation. The scene is humorous due to the clash of cultural codes. Already straining to understand Keitatsu's dialect, Fukunosuke is clearly unprepared for the frank and ribald discussion of female attributes. His discomfort intensifies soon after, as Keitatsu takes Fukunosuke home to stay at his family house.

Arriving home, Keitatsu (erroneously) informs Nanako that Fukunosuke has expressed an interest in her. Fukunosuke denies this, only for Keitatsu to up the ante by casually informing Nanako that "he also said that prefers girls with small tits." By now massively embarrassed, Fukunosuke repeats his denials. Soon after, Keitatsu sits with Fukunosuke and attempts to teach him to play the *sanshin* while Nanako hangs the washing out to dry. As they tune their instruments, Keitatsu continues his less than subtle promotion of his granddaughter's assets, first observing, "look, nice bum, eh?" Striking up a riff on the *sanshin*, Keitatsu improvises a song fragment beginning with two observational lines: "Nanako is doing the washing/She has a cute little butt" before switching to a line sung as if voiced by her, "I have pert tits too." Emboldened by Nanako's lack of adverse reaction to the song, Fukunosuke joins in on the next line as Keitatsu sings "Please fondle them, fondle them now." Rather than reacting angrily to this lyrical harassment, Nanako's response is more amused, as she simply asks (in speech) "Why would I say that?" before the mediated flirtation is cut short by Nabbie's arrival home.

The next day Nabbie meets Sanrâ for the first time in 60 years, and the couple reaffirm their continuing love for each other. While this private scene occurs quietly, accompanied by ambient sounds of the wind rustling grass, it is immediately followed by a further *ute gake* performance of 'Jūku no Haru' by Kadekaru and Ôshiro that reflects the dramatic moment in song, wryly underplaying the previous scene's sincerity with amusing allusions and frank dialogue. Kadekaru opens, skipping the song's first verse and moving to the next three lines and interpolating a fourth:

> *If you want me to make you back into a 19 year old*
> *Look at the dead tree in the garden*
> *If a dead tree could have flowers again*
> *A grilled fish could swim again*

Ôshiro then replies:

> *If you should dump me*
> *I won't let my love for you linger on*
> *While still young*
> *One must live with no regret and blossom tomorrow*

In addition to reflecting the previous scene, the final lines also allude to Nanako's nascent affair with Fukunosuke. In a swerve typical of the film's elliptical progression, the next musical voice presented is McIsaac's, performing an Irish reel in the street that then switches to a nondiegetic accompaniment to the arrival of Nanako's father Keichi on the ferry. The family are returning to the island for an annual festival,[13] which includes divination sessions by the current *yuta*. Commenting on Sanrâ's return to the island, the *yuta* initially decrees that he should be re-exiled but after Nabbie's tearful entreaty she moderates her judgment to forbidding islanders to interact with him. As she leaves she also encounters Nanako and instructs her to marry Kenjii, much to the former's annoyance.

In addition to divination, the festival also includes a concert at the island hall. The film presents three numbers from this in which characters act out aspects of the narrative in song and dance. Opening with an introduction from the show's comperes, two comedians visiting from Osaka, the first number is introduced as a traditional straw hat dance, usually performed by women. On this occasion, and much to the amusement of crowd, a group of young island women are joined by Fukunosuke, dressed in drag. The crowd's laughter intensifies as a bare-chested Kenjii comes onstage and mimes attacking the interloper, driving 'him' off, to crowd applause.

After this Nanako bounces around the stage in a *kawaii* outfit with a bow in her hair (completely unlike her normal appearance in trousers) and sings a pop song in a deliberately girly voice to a pre-recorded backing track, asking a suitor to declare his commitment. During the song, older members of the audience clap along with pleasure with the notable exception of Nabbie who stares off-screen, out the window. Puzzled by this, Nanako's energy fluctuates as she moves across the stage and realizes that Sanrâ is standing outside. As he leaves and walks away, her song shifts to a strong declaration of passion:

Open the door to summer
And take me away somewhere
Summer will invite us in
Summer will embrace our naked bodies

The final number of the concert sequence comprises a performance of a Japanese version of the popular Irish ballad 'Danny Boy' (also known as 'Londonderry Air') sung by the island busker. The song's melody continues as Nanako, her grandparents and Fukunosuke leave the hall and walk away. Cleverly, the rendition of the Irish ballad echoes both the lyrics of Nanako's pop song and 'Jūku no Haru', by stating:

The summer's gone, and all the flowers are dying
'Tis you, 'tis you must go and I must bide
But come ye back when summer's in the meadow
Or when the valley's hushed and white with snow
'Tis I'll be here in sunshine or in shadow
Oh Danny boy, oh Danny boy, I love you so

The concert is a pivotal moment in the film. Later that evening Nabbie writes a letter by candlelight while the scene shifts to the previously discussed version of the 'Habanera' performed outside the shop in a music video-like sequence. As the song reaches its climax, Nabbie's voice begins to read aloud the letter she is writing to Sanrâ, in which she declares her intention to elope with him. The image then cuts to that of Sanrâ finding her note in his fishing boat in the same cove he had been exiled from 60 years before (with the 'Habanera' continuing low in the mix).

The elopement happens soon after, despite Nanako's efforts to prevent it. Overwhelmed with sadness, and exasperated at a marriage proposal from Kenjii, Nanako seeks out Fukunosuke and they share their first kiss. The resolution of the lovers' courtships closes the loop of the narrative and triggers an extended musical sequence where different individuals and groups of islanders exchange lines of 'Jūku no Haru' in a montage that emphasizes their communality as they assemble at Keitatsu's house for a feast. As the song progresses, Fukunosuke reveals the transition he has undergone under Keitatsu's tutelage by singing to Nanako "I'm going to sneak into your bed tonight" and then, unzipping his trousers and dropping them to his ankles, he renders his lust explicit, singing "I hope you'll be wet with dew waiting for me." With the couple's trajectory clear, Keitatsu starts up a fast festive riff on his *sanshin* and sings lyrics from the traditional Ryukyu court song 'Kajadifu bushi' that complements the spirit of *mo-ashibi*:

> *Today is a wonderful day*
> *What can I liken it to?*
> *It's like a flower blooming*
> *With the love of dews*
>
> *Let's dance, you me and everyone*
> *Let's have a good time today*
> *When else can we have more fun?*
> *Let's dance til dawn*

Switching into a 'magic realist' sequence in which time is compressed and juxtaposed, the song continues as the image cuts to Nanako and Fukunosuke, dressed in formal Okinawan marital costume and then leaps forward in time to the image of an older Nanako and Fukunosuke on the porch surrounded by kids watching the dance, which has now spread from the courtyard to the street, embracing and involving the whole community.

Conclusion

Nabbie's Love's use of song material and vocal interaction as key elements of its humour and narrative places musicality at the centre of the film and significantly musicalizes its drama. Drama, intrigue and comedy arise from the cumulative layering and cross-association of song lyrics that parallel and foreshadow the characters' trajectories. The style of film that emerges is distinct from the classic western musical tradition (and other forms such as Bollywood) through the organic/diegetic position of song and vocal-musical interaction within the drama. This does not simply subsume music into everyday narrative. Rather, the 'embedded' series of song performances delivers its own internal commentary on and inflection of narrative and characterization. The switching between musical and non-musical sections and sequences occurs regularly and (seemingly) spontaneously, often in short fragments or overlapping interaction between speech and song modes. Humour is not established and elaborated through deliberately melodramatic or parodic passages but rather through switching to the dialogic lyrical interaction of *uta gake*, whose playful mode allows risqué, direct and or speculative lyrical expression at one remove from more deliberated spoken communications. Referring to the influence of German director Ernst Lubitsch on the silent comedies of Japanese director Yasujiro Ozu, Clifford Hilo commented that the former "could conduct the momentum of flirtation within a single frame" (2008). *Nabbie's Love* exhibits similar deftness by conducting much of the momentum of *its* central flirtation through a single song, continually reworking 'Jūku no Haru' and playing the film's images off its lyrics. Through this, the character, timbre and variable tunefulness of characters' voices interact, resting on the stark and simple *sanshin* riffs that predominate as accompaniment. Humour is intertwined with passion, sadness and a constant awareness of the passing of time and the film's island is bathed in the glow of its music.

Thanks to Sueo Kuwahara for various assistances with my continuing research in Ryukyu and Amami and to Henry Johnson, Danny Long, Junko Konishi and James Roberson for their feedback on earlier versions of this chapter.

Research for this chapter was conducted with funding from Australia Research Council Linkage Grant P0989243 'Sustainable futures for music cultures: Towards an ecology for musical diversity'.

Notes

1. Translations of the dialogue and song texts featured in the film are taken from the Australian SBS TV version, subtitled by Hiroko Moore and Penny Woods, first broadcast in 2001.
2. The film was shot on Aguni Island, located 40 kilometres north west of the Okinawan capital, Naha.

3. Such as those who patronize the wide variety of *shima uta* clubs in the regional capital Naha.
4. Indeed, Nake went on to direct an adaptation of the latter set in the southern islands entitled *Manatsu no Yoru no Yume* in 2009.
5. The *yuta* is a respected female within traditional Okinawan communities who is perceived to have shamanistic and/or divinatory powers.
6. The film's title suggests a linkage to the eponymous popular early twentieth-century song featured extensively in Nakae's film but given that no copies of the film remain I have been unable to gauge the extent of the relationship between the song and Gosho's feature film and whether the former was a direct inspiration for the latter.
7. See Nolletti (2005: 43–62) for a discussion of the film.
8. *Enka* is a style of Japanese post-war music strongly associated with melodrama and nostalgicism that has been compared to US Country music in terms of its emotive qualities and preoccupations.
9. The music is also reprised, less successfully, at the close of the film and over the end credits, where its mood grates with the unbridled festivity of the scene that precedes it.
10. My thanks to Sueo Kuwahara for his information on the song's history (personal communication with the author, May 2010).
11. Yukichi also provides one of the film's only nondiegetic uses of *shima uta*, in the sequence when lines from his rendition of the classic Yaeyama song 'Tsuki nu kaisha' ('The beauty of the moon') accompany images of a large full moon. (Thanks to James Roberson for his information on the song.)
12. See McIsaac (2003) for his own account of his 'colourful' career.
13. While not explicitly referred to in the film this appears to be the Yagan Orimi, which occurs every September on Aguni.

References

Hilo, C. (2008). Against Modernism, In Favor of Tofu: Three Silent Comedies by Ozu. Published online at the University of California Los Angeles Asia Institute archive site: http://asiapacificarts.usc.edu/w_apa/showarticle.aspx?articleID=10160, accessed May 2010.

Ko, M. (2006). 'Takamine Go: A Possible Okinawan Cinema'. *Inter-Asia Cultural Studies*, 7(1), 156–170. http://dx.doi.org/10.1080/14649370500463844

McIsaac, A. (2003). *Fiddling with Disaster: Clearing the Past*. Toronto: Warwick Publishing.

Mitsui, T. (1998). 'Domestic Exoticism: A Recent Trend in Japanese Popular Music'. *Perfect Beat*, 3(4), 1–12.

Nolletti, A. (2005). *The Cinema of Gosho Heinosuke: Laughter through Tears*. Bloomington, IN: Indiana University Press.

Suwa, J. (2007). 'The Space of Shima'. Shima: The International Journal of Research into Island Cultures, 1(1), 6–15, online at http://www.shimajournal.org/issues/v1n1/d. Suwa Shima v1n1.pdf, accessed 15 May 2015.

204 Sounding Funny

Philip Hayward is research advisor in Music and Media Arts in the School of Communication at the University of Technology, Sydney. He has written extensively about screen soundtracks and also researches the music cultures of the Amami and Okinawa archipelagoes of southern Japan and is a member of audiovisual ensemble The Moviolas.

12 A Special Flavour
Comic Song Scenes in the Hindi Cinema

Gregory D. Booth

Introduction

This study offers an overview of relationships among songs, song scenes, comedy and other factors in a repertoire that is both too large and too variable for overviews. The enormous size of the Hindi film repertoire, together with its commercial and inherently eclectic nature, make any interpretive schema vulnerable to possible exceptions resulting from the specific period of production and release, the intertextual identity of the featured actor, character stereotypes, genre, gender and other factors. I base my analysis on the assumption that comedy "tends to involve departures of a particular kind – or particular kinds – from what are considered to be the 'normal' routines of the life of the social group in question" (King, 2002: 5) and offer explanatory models focusing on two sets of core issues. First, I suggest that musical sound has inherent limitations in the Hindi cinema's comic song scenes, but also that comedy's extra-normal nature is enabled by the conventions surrounding those scenes, which are similarly extra-normal. Song scenes have the ability to easily abandon or at least de-emphasize narrative linearity and the conditions of narrative reality; they frequently offer respite from the tensions of the central narrative. These issues are, in a sense, structural: inherent respectively to the nature of musical sound as a symbol system and to the way that Hindi film narrative has conventionally been constructed. Second, I explore the special relationship that comedy in Hindi song scenes has with representations of gender, social class and character type: In some comic song scenes, representations of lower socio-economic groups and of women are "othered", constructed so as to be objects of laughter. I further suggest that the comic song scenes shift back-and-forth between laughter as a subjective and dramatic representation which the audience experiences sympathetically and as an objective incongruity to which the audience responds by laughing. This overview is by no means comprehensive and is limited to the conventional Hindi cinema that dominated the second half of the twentieth century.

Comic events "tend to be different in characteristic ways from what is usually expected in the non-comic world. Comedy lies in the gap between the two, which can take various forms, including incongruity and exaggeration" (King, 2002: 5). The song scene, 'Zara Rukh Ja' ('Stop For a Minute') appeared in the romantic comedy, *Sitaaron Se Aage* (Satyen Bose, 1958).[1] The song begins with a short feature played on an instrument with a single plucked string, attached to a resonating skin membrane at one end and a small handle at the other. The instrument has various names in various languages, but is called *premtal* in Hindi; its construction allows the player to modify the tension of the string and the resonating membrane by pulling, producing a "nonpitched but highly variable sound" (Miner, 2000: 343). In this short section, the principal musical interest is generated by the *premtal*'s ability to produce an exaggerated form of what would be called glissandi in western terms. This type of extreme or exaggerated sliding from pitch to pitch is one of the few relatively consistent musical signs of comedy in the Hindi cinema. In 'Zara Rukh Ja', the melodic and rhythmic pitch manipulations of the *premtal* are not the only musical exaggerations or incongruities. The *premtal* is followed by the entrance of the trumpets, who produce an abrupt four-note phrase in which two noticeably short notes are followed by another two that are longer and connected by more (although more jazz-like) glissandi. The trumpet phrase is repeated twice, each time 'answered' by elaborate passage-work from the violin section. These repetitions are followed by a concluding melodic phrase that is repeated three times, first by a solo trumpet, then by a clarinet, then by a shrill bamboo flute.

The musical introduction lasts roughly 23 seconds and is set ('picturized' in the language of the Mumbai cinema) in what appears to be an idyllic Sunday afternoon in an Indian park, dominated by long-shots of young women and men riding bicycles. The music of this introduction would have at least implied that the coming song scene would a comic one, but that implication is confirmed on the final note of introduction, as the camera shifts to a shot of actor Johnny Walker[2] perched in a tree.

Walker, whose real name was Badr'uddin Jamal'uddin Qazi (1929–1971), acted in well over 100 films, most released during the 1950s and the first half of the '60s. Walker enacted endless variations on the clown, one of the stereotyped characters often encountered in the conventional Hindi cinema. Walker refined this stereotype, acting in a "characteristic style as the hero's comic sidekick within the classic Indian film comedy tradition, relying on his pencil-thin moustache, facial grimaces and nasal drawl" (Rajadhyaksha and Willemen, 1995: 221). Walker's characters changed social class from film to film, but they inevitably provided the convention-breaking, slapstick and farce that remain necessary components of most Hindi films. He was often the focus of specially staged song scenes such as 'All Line Clear' in *Chori Chori* (Anant Thakur, 1956), 'Duniya Gol Hai' in *Chaudvin ka Chaand* (Mohammed Sadiq, 1960) and 'Dil Hamara Husnawalo' from *Baazi* (Moni Bhattacharjee, 1968). He was also the featured star of two comedy films, *Johnny Walker* (Ved-Madan, 1957) and *Mr John* (Inder, 1959).

In 'Zara Rukh Ja' Walker first looks down on the riders and then reaches up to them when he jumps down and crouches in front of his tree. As he sings "stop for a minute" to the passing and oblivious riders, an accordion responds to each of his initial melodic phrases, mimicking the short, abrupt sounds of the trumpets. As the first statement of the song's main melody concludes, Walker pursues two young women in a children's playground as they spin on a small round-about. The glissando-laden *premtal* music of the introduction returns. It is followed by what the Mumbai film music industry called a Hawaiian guitar, a flat guitar-like instrument played with a metal bar sliding across the frets and producing a still more exaggerated version of the sliding from pitch to pitch that has dominated the musical interludes of this song so far. Another trumpet glissando accompanies some reverse-action cinematography, as Walker lands backwards on, and then slides up, a children's slide. The scene continues with a series of comic skits featuring Walker's interactions with individual men, women and couples. Musically, however, the melodies and instruments of this first minute dominate the remaining three minutes of the song. Although certainly not unique, 'Zara Rukh Ja' is one of the more musically expressive comic song scenes in the Hindi cinema.

Music, comedy and popular song

One of the challenges in a consideration of comedy and music in this repertoire is the extent to which the Hindi cinema has adhered to the music-drama form, in which characters express their emotions through song, in scenes that may be more or less formally demarcated from the narrative flow. Conventionally, Hindi films have featured between four and eight song scenes per film, in which actors emote, dance and so forth, while lip-synching to songs specifically composed for the film and recorded by professional singers (called playback singers, Booth, 2008). Song scenes usually offer spectacle (exotic, erotic, fashionable, cultural, religious, etc.); they may introduce characters and their natures, outline central emotional tensions, express or define romantic relationships or, as in the scenes in this study, provide comic interludes. Because they are composed for narrative use, conventions regarding songs' functions and placement have also informed the way songs are composed. Most required specific kinds of instrumental interludes in which narrative action – such as the slapstick routines that Walker performs in 'Zara Rukh Ja' – could occur.

In addition to their narrative/cinematic importance, Hindi film songs have also completely dominated India's popular music culture during most of the twentieth and twenty-first centuries. In the process of producing India's cinema hits, film producers were simultaneously producing India's popular music hits and often ensured that their songs reflected current musical fashions. This was crucial given the range of extra-cinematic contexts in which film songs were consumed. Film songs were sold on discs (and later cassettes), broadcast on the radio and television, played in shops, restaurants and nightclubs. Consequently, this study is an enquiry into the relationship not only between narrative comedy and music as such, but also between narrative comedy and popular song. Significantly, the production of musical meaning, especially in popular song, is a process less suited to the inclusion (or even the production) of the kinds of musical incongruity – exaggeration, disjunction or other features – that might musically reinforce the comic nature of a song scene.

Throughout 'Zara Rukh Ja' Johnny Walker provides comedy based on incongruity and slapstick through pose, gesture, behaviour, facial expressions and so on. In his interactions with other characters in the scene he consistently invades personal space and generally ignores many of the rules for inter-personal and gendered social behaviour in post-colonial India. Aside from the uniquely bicycle-based antics, the scene is a typical comic song scene of its period. In addition, and again quite typically, the situation offers some opportunity for erotic display by featuring a number of bicycle-riding women in quite abbreviated shorts (an unusual sight for the time) who become the objects of Walker's special attention.

One of Walker's many comic scenes, 'Zara Rukh Ja' immediately succeeded another popular song scene from *Pyaasa* (Guru Dutt, 1957) entitled 'Sar Jo Tera Chakaraye' ('If Your Head is Dizzy'), in which Walker played the role of an itinerant head masseur, such as were still frequently encountered in the India of the 1950s. Somewhat coincidentally, both songs were by film composer S.D. Burman, featured many of the same musicians and were sung by the same playback singer, Mohamed Rafi.

In semiotic terms, both 'Zara Rukh Ja' and 'Sar Jo Tera' offer slapstick, farce, and other unexpected conjunctions through the deployment of symbolic (in the Peircian sense) and iconic signs of distortion, exaggeration and so on. The iconic and symbolic signs of comedy that appear on the screen and in the lyrics are enabled by the conventions of the song-scene context and by the generally lively and upbeat musical nature of these songs. In addition, these specific songs include musical elements that explicitly reinforce the scene's comedy, but the fundamentally ambiguous nature of musical sound's semiotic potential limits the ways and means by which music can be used as a sign of anything so specific as comedy.

Musical sounds are signs of direct and immediate experience (Turino, 1999); their relationships to referential meanings are most frequently indexical, that is, constructed through experienced concurrence. The specific and inherently meaningless musical sounds of 'Sar Jo Tera' and 'Zara Rukh Ja' are transformed into potential signs of comedy through their repeated concurrence with iconic/symbolic signs of comedy that Walker and other actors produce. Generally, "the meanings of indices are dependent on the experiences of the perceiver ... and thus can be quite fluid and varied" (Turino, 1999: 228). Such variability of meaning is limited in the cinema, however, because of the relative uniformity of the audience's narrative experience. A theatreful of viewers watching *Pyaasa* would subsequently be more likely to agree on the comic 'meaning' of the sounds in 'Zara Rukh Ja' even without the words and images. Furthermore, because of the cultural dominance of the Hindi cinema and its songs, a remarkably large national audience would have come to assign relatively fixed meanings both to musical sounds and to songs through repeated exposure to similar sounds in narrative and emotional cinematic contexts.

Sounds and songs come to be endowed with referential meaning through repeated association. Film composers, especially those concerned with background music, have often sought to identify (and make use of) the implied iconicity of what remain fundamentally indexical musical signs. The upward-gliding trumpet sounds that are synchronized with Walker's backwards leap to, and then up, the playground slide in 'Zara Rukh Ja' do indeed appear as iconic signs of his movement, but the specificity of their meaning remains dependent on our concurrent experience of both sound and image. The synchronicity of Walker's movements (as he administers a massage in 'Sar Jo Tera') with a series of accompanying percussive sounds makes use of an implied iconicity, based on the direct physical correspondence between the images of the actions, and the kinds of actions that produced the percussion sounds on the sound track. There is also an implied comic relationship between the customer's head and some of the musical instruments being heard[3] (drums and other hollow, struck bodies), but these constructed musical signs reinforce, at best, the iconic and symbolic signs of comedy on the screen.

The imposed synchronicity of inherently asynchronous sounds is the basis for all sound cinema, but it plays a special role in the production of comedy because it transforms musical sounds into quasi-iconic signs of comic action. The song 'Chal Shuru Ho Jaa' ('Come On, Let's Start') was featured in a comic fight scene in *Humjoli* (Ramanna, 1970). The percussive 'sounds' of fisticuffs are transformed into musical sounds by their regular repetition and rhythmic positioning in the context of both the song as music and the song as the soundtrack for what becomes a poolside brawl initiated by the film's two heroes, actors Jitendra and Mehmoood. The inherently abstract musical sounds are repeatedly transformed into iconic signs of comic action. The unexpected and farcical juxtaposition of the musical sounds and images, and the timing of those juxtapositions as expressive musical as well as comic content, transform musical sounds into indexical signs that reinforce comedy.

In addition to the plethora of percussion sounds timed to coincide with our heroes' blows, glissandi played on xylophone and trombone also appear to iconically represent flying bodies. The scene is an outstanding example of the close cooperation between song composer and director, resulting in a carefully staged, comic and highly musical brawl, but it is instructive to compare *Humjoli*'s musical brawl with a similarly comic musical brawl in *Chandini Chowk to China* (Nikhil Advani, 2009). In 'India Se Aaya Mera Dost' ('I've Come From India My Friend'), the hero (played by Akshay Kumar) drunkenly and unknowingly survives an attack by a gang of black-clad 'kung-fu assassins', ultimately allowing them to defeat themselves. Kumar's obliviousness to the deadly army and his inadvertent success provide many opportunities for slapstick humour.[4] 'India Se Aaya' is, if anything, even more carefully staged than the ultimately chaotic 'Chal Shuru Ho Ja', but there are no musical sounds that reinforce the comedy in this more recent scene.

Musico-comic practice is inconsistent in the Hindi cinema, as these examples suggest; but that inconsistency is a result of music's secondary role in the production of comedy. The level of musical exaggeration or distortion necessary, perhaps, to act as direct musical signs of comedy rarely make for good popular songs. As a result, many of the songs from comic scenes do not directly reinforce the comedy of the scene. These examples also suggest that when music does reinforce comedy, it is most likely to do so during the instrumental interludes of these popular songs.

It is the extent to which musical sounds simultaneously act as musically significant signs and quasi-iconic signs of comedy that makes slapstick scenes such as these successful. In such instances, the sounds are uniquely both elements of musical expression and expressions of the scenes' narrative/emotional meaning (comedy). In 'Sar Jo Tera', Johnny Walker's first interaction with his victim's head is accompanied by a lovely folk-style percussion cadence (a rhythmic phrase repeated three times), in which the last beat coincides with his plucking of a hair from his victim's head. Comedy is heightened here by the successful conjunction of two independent expressive systems, as explicitly musical gestures and content (with widely understood musical meanings) are apparently and incongruously performed on a human head in the course of a massage. Nevertheless, the contributions of the referential iconic features (actions, costumes, gestures, behaviour) and the symbolic content (song lyrics and narrative context) will always be the dominant symbols in a Hindi song scene.

The emotional representation or production of comedy

In the Hindi cinema, slapstick, farce, parody, and other forms of exaggeration, distortion and boundary-testing are standard features of comic song scenes, but they appear in two potentially distinct modes of emotional representation and response. Differences between these modes may affect music's ability to reinforce comedy. Of the two, one appears to have a closer connection to the aesthetic theories of classical Sanskrit drama, while the other is more commonly encountered in what might be called 'folk' dramatic forms.

Comedy in classical theories of dramatic narrative (as set out in the Sanskrit text, the *Natyashastra*, c. 200 CE) was considered one of eight core emotional moods (*bhava*) that could dominate a narrative scene and be represented through the expressions and gestures of actors. In this conceptualization of emotional representation and response, viewers experience the corresponding taste (*rasa*; lit. juice or essence). The emotional mood, *hasa*, is translated as mirth (Lutgendorf, 2006) or laughter (Rowell, 1992). The corresponding taste, *hasya*, is the experience of the comic. Booth (1995) and Lutgendorf (2006) both argue that classical aesthetic theory has some relevance to the Hindi cinema. Although the Hindi cinema has also borrowed from Hollywood cinema with enthusiasm and from Indian folk and urban narrative forms, this classical vision of comedy contributes to an understanding of some comic song scenes.

In the distinction between emotional representation by actors and emotional experience by viewers, the audience's experience of comic is not the reality of the comic emotion (laughter). At best it is a sympathetic response to the actors' emotional representations. Consequently, the *bhava-rasa* system triply mediates viewers' emotional experience, through the cinematic medium, the characters' identities (as those who are 'feeling' the emotions) and the actors' expressions and gestures (and words). Laughter or mirth may be a core emotional mood, but laughter is the physical 'business' of the actors who, by laughing, represent that mood for the audience to experience. This mediated practice of the comic is illustrated in the song scene, 'Wah Wah Ramji' ('Lord Ram, You've Done Well'), from the blockbuster *Hum Aapke Hai Kaun* (Sooraj Bharjatiya, 1994).

'Wah Wah Ramji' is picturized on the family celebration of an engagement between the elder siblings (named Rajesh and Pooja) of the main hero and heroine (Prem and Nisha). The event is staged in a studio-set version of a Hindu temple complex; the song lyrics praise the temple deity, Ram or Ram-ji, for bringing the couple together and express the families' happiness at the confirmation of the relationship. Thus, over the four-plus minutes of the scene, Rajesh and Pooja are engaged, the ring is placed on Pooja's finger, all the attendant rituals are performed, and the incipient flirtation between Prem and Nisha is advanced.

The music of 'Wah Wah Ramji' displays almost no signs of comedy. Mumbai's famous string section delivers a suitably exuberant flourish, leading to a strongly percussive introduction. The song itself offers a lively tempo and short, syllabic melodic phrases. The synthesized sound of *shahanai* (an instrument traditionally associated with weddings) provides appropriate atmosphere in one interlude. The synthesizer also produces a bass glissando-like pitch manipulation. Although this instance is more subtle than those in scenes discussed above, this tentative gesture towards the musical reinforcement of comedy stands out against the song's otherwise bland jollity.

'Wah Wah Ramji' begins with slapstick comedy, when Prem's antics cause Pooja to spill paint over Rajesh's white shirt, at which everyone in the scene laughs. Subsequent scenes intersperse signs of family happiness (singing and dancing, the eating of sweets, religious rituals) with other comic skits or gags, all of which involve Prem and inevitably provoke laughter in the other characters because they portray the distortion of social norms that are possible in these kinds of celebratory events. Overall, the scene offers an idealized representation of family relations in the enjoyment of a happy and auspicious occasion.

Happiness, however, is not one of the eight emotional moods set out in the *Natyashastra*. In this paradigm, it is not possible to distinguish between happiness (which might be a better description of the emotional mood of this scene) and mirth or laughter (which may be the physical manifestation of happiness). Instead, happiness is here subsumed within humour's theoretical and representational role. Laughter is the business of the actors; the audience must settle for the experience of the comic.

This form of emotional representation, in which happiness is mixed with comedy and in which the two are collectively represented as laughter, was a prominent feature of comic song scenes in many Rajshri films from *Maine Pyaar Kiya* (Sooraj Bharjatiya, 1989) through *Vivah* (Sooraj Bharjatiya, 2006). This representational mode is also found in the song, 'Oh Meri Maina' ('Oh, My Myna-bird'), from the film *Pyaar Kiye Ja* (C.V. Sridhar, 1966), whose songs highlight India's fascination at that time with rock'n'roll. 'Oh Meri Maina' is another scene of happiness and laughter in which the narrative's two heroes (actors Shashi Kapoor and Mehmood) are shown listening to a record (the disc and player are physically present) that we are meant to understand as one of western pop music (although it is actually a Hindi film song 'in the style of' western pop). Mehmood's girlfriend, played by Mumtaz, also participates.

Mehmood, who is both second hero and clown, provides considerable slapstick humour, which is reinforced by Mumtaz's distinctively Indian and noticeably frenzied interpretation of western rock'n'roll dancing. Her western-style knit top and stirrup pants make her an appropriately stylish source of erotic display as well. There are musical style elements (horn lines and drum set solos) that were routinely deployed by Mumbai's composers as musical signs of westernness and that justified the unusual dance gestures and the western clothing of the scene, but musical sound does not reinforce the comedy.

A spectrum of comic representation

In scenes such as 'Wah Wah Ram-ji' and 'Oh Mere Maina', the iconic signs of laughter (as an emotional mood) are displayed by the narrative protagonists who are the focus of the these scenes. In the two comic fight scenes discussed above, the heroes do not laugh as such, but they are depicted as enjoying themselves. The heroines in these scenes laugh; but their laughter is directed equally at the heroes' slapstick antics and the equally slapstick fates of their adversaries. In the two Johnny Walker scenes above, however, one is hard-pressed to locate signs of laughter in any form. Walker, who is neither a hero, nor a clown/hero (as Mehmood is in the two scenes above) in these scenes, is constructed as the object of the audience's laughter; he himself offers what could best be described as grimaces.

Collectively, these song scenes offer a range of relatively distinct comic experiences. In the mutual happiness and laughter of 'Wah Wah Ram-ji', we taste comedy in its mediated form, just the way we taste representations of romance or sorrow as experienced by the narrative characters. Walker's scenes, on the other hand, exploit comedy's potential to be a relatively unmediated and directly experiential phenomenon; the signs of incongruity, distortion, exaggeration and so forth (both musical and iconic) are intended to produce laughter, not merely the taste of the comic, in the audience. These extremes of comic representation occupy opposite ends of a loosely constructed spectrum, ranging from the audience's mediated experience of the comic as sympathetic response to signs of the comic (laughter, etc.) to their relatively antipathetic laughter in response to signs of distortion, incongruity and so forth.

In the scenes that I locate at both extremes of my proposed spectrum, relative socio-economic status is clearly and distinctly represented: the social equality and mutual happiness shared by those celebrating a family wedding stands in stark contrast to the annoyed looks most other characters direct at Johnny Walker (especially in 'Sar Jo Tera'), who is socially separated from the other characters in his scenes by his dress and behaviour and who is ignored by those who have no desire for his attentions. This social disparity is part of the comedy and is also an excuse for it. It is the distance required, perhaps, to facilitate the objectification of Walker's characters for the audience's laughter. They laugh at the incongruity in the scene, but also at the slapstick circumstances of discomfort that Walker's behaviours cause both for himself and others.

The two comic fight/song scenes I describe above focus on their narratives' heroes (and the clown/heroes played by Mehmood). These heroes' condition as objects of laughter is a temporary condition, however, one that in no way imperils their ultimate victory, an inevitable condition of their heroism. The pair in 'Chal Shuru Ho Ja' are so clearly superior to the villains that the brawl lacks the tension usually found in fight scenes. To reinforce the heroes' temporary comic status, they end up fighting in their underwear, a source of humour to which the watching heroines respond with laughter, even as they also laugh at the fates of the villains. In 'India se Aaaya', Akshay Kumar's hero is so drunk that he remains unaware of the dangers of his situation; his drunken gestures and movements save him from all the efforts and expertise of the ninja horde.[5] These scenes are thus located somewhere in the middle of my proposed spectrum. Each one of these scenes, however, clearly responds to a concern for the nature of comedy as it interacts with social class and the conventions of heroism.

Clowns, comedy and heroism

Neither clown nor hero characters are tied specifically to social class, but clowns must possess traits that make them suitable objects of laughter and that distinguish them from their more serious, heroic companions. Johnny Walker's elite characters, in films such as *Chaudvin ka Chaand* or *Mere Mehboob* (H.S. Rawail, 1963), were clearly non-heroic and were represented as permanently and especially foolish. Despite the ambiguities, "comedy has been judged as a form of low art, as a genre inferior to tragedy, as appropriate only to the trials and tribulations of the lower classes" (Trahair, 2007: 15). The general silliness, the distortions, exaggerations or even transgressions necessary to comedy have often been unsuitable to the intense love, anger, pathos, melancholy and overall seriousness of purpose that have been the emotional provenance of Hindi film heroes. Because of the interaction between heroism, class, clowns and comedy, the phenomenon Trahair explains in terms of class must also be viewed from the perspective of narrative conventions and character construction. Some South Asian clown character-types have less to do with the lofty themes of heroic characters and more to do with the everyday concerns (including sexuality and social norms) of the common people (GoldbergBelle, 1989), but while comedy is not necessarily low class, it is consistently non-heroic. Like all such conclusions about the Hindi cinema, the power and nature of the comic-heroic interaction has shifted across time and from actor to actor.

Song scenes, which heighten/intensify emotional content, have been one of the central locations for the negotiation (or not) of the distinctions between comic heroes and clowns. 'Awaara Hoon' ('I'm a Tramp'), the title song of *Awaara* (Raj Kapoor, 1951), featured actor/director Raj Kapoor in one of his variations on the Charlie Chaplin image that obsessed him during this period. The scene divides rather neatly in half. The first half offers a series of skits: Kapoor's character picks pockets, is pursued by angry victims, steals a bicycle and is forced to jump from the back of a moving truck as he wanders through a studio-set urban market and its associated (though real) suburban housing blocks. His ragged clothes and behaviours distance him from the other, more well-to-do and law-abiding, characters in this part of the scene. These Chaplinesque, slapstick skits do not offer the representation of comedy as an emotional mood within the narrative. Instead, Kapoor's character is the object of our laughter, which is a response to his antics and misfortunes.

The music of 'Awaara Hoon' could be said to be cheerful, but there are no even vaguely exaggerated musical features or quasi-iconic comic sounds. This is appropriate, perhaps, because midway through 'Awaara Hoon' the slapstick disappears (and the comedy with it) as Kapoor's character wanders into a poorer section of the city. Instead of well-to-do businessmen, he encounters women and children. His smiles become more genuine, his interactions with other characters more positive, and the lyrics take a more positive, if philosophic, approach to his situation and to humanity. The exaggerated glissandi of 'Zara Rukh Ja' or the percussive silliness of 'Sar Jo Tera' would have seemed out of place by the conclusion of 'Awaara Hoon'.

'Awaara Hoon' and its parent film addressed ambiguities connected to notions of class and the 'nature v. nurture' debate. Kapoor, of course, was not a clown like Johnny Walker (or even like Mehmood). Although he often represented himself as a semi-comic wanderer, his downtrodden or lowly situations were usually narratively constructed and were often resolved by the end of the films in which he was routinely the hero, never the sidekick. In the same period that Kapoor was negotiating issues of class and heroism (and comedy), however, another actor, Bhagwan, was discovering that a serious commitment to comedy (which Kapoor never made) ultimately disqualified him from heroic roles.

Albela (Bhagwan, 1951) was the third-highest grossing film of 1951 (*Awaara* was highest) and epitomizes Bhagwan's attempt to be both clown and hero. The film is replete with comic and semi-comic songs, the most clearly 'clown-ish' of which is 'Oh Beta-ji' ('Oh Son'), in which Bhagwan, having been hired as a dishwasher in the heroine's house, brings an entire shelf of metal kitchen utensils down on his head and then comically and delightedly discovers that he can bang out a melodic rhythm on them that introduces the song. In each of the subsequent musical interludes we find music that Bhagwan appears to produce from a series of kitchen utensils. These sounds and actions reinforce the comic emotions of the song scene. The popularity of the film's songs was understood to have made the film a hit, but *Albela's* success was never repeated. Bhagwan was largely relegated to lower-class clown roles thereafter. In the early colour hit *Jhanak Jhanak Payal Baje* (V. Shantaram, 1955) he plays a clown/servant whose low-class music and dancing (in a solely instrumental music and dance scene) are an explicit source of narrative tension.

The clown-hero interaction has been most successfully managed, perhaps, by actor Kishore Kumar, who, only a few years after Bhagwan, was able build a highly successful career as a hero who could also play the clown. Like Bhagwan, however, Kumar aligned himself with lighter (and originally western) popular music styles. This is demonstrated in a host of jazzy song scenes such as 'Hum The, Woh Thi' ('I Was There, She Was There') in *Chalti Ka Naam Hai Gaadi*, (Satyen Bose, 1958), in which Kumar tells his brother about the circumstances in which he fell in love.

Kumar introduces the lyric in a staged whisper and puts his fingers to his lips to whistle, but the sound is actually that of a toy slide whistle. It is the first of many instrumental sounds that reinforce the slapstick humour of the scene. Other humorous sounds include an old-fashioned rubber-bulb car horn, played both as a car horn, and later (without the bulb) used by their assistant (who is the film's only unambiguous clown) as an 'air trumpet' to mime the actual jazz trumpet sounds coming from the sound track. As when Kumar's brother 'plays' a flashy jazz drum solo on the hood of car, the apparent production of musical sound from the prosaic materials of the garage add to the scene's comedy.

The conventions of character type have clearly been subject to alteration throughout the cinema's history, in response to the particular time and the abilities of the actor in question. By the 1970s and 80s, those conventions seemed to have reached a point where even clearly non-comic heroes (and heroines) could be featured in comic set pieces in films whose overall orientation was much more violent and action-oriented. Actor Amitabh Bachchan, certainly the angriest of the 'angry young man' heroes of this period, displayed a talent for comedy in song scenes such as 'Mere Angne Mein' ('In My Courtyard'), found in *Lawaaris* (Prakash Mehra, 1981), in which Bachchan enacted a series of cross-dressing roles, miming to a song whose music shows that pitch manipulation as a means of reinforcing comedy remained an important musical sign of comedy in the 1980s.

'Mere Angne Mein' is a comic interlude in a film that is focused on action and revenge. Many such scenes in the 1970s and 80s – including another classic Bachchan comedy song scene, 'My Name is Anthony Gonsalves' (*Amar, Akbar, Anthony,* Manmohan Desai, 1977) – were contextualized as indirect confrontations with narrative villains, in which heroes used comedy (and sometimes disguise as well) to deflect the otherwise aggressive nature of such confrontations. In these scenes, the villains at whom such comic aggression is directed remain unamused by the hero's antics, while other onlookers (often including the heroines) laugh happily, apparently unaware of the aggressive subtext. Such comic song scenes may thus more consistently engage with their narrative's central concerns and incorporate a degree of tension (Will the villain lash out? Will the hero be recognized?) into what remain comic scenes. The comic song here becomes a weapon in the hero's battle against structurally more powerful enemies.

Gender and erotic display in comic song scenes

As I suggested at the beginning of this study, gender and gender relations also interact with comic song scenes. This is already clear from the above discussion of heroism, a characteristic that is inherently masculine in the Hindi cinema and that has an ambivalent relationship to comedy. In the production of comedy, however, gender (especially as constructed on female bodies) becomes an additional basis for 'othering' characters (including heroines) so that they can serve as objects of our laughter. A focus on heroines in comic song scenes, however, is further complicated by the long-standing function of heroine-based song scenes as primary sites for the production of erotic display. As we have already seen in 'Oh Mere Maina', eroticism may be part (and even a dominant part) of comic song scenes involving heroines. Sri Devi, an actress routinely featured in erotic song scenes, also demonstrated a talent for comedy and the comic/erotic interaction in *Mr India* (Shekhar Kapoor, 1987), in the song scene 'Kehte Mujh Ko, Hawa Hawaai' ('They Call Me Hawa Hawaai').

Sri Devi appears in an elaborate and tight-fitting gold lamé gown, pretending to be an entertainer in the villains' lair. The introductory music includes a long descending violin glissando, which playback singer Kavita Krishnamurthy echoes twice in an exaggeratedly shrill voice. This is followed by a longer introduction in which a nonsensical text, composed of homonymous English words and phrases, is set to a unmetered, glissando-laden and exaggeratedly melodramatic melody. After this musically comic introduction, however, the rest of the scene's comedy is symbolic and iconic. Sri Devi's gown and the choreography simultaneously produce considerable erotic display, but her facial expressions, bizarre make-up, interactions with the villains and even their growing realization that she is an imposter make it a rather slapstick vision of eroticism.

The comic eroticism of 'Hawa Hawaai' is more extreme than that found in 'Oh Mere Maina' or 'Zara Rukh Ja'. The relatively explicit sexuality and comedy both reflect changing times and aesthetics. The 1980s to mid-1990s were dominated by a circular commercial logic based on the interactive perceptions that many members of India's growing urban upper and middle classes were staying away from India's increasingly aging theatres that were showing increasingly formulaic, violent, and sexualized films in order to appeal to the less sophisticated audience of generally lower socio-economic standing that was seen as making up the majority of the audience. A blatancy of both comedy and erotic display are quite firmly entwined in films of this period because producers assumed these were necessary given the nature of their audience.

This rationale also explains the song scene 'Rana-ji Maaf Karna' ('Lord, Please Forgive Me') appearing in the action and revenge-focused *Karan-Arjun* (Rakesh Roshan, 1994). 'Rana-ji' features actress Mumta Kulkarni accompanied by a troupe of female dancers, all in stylized and relatively revealing versions of Rajasthani folk costume. The song's lyrics, staging and delivery also imitate Rajasthani folk culture, but offer a comic scenario not dissimilar to the comic/pornographic songs sung primarily in the Bhojpuri language that flourished in the late 1980s with the growth of India's cassette industry. In 'Rana-ji', an elder woman berates a younger married woman for sexual promiscuity, while the latter bemoans her fate, asks for forgiveness (not from the older woman or from her husband, but from the local landowner, the *thakur*, or as the song calls him, 'Rana-ji') and protests her innocence, having managed to spend the night with her brother-in-law (rather than her husband) in a case of mistaken identity.

Especially in films of the 1980s and early 1990s, eroticism and comedy are often weighed down by a deep-seated, if sometimes implicit, misogyny. In 'Rana-ji', humour is produced by the situation (the heroine is using erotic display to distract the villains for the heroes' benefit), but also by our response to the plight of the imagined village woman and Kulkarni's portrayal of her. In this context, her apparent inability to distinguish between the two men is laughable, as is the implication that her 'mistake' may not have been entirely unintentional. Other iconic signs of comedy arise from the disjunction apparent in the juxtaposition of Kulkarni's exaggerated expressions of distress and her erotic dance gestures. Johnny Lever, the most famous clown in the Hindi cinema of the 1990s, is also featured in this scene, disguised as one of the dancing girls in the group; the incongruity of his intentionally female dress, distorted face and bass-voice injections, as well as his interactions with other actors in the scene (who do not know him to be disguised) also contribute to the comedy of the scene. The music of the scene reflects the contemporary fad for 'ethnic' or 'folk' music and costume, but does nothing to reinforce the largely symbolic signs of comedy in the scene.

A whole subset of comic or semi-comic song scenes in this period base their humour on this rather misogynistic approach to gender relations through a stylized form of gendered or sexualized harassment (which the Indian press of this period routinely referred to as 'eve teasing'), in which heroines were the objects of unwanted attention by heroes, usually before their romantic relationship had been established or as a means of resolving romantic disputes. The smiles and laughter in 'Aa Aa Ee Ee, Oh Oh, Mera Dil Na Tordo' ('Ah, Ee, Oh, Don't Break My Heart'), in *Raja Babu* (David Dhawan, 1994) are all on the part of the hero, played by Govinda, who successfully constructed and maintained a comic/heroic persona throughout the 1990s. He is assisted by actor Shakti Kapoor (who made a transition from villain characters in the 1980s to clown characters in the 1990s and who keeps losing his pants in this scene) and a chorus of quite sexualized school girls. Collectively they pursue, harass and generally manhandle an unhappy-looking Karishma Kapoor, who resists and seeks to avoid their attentions. 'Aa Aa Ee Ee' was a hit song in 1994, but (or, perhaps, 'consequently') the music provides few clues regarding the nature of the scene.

Govinda developed a widely-received reputation as a star whose most significant audience was drawn from the more rural regions and from audiences that were (and still are) less globalized. Govinda is consequently one of those heroes whose particular version of comic heroism "may be very popular in India, but have no fan following abroad" (Bose, 2006: 27). In India's rural theatres, at least, Karishma Kapoor's plight and the song scene in general would have been received as comic, although the scene would perhaps have been less popular with educated urban audiences.

Govinda is by no means the only hero to be featured in song scenes in which comedy is based on sexual harassment, but the long-term viability of his version of comic heroism and of this particular vision of the comic song scene were again demonstrated almost 10 years later in *Khullam Khulla Pyaar Karen* (Harmesh Malhotra, 2005). 'Challa Challa' ('It Went') replaces Karishma Kapoor with actress Preity Zinta and the female chorus with a male one, but the song scene replicates the physically aggressive approach to gender interaction, the lack of iconic signs of happiness or laughter (especially by heroines), and the absence of musical signs or reinforcements of comedy that are found in 'Aa Aa Ee Ee'.

Conclusion

This overview has made clear that song scenes, an omnipresent feature of the conventional Hindi cinema, have been fundamental sites for the production of comedy. Their central focus on emotional content and their potentially independent position within the narrative not only enabled comedy in general, but allowed the construction of comic interludes in films outside the comedy genre. The nature of comic interludes and their featured actors have both interacted with the importance of spectacle in song scenes, which has clearly encouraged an interaction with sexuality and erotic display. It has also allowed the development of the representational/sympathetic mode of comic song scene in which – following classic aesthetic understandings – the audience experiences only the taste of the actors' laughter. Comic song scenes have featured heroes, especially in such representational/sympathetic scenes, but comic song scenes have more commonly been the domain of clown actors, especially in scenes that seek to provoke laughter at the events and characters on the screen.

Despite the centrality of the song scene for the production of comedy, it will also be clear that comedy and musical sound have a complex and highly variable set of relationships in the Hindi cinema. I have argued that music's ability to produce or reinforce comedy is inherently limited and dependent upon a set of cinematic-musical conventions that combine local and global practices. The cinema's ability to generate collective and broadly similar emotional experiences and the repeated uses of similar sounds in similar cinematic/narrative situations have produced seemingly iconic musical signs that are understood as both signs of comedy as mediated emotion and signs of the comic as direct emotional experience. Equally significant is the impact of the dual role of the songs in these scenes. This has imposed limitations on the musical production, or even reinforcement, of cinematic comedy. Exaggeration, distortion and incongruity, as musical and potentially comic phenomena, have been largely constrained in both degree and placement by their pop song contexts. While some songs have deployed musical signs to reinforce comedy, others have ignored the comedy-music relationship.

In terms of musical sound, the sliding-pitch phenomenon referred to early in this chapter has reappeared in numerous scenes across a relatively wide set of historical examples. It appears to be literally the only purely musical sign of comedy that has been routinely (if inconsistently) used in the Hindi cinema. The other consistent feature directly connecting musical sound and comedy has been the conjunction of semi-iconic (and largely percussive) musical sounds with actors' percussive gestures. Drum solos have been played on human heads, kitchen pots and automobiles. The apparent conflation of two different modes of expression (of which one is musical) seems to amplify the comedy in these scenes. These musical practices, however, now appear somewhat old fashioned; prominent in the 1950s and even 1960s, they are much less part of twenty-first-century cinematic and musical practice.

In this study I have moved from quite detailed examination of musical instances, specific sounds and carefully choreographed moments to broader patterns and to interactions between cultural and ideological positions on gender, heroism and social class, on one hand, and comedy, music and narrative conventions on the other. More than specific musical sounds, it is the fundamentally emotional nature of the Hindi cinema's song scenes that has been a crucial element connecting music (song, to be more specific) to the production of comedy. Although there have been many non-musical comic scenes in the Hindi cinema, it is comedy's place in song scenes that has given it the unique flavour and that has determined much of this cinema's production of emotional response.

Notes

1. In this study, titles of films are italicized, titles of songs are placed in single quotation marks. This song scene and the majority of examples referred to in this study can frequently be located on YouTube or similar video websites.
2. In writing on the Hindi cinema, names of characters are less commonly used than names of actors, as in this case. I will use one or the other as suits the example being discussed and will make clear which practice I employ in each case.
3. Moreover, there are subtleties of social or class critique that comic songs allow for, and in this instance the film plays with the idea that a head masseur has the power – in that moment – to make fun of his clientele (drumming on their heads) even though he is of a lower social standing.
4. 'India Se Aaya Mera Dost' is an intertextual reference to another older comic song, 'Bambai Se Aaya Mera Dost', from the film *Aap Ki Khatir* (1977).
5. In a clear example of the flexibility of these matters in response to the particularities of actor, narrative conventions, and screen play, Kumar's hero is largely "non-heroic" throughout the majority of the narrative.
6. Film titles in Hindi are translated so as to make sense as titles in English. Titles consisting solely of proper nouns are not translated.

References

Booth, G. (1995). 'Traditional Content and Narrative Structure in the Hindi Commercial Cinema'. *Asian Folklore Studies*, 54(2), 169–190. http://dx.doi.org/10.2307/1178940

Booth, G. (2008). *Behind the Curtain: Making Music in Mumbai's Film Studios*. New York: Oxford University Press. http://dx.doi.org/10.1093/acprof:oso/9780195327632.001.0001

Bose, D. (2006). *Brand Bollywood: A New Global Entertainment Order.* New Delhi: Sage Publications. http://dx.doi.org/10.4135/9788132102786

GoldbergBelle J. (1989). Clowns in Control: Performances in a Shadow Puppet Tradition in South India. In S.H. Blackburn, P.J. Claus, J.B. Flueckiger, & S.S. Wadley (Eds.), *Oral Epics in India* (pp. 118–139). Berkeley, CA: University of California Press.

King, G. (2002). *Film Comedy.* London: Wallflower Press.

Lutgendorf, P. (2006). 'Is There an Indian Way of Filmmaking?' *International Journal of Hindu Studies,* 10(3), 227–256. http://dx.doi.org/10.1007/s11407-007-9031-y

Miner, A. (2000). Musical Instruments: Northern Area. In A. Arnold (Ed.), *The Garland Encyclopedia of World Music: Vol. 5, South Asia: The Indian Subcontinent* (pp. 331–349). New York: Garland.

Rajadhyaksha, A., & Willemen, P. (1995). *Encyclopaedia of Indian Cinema.* New Delhi: Oxford University Press.

Rowell, L. (1992). *Music and Musical Thought in Early India.* Chicago, IL: University of Chicago Press. http://dx.doi.org/10.7208/chicago/9780226730349.001.0001

Trahair, L. (2007). *The Comedy of Philosophy: Sense and Nonsense in Early Cinematic Slapstick.* Albany, NY: State University of New York Press.

Turino, T. (1999). 'Signs of Imagination, Identity, and Experience: A Peircian Semoitic Theory for Music'. *Ethnomusicology,* 43(2), 221–255. http://dx.doi.org/10.2307/852734

Filmography[6]

Albela (*A Jolly Person*) (Bhagwan, 1951)
Amar, Akbar, Anthony (Manmohan Desai, 1977)
Awaara (*Loafer*) (Raj Kapoor, 1951)
Baazi (*Indulgence*) (Moni Bhattacharjee, 1968)
Chalti Ka Naam Hai Gadi (*If It Runs, It's Called a Car*) (Satyen Bose, 1958)
Chandini Chowk to China (Nikhil Advani, 2009)
Chaudvin ka Chand (*Four Quarters of the Moon*) (M. Sadik, 1960)
Chori Chori (*Thievery*) (Anant Thakur, 1956)
Hum Aapke Hai Kaun (*Who Am I to You?*) (Sooraj R. Barjatya, 1994)
Humjoli (*Companion*) (Ramanna, 1970)
Jhanak Jhanak Payal Baje (*Jangle Jangle Sound the Anklets*) (V. Shantaram, 1955)
Johnny Walker (Ved-Madan, 1957)
Karan-Arjun (Rakesh Roshan, 1994)
Khullam Khulla Pyaar Karen (*Show Your Love Publicly*) (Harmesh Malhotra, 2005)
Lawaaris (*Without an Heir*) (Prakash Mehra, 1981)
Mere Mehboob (*My Beloved*) (H.S. Rawail, 1963)
Maine Pyaar Kiya (*I Fell in Love*) (Sooraj R. Barjatya, 1989)
Mr India (Shekhar Kapoor, 1987)
Mr John (Inder, 1959)
Pyaar Kiye Ja (*Fall in Love*) (C.V. Sridhar, 1966)
Pyaasa (*Thirst*) (Guru Dutt, 1957)
Raja Babu (David Dawan, 1994)
Sitaaron Se Aage (*Beyond the Stars*) (Satyen Bose, 1958)
Vivah (*A Journey from Engagement to Marriage*) (Sooraj R. Barjatya, 2006)

Gregory D. Booth is an Associate Professor of Ethnomusicology in the Department of Anthropology at the University of Auckland and has been engaged in the study of Indian music and culture for more than 30 years. He is the author of two books, *Behind the Curtain: Making Music in Mumbai's Film Studios* (OUP, 2008) and *Brass Baja: Stories from the World of Indian Wedding Bands* (OUP, 2005), and numerous articles on music, film, industry and culture in South Asia. He recently edited *More than Bollywood: Studies in Indian Popular Music* (Booth & Shope, OUP, 2013) and is currently studying aspects of India's music and film culture industries, focusing on a wide range of factors including intellectual property, technology, industrial structures, and the music-film relationship.

13 Humour Between the Keys
A Detailed Analysis of The Cat Concerto

Peter Morris

Introduction

MGM's *The Cat Concerto* (1947) was the 29th in the Tom and Jerry series and was released theatrically on 26 April 1947. It won the Academy Award for Best Cartoon for 1946[1] and was the fourth Oscar in a row for the Tom and Jerry creative team. The directors of *The Cat Concerto* were William Hanna and Joe Barbera, who oversaw all the Tom and Jerry cartoons from 1940 to 1958 and subsequently set up an independent company primarily for television, producing budget cartoons featuring the titular Huckleberry Hound, Yogi Bear, Flintstones and Scooby-Doo. As with all but one of the Tom and Jerry cartoons from 1940 to 1958, the musical director was Scott Bradley.[2]

As has been established elsewhere,[3] the functions of music in Hollywood cartoons are as complex as in live action films: the music is subservient to the narrative and, in the case of animated works, to the mechanistic construction process. Unlike the earliest sound cartoons, when the rhythmic phrasing of the animation was mapped onto the strict metre of popular song, from the late-1930s cartoons were emerging from pre-imposed rhythmic and melodic structure and starting to develop their own musical language and sense of cadence.

The use of classical music in cartoons

Cartoon music in this period is mainly a postmodern plundering of assorted musical styles. The rapid changes of emotion, action and characterization in cartoon narrative mean that this is a world of musical fragment and quotation, not extended melody. The classical repertoire is very much a member of the candidate set and is treated with no more respect than any other type of music – arguably, it is treated with less respect. As well as the classical canon being included as individual quotes within broader scores (e.g., Goldmark reports more than a dozen uses of Mozart's C major piano sonata K.545 in

Warner Brothers works (2005: 7), there are examples of entire cartoons based on classical music.

Although it may be thought unusual to find a cartoon solely based on classical music, there are many precedents, of which the most significant was Disney's feature length *Fantasia* (1940). Unlike *Fantasia*, based on multiple scores as befits its 125-minute running time, *The Cat Concerto* is based on just one work – Liszt's *2nd Hungarian Rhapsody* (1847). Interestingly, Liszt's work has been a regular in cartoons and significant parts of it can also be found in *An Optical Poem* (1937), *Rhapsody in Rivets* (1941), *Rhapsody Rabbit* (1946),[4] *Colour Rhapsodie* (1948), *Who Framed Roger Rabbit* (1988), *C Flat or B Sharp* (1990) and, in lesser amounts, in many cartoons e.g. *Back Alley Oproar* (1948), *What's Up Doc* (1950) and a dozen live action movies. As a parody of the cartoon style, the *Rhapsody* is also used in *Who Framed Roger Rabbit* (1988, Alan Silvestri) in which Donald Duck and Daffy Duck fight to outdo each other in a 'duelling pianos' contest, delivering ever more dazzling, virtuoso performances. In pulling together these characters (one Disney, the other Warner Brothers) and this piece of music, the director, Robert Zemeckis, seems to be making a point that the *Rhapsody* is the apotheosis of non-original cartoon music. Theories explaining its popularity will be suggested in a later section.

It is, perhaps, no surprise that *William Tell*, *The Hebrides*, *Tales from the Vienna Woods*, *Carmen*, *The Barber of Seville* and so on should find their way into cartoons. As Chuck Jones (probably the most famous of all animators) points out: "The average cartoon musician was a theater organist in the silent era and so William Tell takes quite a beating in the average cartoon" (Jones, 2002: 94). These works would have been well known to the adaptable and skilled silent era musicians. However, classical music as a source was not only confined to being subordinate to the animation. As early as 1928/29, Carl Stalling and Walt Disney debated the relative importance of music and animation. As a sop to Stalling's complaint about his music being secondary to the animation in the main Disney shorts, Disney created a series of cartoons (the *Silly Symphonies*) in which the music was written first and the animation created to support the music. The earliest of these – *The Skeleton Dance* (1929, Stalling) – apparently owes much to Saint-Saëns' *Danse Macabre*, though Stalling denies direct quotation. This style of using large sections of original or source music is found in many later cartoons, including much from Warner Bros. – *A Corny Concerto* (1943), *Rhapsody Rabbit* (1950) and *The Rabbit of Seville* (1950) – all with scores by Carl Stalling.

What's Opera Doc? (Franklyn, 1957)[5] was perhaps the most ambitious of these, basing plot, animation style and music around several of Wagner's operas[6] and provided both a vehicle and a pastiche. Chuck Jones (director and lead animator) did not try to abbreviate Wagner's storylines but instead created a work based on standard operatic building blocks: overture, villain, dramatic hero, heroine, love scene, death of the hero and denouement. Of course, Wagner's extended melodic style could never be used due to the seven-minute limitation of the cartoon, and Jones/Franklyn chose to take paradigmatic excerpts from the originals, providing as much a pastiche of the music as of the operatic style.

It was, of course, the lampooning of high art in the new temple of entertainment called the cinema that makes the cartoon especially funny: Elmer Fudd as Siegfried performing a balletic love duet with Bugs Bunny as Brunhilde, "Kill the wabbit" set as lyrics to the main motif of *The Ride of the Valkyries*. Even the ending, when Bugs Bunny dies, takes a swipe at the supposedly dull operatic world. Bugs comes back to life and announces "Well, what did you expect in opera, a happy ending?"

Everything, from the opening credits, with their mock proscenium arch, to the costumes and pseudo-scenery, makes a point. The old world has made way for the new and Bugs' triumphal resurrection is not a victory over Elmer Fudd as much as it is over opera itself. However, the issue here is not pro-cartoon or anti-opera, it is rather about the use of classical music as a tool in the postmodern toolset of the cartoon composer. Whether the music is played by a swing band (typically modelled on Raymond Scott's quintet) or by a full symphony orchestra, classical music was exposed to the cartoon audience in a subliminal way, bringing classical music to an audience that might not have otherwise experienced it.

The plot

The plot of *The Cat Concerto* is as slight as most of the Tom and Jerry cartoons. This is not the world of *The Simpsons* where the audience is meant to understand both cultural and satirical references and follow a plotline through 24 minutes. Tom and Jerry cartoons are home to the chase, the sight gag and the anti-heroicism of David and Goliath, compressed into seven minutes. As with most animated shorts, the situation is more important than the book.

What plot there is revolves around Tom, as a concert pianist, trying to perform Liszt's *2nd Hungarian Rhapsody* on a piano in which a mouse has set up home. Tom's major desire is to play the piece without interruption; Jerry's to live in peace. Thus the situation of this cartoon is not the classic chase or mutual doing of harm: Jerry tries to stop Tom from playing while Tom wants rid of the mouse without skipping a beat. Thus when Jerry manages to stop Tom (such as the mousetrap gag at 0:04:06) Jerry continues the music in a mock triumphal way by running up and down the keyboard. It is not the harm that is done that pleases Jerry, it is that the ownership of performance has changed hands. The same is true of 'On the Atchison, Topeka and the Santa

Fe' at 0:04:39, where Jerry dances in delight on the hammers, causing them to play. This is affirmed in Jerry's formally taking the bows at the end of the piece, having commandeered the final section.

In each case, music plays a pivotal role. Jerry's motif after the mousetrap is a clearly articulated, skipping arpeggio figure; the 'On the Atchison, Topeka and the Santa Fe' routine is all his own doing, introducing music that is outside the classical norm, thereby hijacking it completely; the finale sees Jerry no longer reacting to Tom but driving the situation by forcing the pace and, via a series of false endings, the shape of the music. Many similar gags simply would not work 10 seconds later or earlier. They are mapped onto music in its predefined format and it is the animation that had to make way, not the score.

Having made that point, there is evidence that music and storyboards were worked on together, rather than have either one worked on in advance of the other. The repeated bouncing that Jerry receives at 0:02:08 meant that the music had to be extended from the original five repeated notes to 17, improving the comedy. In the same way, extending cadenzas and conformance to the macro structure (see later) meant that the music had to be adapted. What remains, however, is a score that stands in its own right. There is nothing un-Lisztian about the resulting soundtrack. The phrase lengths, rhythmic shape and cadence are all within romantic conventions, leaving the animators with limited freedom to time the movement and gags.

Detailed analysis

Scott Bradley arranged and conducted the music in *The Cat Concerto* for piano duet and orchestra with John Crown (Head of Piano at the Southern University of California) playing the upper, virtuosic part and Arthur Schutt, an MGM session musician, playing secundo. The score comprises the major part of Liszt's original plus a fragment from 'On the Atchison, Topeka and the Santa Fe' (Warren/Mercer, 1946)[7] played on piano by Calvin Jackson.[8] The Liszt arrangement is reasonably faithful to the original score, albeit with a small number of cuts and some repeats. Although a couple of cadenzas have been extended, arguably in the style, only one section is newly composed: a cadenza at 0:04:59, replacing bars 260 to 269. As with the cadenzas, repeated sections (cues 0:02:11, 0:04:45 and 0:06:06 to the end), are done for comedic purposes, allowing reinforcement of a single gag or to extend a gag with variants. Despite these changes, however, the piece is almost entirely in its original shape.

Much as is the case with live action films, a plot is created on storyboards, which highlight the individual shots required and key action moments within those shots. There are, of course, no actors to improvise, interpret or happen on those chance comedic moments. It is the job of the director and the animators to plan every single movement, every hair disturbance, all moves of the virtual camera, depth of field and focus. Moments such as camera shake (0:05:09), and repeated panning to follow a disorientated Jerry (0:05:53 et seq.) are constructed at storyboard stage.

It is easier in animation to create more shots or takes than it is to pan, dolly or zoom. Ordinarily, the background artist will produce a single cel against which the character and foreground artists will create detailed animation. A static shot requires only one background cel for a shot that may be 15 seconds long. Moving the camera can mean extra work for the background artists who have either to produce a much larger background or multiple background cels, something that the producer would be loath to fund unless essential for the plotline. Chases in particular demand as much variety in the background as they do foreground.[9]

What follows is an analysis of the shots in *The Cat Concerto*, looked at from the point of view of comedic structure. Cue points are given in h:mm:ss format and bar numbers are numeric, unless greater accuracy is required, in which case they may be annotated x.y.z, where x is the bar number, y is the beat number and z is the subdivision within the beat.

Cue: 0:00:00	Shot: 01	POV:	Bar:
Description: MGM title card			
Commentary: T&J opening fanfare.			

Cue: 0:00:04	Shot: 02	POV:	Bar:
Description: FTB (Fade to black)			
Commentary: Piano & orchestra arrangement of the final section of Chopin's D minor prelude, Op. 28 No. 24.			

Cue: 0:00:06	Shot: 03	POV:	Bar:
Description: Fade to Academy Award title card			
Commentary:			

Cue: 0:00:08	Shot: 04	POV:	Bar:
Description: Dissolve to main title card			
Commentary:			

Cue: 0:00:15	Shot: 05	POV:	Bar:
Description: Dissolve to credits title card			

Humour Between the Keys   229

Cue: 0:00:15	Shot: 05	POV:	Bar:
Commentary:			

Cue: 0:00:20	Shot:06	POV:	Bar:
Description: Dissolve to producer title card			
Commentary:			

Cue: 0:00:23	Shot: 07	POV:	Bar:
Description: FTB			
Commentary:			

Cue: 0:00:24	Shot: 08	POV: Audience in dress circle	Bar:
Description: Fade to establishing shot			
Commentary: The first shot places the audience firmly within a concert setting. LS of stage with grand piano in centre and, although not clear, the orchestra may be in a pit in front of the stage. The music playing (forming a seamless continuation of the opening titles) is the final part of Chopin Preludes Op. 28 No. 24, arranged by Bradley for piano and orchestra with flowing arpeggios and declamatory style.			

Cue: 0:00:29	Shot:	POV:	Bar:
Description: Pan left, dolly in to stage right entrance			
Commentary: Preparation for Tom's entrance.			

Cue: 0:00:33	Shot: 09	POV: Audience in front stalls	Bar:
Description: Dissolve to LS stage right for T's entrance			
Commentary: Chopin stops. Tom enters. Tracking shot to R as T walks to piano. T receives applause. Strauss (2002, p10) reports that finger and wrist movements were based on Vladimir de Pachman (1848–1933).[10] Tom, as haughty character, walks with eyes closed and bows establishing the concert as being remote, elite, intellectual, slow and for a serious audience. Creating these presuppositions allows the later contrast with upstart, Jerry.			

Cue: 0:00:44	Shot: 10	POV: Front stage left	Bar:
Description: MS T at piano			

Cue: 0:00:44	Shot: 10	POV: Front stage left	Bar:
Commentary: The orchestra tunes up and Tom goes through the formalized ritual of preparing to play: adjusting piano stool, wiping hands and waiting patiently with hooded eyes. Conductor taps baton.			

Cue: 0:00:56	Shot: 11	POV: Looking down keyboard	Bar:
Description: MS T at piano			
Commentary: T raises arm to play.			

Cue: 0:00:58	Shot:	POV:	Bar: 1
Description: Start of Rhapsody			
Commentary: T plays mostly with eyes closed, half opening at the beginning of each gesture, head upright, flowing arm movement. T plays only melodic right hand part with orchestra playing the left hand accompaniment.			

Cue: 0:01:16	Shot: 12	POV: Within piano	Bar: 5.2
Description: MS T through lid			
Commentary: T is framed within piano and lid. Head nodding and much gestural moving of torso. T is not just a cat; he is a serious concert pianist.			

Cue: 0:01:24	Shot:	POV:	Bar: 7.2
Description: End of T's opening section			
Commentary: Having played the opening section, T opens eyes and looks forward (presumably at the conductor).			

Cue: 0:01:25	Shot: 13	POV: Front stage left	Bar: 7.2
Description: MS T at piano			
Commentary: Front stage POV allows T's gestures to be seen more clearly.			

Cue: 0:01:26	Shot:	POV:	Bar: 8
Description: T prepares for *Andante mesto* while the orchestra continues			
Commentary: T wipes hands, plays with collar and tie and raises left hand to play.			

Cue: 0:01:31	Shot:	POV:	Bar: 8.2.2.2
Description: T's shirt front falls open			

Humour Between the Keys 231

Cue: 0:01:31	Shot:	POV:	Bar: 8.2.2.2
Commentary: T made to look foolish by having his starched shirt front fall open. Bathos is used to ridicule T's otherwise perfect dress sense.[11] The sight gag is positioned just before the next section of music (on the paused A in the cellos), using timing as the musical indicator, rather than melody or harmony. It was an inappropriate moment for the wardrobe malfunction and taps into Morreall's superiority theory of laughter.			

Cue: 0:01:32	Shot:	POV:	Bar: 8.2.2.3
Description: T pushes up shirt front			
Commentary: Other than pushing the shirt up again, T does not acknowledge that there is a problem. The repair is done on the final G♯ demisemiquaver before the *Andante mesto*, acting as an upbeat.			

Cue: 0:01:33	Shot:	POV:	Bar: 9
Description: *Andante mesto*			
Commentary: Orchestra drops out (doesn't reappear until 0:05:30). T has piano solo, full of gestures and all goes well, as it needs to, to set up first sight of Jerry. Music is strong, minor key and *molto expressivo*, allowing the animators to make corresponding body movements to the free style of the music.			

Cue: 0:01:35	Shot: 14	POV: Looking down keyboard	Bar: 10
Description: MS T at keyboard			
Commentary: T looks sombre and elegant, bottom lip sticking out.			

Cue: 0:01:44	Shot:	POV:	Bar: 13.2
Description: T opens eyes and smiles at camera			
Commentary: T's acknowledgment of camera brings sense of reality to his character. Apart from the smile, T wobbles his head on the double grace note, setting up a musical/gestural link repeated later. Despite the music still being in C♯ minor, the gesture overrules the tonality; it is a happy moment.			

Cue: 0:01:46	Shot: 15	POV: Front stage left through piano lid	Bar: 14.2.2
Description: MS T at keyboard			
Commentary: Music changes to relative major, though T's attitude is the same.			

232 Sounding Funny

Cue: 0:01:50	Shot:	POV:	Bar: 16.2
Description: Continuation of previous shot			
Commentary: Dolly back to reveal 3/4 of piano.			

Cue: 0:01:53	Shot:	POV:	Bar: 17.2
Description: Continuation of previous shot			
Commentary: Repeat of smiling/head movement found at 0:01:44 on double grace note, though T's eyes open a second time, allowing the forced change back to relative minor to have greater contrast.			

Cue: 0:01:54	Shot:	POV:	Bar: 18.2
Description: Return to stern demeanour			
Commentary: Coincident with strong dominant 7th of C♯ minor, forcing the modulation.			

Cue: 0:01:57	Shot: 16	POV: Above treble strings	Bar: 19.1.2
Description: CU hammers			
Commentary: T is secondary to shot of the hammers. Preparatory shot for dolly to J.			

Cue: 0:01:59	Shot:	POV:	Bar: 20.2
Description: Fast dolly right to J 'at home'			
Commentary: J is asleep in a makeshift house. Curtains, lampshade and washing (including shorts and a towel monogrammed with J.M.) hanging out provide the incongruity. In addition, J is asleep and smiling, despite the noisiest part of the music so far.			

Cue: 0:02:02	Shot:	POV:	Bar: 21
Description: Hammers move around J asleep			
Commentary: Hammers around J move, creating tension that J will be hit (see 0:03:44 and 0:04:02 for similar gags constructed in same way). Rhythms from the right hand appear in the bass notes, indicating that the gag is more important than note accuracy.[12] Gags such as this create tension, contributing to humour through relief theory.			

Cue: 0:02:05	Shot:	POV:	Bar: 22.2
Description: J's blanket raised			

Cue: 0:02:05	Shot:	POV:	Bar: 22.2

Commentary: Key change via strong secondary dominant. This pivot is reflected and timed by J's blanket being projected up by a hammer. Pillow raised on 23.2 in anticipation of cadenza.

Cue: 0:02:07	Shot: 17	POV:	Bar: 24

Description: J moved by wave of hammers

Commentary: The G♯ minor flourish in the scored cadenza is extended to allow the sleeping J to be moved up and down the inside of the piano. J is still asleep until end when he is bounced partly out of shot and looks surprised. Although the cadenza is extended, it is the kind of extension that would commonly be used in playing a Liszt piece.

Cue: 0:02:08	Shot:	POV:	Bar: 24

Description: J bounced on repeated B

Commentary: Having awoken, the surprised J is bounced several times on a repeated B. Liszt's score has 5 Bs but the cartoon uses 17, the last of which pauses to allow J to be projected completely out of shot for 17 frames (0.75s) at 0:02:13. While J is out of shot, there is no subject and no music, creating comedic tension.

Cue: 0:02:14	Shot:	POV:	Bar: 25

Description: J lands on head between strings

Commentary: Returning from out of shot, J somersaults and lands with his head jammed between two strings. He falls over onto his back. Both landing and falling are on down beats (25 and 26), the music of which represents closure of the cadenza passage. The tension created by 0:02:08 is resolved by physical comedy (slapstick) as much as the simple release of tension, a combination of farce and relief theory.

Cue: 0:02:19	Shot: 18	POV: MS T through piano	Bar: 27

Description: MS T

Commentary: Unlike previous sections, where the score uses the minor/major pattern, the *dolce con grazia* section starts with major. Played highly rubato, T uses florid gestures to represent delicacy and smiles in accord with the change to the major key. However, in the scheme of Cat and Mouse chase, J has just lost and T's smile can be taken as one of unwitting triumph, creating a sympathy towards J.

| Cue: 0:02:24 | Shot: 19 | POV: Keyboard into piano | Bar: 29 |

Description: MS piano strings

Commentary: J peeps out of the piano and sees T playing. J does double take on down beat of 30. J is delighted to see T, as if greeting an old friend and warning the audience, by association, of action to come.

| Cue: 0:02:27 | Shot: 20 | POV: Front centre stage | Bar: 30.2 |

Description: MS T

Commentary: T opens his eyes and sees J. Music returns to minor with T doing double take on down beat of 31. T is shocked to see J, reinforcing emotional roles of major/minor tonalities.

| Cue: 0:02:29 | Shot: | POV: | Bar: 31.2 |

Description: Dolly R to J conducting

Commentary: J is lying on his side conducting with eyes closed, apparently enjoying the music but his closed eyes indicate mimicry (varied restatement).

| Cue: 0:02:30 | Shot: 21 | POV: Keyboard | Bar: 32 |

Description: FS low-angle at J conducting

Commentary: CU J, smiling, cross-legged leaning on one arm, eyes closed. J is taking advantage of T playing and thinks himself immune. J conducts with one finger.

| Cue: 0:02:34 | Shot: 22 | POV: Keyboard | Bar: 33 |

Description: MS 2-shot

Commentary: T turns from surprise to anger and flicks J off the piano exactly on 34.2 (the last beat before the capriccioso).

| Cue: 0:02:37 | Shot: | POV: | Bar: 35 |

Description: Dolly to MS T

Commentary: T resumes composure, smiles and closes eyes for capriccioso, played in highly mobile manner. The style of music reflects T's mood at having rid himself of J.

Humour Between the Keys   235

Cue: 0:02:40	Shot: 23	POV: R of T	Bar: 38
Description: FS J			
Commentary: J appears under key at top of keyboard, looking indignant.			

Cue: 0:02:41	Shot: 24	POV:	Bar: 40
Description: 2-shot T & J staring at each other			
Commentary: Face off between T & J. T can't do anything to interrupt the flow of music.			

Cue: 0:02:42	Shot:	POV:	Bar: 59
Description: Dolly/zoom 2-shot			
Commentary: Music cut bars 41–58 inclusive to double-handed trill at 59. T uses one finger to repeatedly hammer key above J's head in keeping with highly percussive piano part. T looks determined to save his performance. The repeated striking of J is clearly timed for the music, which in turn sets the agenda and structure of the build-up to this point. This is an immovable sight gag.			

Cue: 0:02:44	Shot:	POV:	Bar: 61
Description: Pan with J running under keys			
Commentary: J runs up and down under the keys to try and escape. It is J, not T, who plays this cadenza.			

Cue: 0:02:48	Shot:	POV:	Bar: 79
Description: T plays big chord squashing J			
Commentary: Music cut bars 62 to 78 inclusive. Extra tonic chord inserted on downbeat of 79 for T squashing J.			

Cue: 0:02:50	Shot: 25	POV: Front stage left through piano	Bar: 81
Description: LS T			
Commentary: T looks satisfied and is back to playing as before. Double grace note at 0:02:54 repeats head wobbling gesture from 0:01:44. Exaggerated movement for chords at 82.2–83.			

Cue: 0:02:59	Shot: 26	POV: Stage right of top of keyboard	Bar: 84
Description: MS T			

Cue: 0:02:59	Shot: 26	POV: Stage right of top of keyboard	Bar: 84
Commentary: T smiles while playing cadenza. T plays with great elegance and looks ecstatic when playing trill (0:03:02).			

Cue: 0:03:04	Shot:	POV:	Bar: 84
Description: Continuation of previous shot			
Commentary: T stops playing trill but it continues, substantially expanded compared to the score. T does double-take (0:03:05).			

Cue: 0:03:06	Shot: 27	POV: above treble strings	Bar: 84
Description: CU hammers FS J moving hammers			
Commentary: T looks into piano and sees J moving hammers up and down continuing the trill. T grips keyboard lid, peers over, raises eyebrows and blinks. T reaches for tuning lever and hits J on head (0:02:11).			

Cue: 0:03:13	Shot:	POV:	Bar: 84
Description: Zoom in FS J moving hammers			
Commentary: Delayed reaction from J who continues trill until pain sets in. Over 3 seconds of silence (other than thud of J falling over cross-eyed) but pause is just before pick-up to *dolce* at 85, making the silence a musical teasing gesture before modulating to the relative major. This modulation and preceding filigree anacrusis offer great scope for delicacy in the following section.			

Cue: 0:03:15	Shot: 28	POV: Stage right of top of keyboard	Bar: 84
Description: MS T at keyboard			
Commentary: T looks self-satisfied and plays this *dolce* much as he played the *dolce con grazia* at 0:02:19. The extra sweetness and florid gestures are to provide contrast to 0:03:33.			

Cue: 0:03:24	Shot: 29	POV: Downstage right of keyboard	Bar: 87
Description: CU treble end of keyboard lid			
Commentary: J appears from behind lid, looks indignant and slams keyboard lid on T's fingers.			

Cue: 0:03:33	Shot: 30	POV: Low-angle, top end of keyboard	Bar: 118
Description: Medium CU T grimacing			
Commentary: Music cut 91 to 117 inclusive. T is in pain but has to continue playing. Bang of lid coincident with first beat of Friska section. This is the first time J has inflicted pain on T and the Friska marks the start of joint hostilities. The initial key is relative minor of the key established at bar 85 (F# minor).			

Cue: 0:03:34	Shot: 31	POV: Centre of keyboard	Bar: 120
Description: XCU T's hands flattened			
Commentary: The lid has flattened T's hands and he is incapable of playing fast or florid music. Relative to the extreme rubato of 85 to 92, the contrasting static nature of the score at the start of the *Vivace* supports the gag.			

Cue: 0:03:38	Shot: 32	POV: Centre of keyboard looking up keyboard	Bar: 150
Description: CU top of keyboard			
Commentary: Music cut 126 to 149 inclusive. J opens archetypical mouse hole shaped door in keyboard lid. This is clearly a normal entrance since there is a mat inside the door, making it doubly incongruous. J looks up joyously at T playing.			

Cue: 0:03:41	Shot:	POV:	Bar: 158
Description: J returns inside door			
Commentary: Music cut from 154 to 157 inclusive. J's head disappears exactly on downbeat of 158, tightly choreographed, indicating firm action. Returns with scissors.			

Cue: 0:03:44	Shot:	POV:	Bar: 166
Description: J tries to snip T's finger			
Commentary: Music cut 162 to 165 inclusive. As T plays top C# (166 *et al.*), J tries twice to cut off T's finger with scissors.			

Cue: 0:03:47	Shot:	POV:	Bar: 174
Description: Continuation of previous shot			
Commentary: Music cut 170 to 173 inclusive. Repeat of attempted finger snipping gag at 0:03:44 but at double speed since high C# now every bar instead of every two bars. Music changes to F# major.			

238 Sounding Funny

Cue: 0:03:50	Shot: 33	POV: 3/4 up keyboard at J	Bar: 178
Description: FS J looking exhausted			
Commentary: Snipping at double speed has left J exhausted. *Tempo giusto* section seems to laugh at J's attempt. J changes plans.[13]			

Cue: 0:03:57	Shot:	POV:	Bar: 194
Description: Zoom out to CU top octave			
Commentary: Music cut from 186 to 193 inclusive. J walks to the tempo of the music to collect some keys from the top of the keyboard and replaces them with a mousetrap. This section, animated to broken IV-I arpeggios with straight quavers, denotes determination, which works to contrast with 0:04:09, where this gag will end. Having laid the trap, J leans against the piano to watch it spring.			

Cue: 0:04:02	Shot: 34	POV: Keyboard lid looking at upper keyboard	Bar: 202
Description: XCU mousetrap & T's right hand/paw			
Commentary: T plays notes on either side of the mousetrap. Music is now semiquavers with chromatic neighbour notes within a dominant 7th, creating tension through dissonance and appoggiaturas.			

Cue: 0:04:06	Shot:	POV:	Bar: 208.2
Description: T's finger gets trapped			
Commentary: In keeping with the tightly choreographed animation, the trap springs on a dominant/tonic resolution. This is another gag that could not slip by eight bars; the clear determination of J at 0:03:57 and the music at 0:04:02 are essential to the structure of the composite humour.			

Cue: 0:04:07	Shot: 35	POV: Centre piano through lid at T	Bar: 210
Description: T looking at trap on finger			
Commentary: T stands, stops playing and looks at finger. T notices that the music is continuing.			

Cue: 0:04:09	Shot: 36	POV: Downstage centre towards keyboard	Bar: 212
Description: J dancing on keys			

| Cue: 0:04:09 | Shot: 36 | POV: Downstage centre towards keyboard | Bar: 212 |

Commentary: J is dancing up and down the keyboard, playing the music that T has stopped. It is not clear whether J wanted to hurt T or just to cause him to stop playing. Whatever, the reason, J's appearance is triumphal. This is the same harmonic pattern (IV-I) as at 0:03:57, and closes the gag started at that point. The semiquavers here are not based on a 7th chord, as at 0:04:02 and the simplicity of the chords reinforce J's delight.

| Cue: 0:04:12 | Shot: 37 | POV: Centre of piano through lid | Bar: 218 |

Description: Medium CU T, trying to catch J

Commentary: T tries to catch J using both hands. When grabbing, T misses but apparently grabs fistfuls of wrong notes, represented by the chromatic, semitone acciaccaturas in the left hand.

| Cue: 0:04:16 | Shot: 38 | POV: Downstage centre looking at keyboard | Bar: 224 |

Description: FS 2-shot

Commentary: J has bounced up into the body of the piano and T climbs up to find him. Music is now played with feet but when T can't find J, T climbs down again, playing with feet and hands seamlessly. This is an immensely funny moment where the continuity of the music, with a slight decelerando, shows T to be equally capable of playing with hands or feet. The humour here is, in some part, based on incongruity but is mainly the same delight that comes from extreme virtuosity, edging on disbelief.

| Cue: 0:04:25 | Shot: 39 | POV: Above keyboard lid at bass end | Bar: 232 |

Description: CU T's hands and right up keyboard

Commentary: Although T's face is not seen, we assume he is back to his more controlled self, indicated by the music slowing down and marking the end of the previous section. The camera shot is set for the 'stretching finger' sight gag. To play notes at the top of the keyboard (bars 234 and 236), the animators stretch T's little finger by two and a half octaves (far more than the stretch in the score). The gag is repeated.

| Cue: 0:04:32 | Shot: 40 | POV: Inside treble end of piano, looking at T | Bar: 237 |

Description: MS T playing

| Cue: 0:04:32 | Shot: 40 | POV: Inside treble end of piano, looking at T | Bar: 237 |

Commentary: Music cut from 239 to 249 inclusive. T is looking happy as he thinks himself to be back in control. The relative calm and grace of the music and Ts expression create the illusion that all is well. As an audience, we know that not to be so and the smile seems to alert us to upcoming trouble rather than to soothe us.

| Cue: 0:04:34 | Shot: | POV: | Bar: Insert |

Description: Continuation of previous shot

Commentary: T opens eyes. He is apparently playing a boogie-woogie version of 'On the Atchison, Topeka and the Santa Fe'. T is enjoying it and loosens up from his formal style until he realizes something is wrong and stops playing.

| Cue: 0:04:39 | Shot: 41 | POV: Inside treble end of piano, looking at hammers | Bar: Insert |

Description: CU hammers, FS J

Commentary: J is doing a jazz/tap act on the hammers, causing them to play the wrong music. J's expression is one of delight.[14]

| Cue: 0:04:45 | Shot: 42 | POV: Stage right of top of keyboard | Bar: 250 |

Description: MS Tom

Commentary: Bars 250 and 252 contain sforzando chords on the downbeats. T uses these strong beats to thump the keys and bounce J into the air so as to catch him. Bars 250 to 253 are repeated so as to allow J to do four cameos, one for each time he is bounced.[15]

| Cue: 0:04:54 | Shot: 43 | POV: Down stage centre | Bar: 254 |

Description: CU Piano stool

Commentary: T puts J in piano stool. Tom is seamlessly playing with left hand alone while holding J in right hand.

| Cue: 0:04:56 | Shot: 44 | POV: Downstage of piano | Bar: 258 |

Description: Low angle FS T and piano stool

Humour Between the Keys   241

| Cue: 0:04:56 | Shot: 44 | POV: Downstage of piano | Bar: 258 |

Commentary: This is a set-up scene for the piano stool rising. Bars 258–259 are repeated over a half diminished chord, slowing down in preparation for the cadenza. Tom still has time to flick his tails into position before sitting down again, setting up the falsehood that he is in control.

| Cue: 0:04:59 | Shot: 45 | POV: Downstage of piano | Bar: Insert |

Description: CU piano stool

Commentary: Start of non-original four part cadenza (rolling scales, rising passage, trills, final flourish). During rolling scales, J looks up at T and start to raise piano stool

| Cue: 0:05:01 | Shot: 46 | POV: Over piano from downstage left | Bar: Insert |

Description: MS T

Commentary: During rising passage, piano stool is lifted to an abnormal height.

| Cue: 0:05:02 | Shot: | POV: | Bar: Insert |

Description: Zoom out

Commentary: Zoom used to give visual impression of distance being stretched. T is unaware and carries on playing, eyes closed and holding on by toes while tailcoat falls around his head.

| Cue: 0:05:05 | Shot: | POV: | Bar: Insert |

Description: T at highest extent, plays two-handed trill with crossed hands. With tails over his head, T realizes that something is wrong and trill gets slower as he looks upwards at feet. Change of speed provides contrast for falling.

Commentary:

| Cue: 0:05:06 | Shot: 47 | POV: Downstage left of piano stool | Bar: Insert |

Description: XCU piano stool & FS J

Commentary: J lowers the stool rapidly. Cadenza flourish starts downwards (i.e. stool is falling from J's POV).

| Cue: 0:05:07 | Shot: 48 | POV: Over piano from downstage left | Bar: Insert |

Description: FS T suspended by feet

Cue: 0:05:07	Shot: 48	POV: Over piano from downstage left	Bar: Insert
Commentary: Cadenza moves upwards as T realizes he is suspended in mid air. The rising figure reflects J's interest in what should be up (contrast with J's interest in stool coming down which is under falling figure). After stool has fallen, silence is used to heighten anticipation during which T looks down at stool and up at feet before succumbing to the temporarily suspended laws of gravity.			

Cue: 0:05:09	Shot:	POV:	Bar: 270
Description: Camera shake			
Commentary: Music cut 260 to 269 inclusive. T falls back but lands on keyboard, apparently causing the camera to shake, and plays slow octaves version of 270–273.1.1.			

Cue: 0:05:12	Shot: 49	POV: Above top of keyboard	Bar: 271
Description: CU T			
Commentary: T picks up J and continues to play the octave passage one-handed.			

Cue: 0:05:13	Shot:	POV:	Bar: 272
Description: Zoom in on 2-shot			
Commentary: T holds J in fist nose to nose. Zoom in reflects T's anger. J looks scared.			

Cue: 0:05:14	Shot: 50	POV: Above top end of pianos string	Bar: 272
Description: XCU hammers T partly in shot top left			
Commentary: T jams J between hammers. Silence afterwards creating tension. Pause after 273.1.1			

Cue: 0:05:16	Shot: 51	POV: Stage right of top of keyboard	Bar: 273.1.2
Description: MS T			
Commentary: T looks evil, deliberately planning on harming J. Music is now regular and strong and remains so until the end of this slapstick section (0:05:51)			

| Cue: 0:05:19 | Shot: 52 | POV: Treble string to hammers | Bar: 277 |

Description: XCU hammers with J trapped

Commentary: J looks nervous and is repeatedly hit by hammers. This section is pure slapstick with J being stretched, hit, flattened, etc. supported by a brash statement of the theme that feels somewhat like circus music, akin to March of the Gladiators (Julius Fucik, 1872–1916) because of its combination of chromatic lines and simple chord structure.

| Cue: 0:05:22 | Shot: 53 | POV: Piano strings to hammers | Bar: 344 |

Description: XCU hammers & J

Commentary: Music cut 282 to 343 inclusive. Dolly left as J moved up hammers by rising quaver figure. J is contracted and expanded every bar in strict rhythmical pattern. The chromatic movement mirrors J's sideways movement.

| Cue: 0:05:27 | Shot: | POV: | Bar: 351 |

Description: Zoom out

Commentary: XCU needed for J moving but coming shot needs more space. Rather than new shot, zoom out creates sense of new gag coming (used also at 0:05:02). Music cut from 354 to 357 inclusive. J is repeatedly spanked by hammer on the repeated B♯/C♯ section.

| Cue: 0:05:28 | Shot: | POV: | Bar: 351 |

Description: Continuation of previous shot

Commentary: Music cut from 354 to 357 inclusive. Bar 358 repeated. J is repeatedly spanked by hammer on the extended B♯/C♯ section in 358.

| Cue: 0:05:30 | Shot: | POV: | Bar: 360 |

Description: J set up for golf shot

Commentary: End of chromatic quaver passage marked by J being wedged into the hammers on downbeat of 360. Orchestra returns for first time since 0:01:33. J is hit as if a golf ball on sforzando downbeat of 362 (second bar of phrase). The quasi-circus music is reinforced by J's involuntary acrobatics.

| Cue: 0:05:32 | Shot: 54 | POV: Mid range strings looking up hammers | Bar: 362 |

Description: XCU hammers, J bouncing down

| Cue: 0:05:32 | Shot: 54 | POV: Mid range strings looking up hammers | Bar: 362 |

Commentary: J bounces down hammers turning somersaults. Pan right with J's movement. Final somersault jams J ready for next golf shot.

| Cue: 0:05:33 | Shot: 55 | POV: Above strings towards hammers | Bar: 365 |

Description: CU hammers & J

Commentary: J is hit as if a golf ball on sforzando downbeat of 365 (second bar of phrase). This is a straight repeat of the gag at 0:05:30.

| Cue: 0:05:34 | Shot: 56 | POV: Bass strings looking up hammers | Bar: 366 |

Description: XCU hammers, J bouncing down

Commentary: J bounces down hammers turning somersaults. Pan right with J's movement. Final somersault leaves J lying flat on non-moving hammers, setting up next gag.

| Cue: 0:05:36 | Shot: 57 | POV: Centre keyboard lid towards hammers | Bar: 369 |

Description: CU hammers. MS J

Commentary: J rides hammers rodeo-style and is hit repeatedly in crotchet rhythm. 373–376 is straight repeat of 369–372 so slapstick repeated.

| Cue: 0:05:40 | Shot: 58 | POV: Keyboard lid towards hammers | Bar: 377 |

Description: CU hammers, FS J

Commentary: 377–380 comprises 4 falling demisemiquaver figures and rapidly rising scale. These are used to propel J down the notes and ride a wave of hammers to the top again. J stops a stationary hammer at top of scale (380.2). 381 to 384 are a straight repeat of 377–380 and gag is repeated.

| Cue: 0:05:45 | Shot: 59 | POV: Bass end of keyboard lid | Bar: 385 |

Description: MS Hammers & J

Commentary: Music has same patterns as 377–384. This time, J turn somersaults on demisemiquavers and is projected up the keyboard on rising scale. Zoom out on first scale to give sense of distance and enhance the gag. His trapped tail pulls him bask to hit static hammer on final note of each scale (388.2, 392.2).

Humour Between the Keys   245

Cue: 0:05:50	Shot:	POV:	Bar: 393
Description: XCU hammers			
Commentary: Zoom in to XCU of hammers which have squashed J, who is dizzy and disoriented. J staggers to rapid repeated notes and slowing tempo with repeated C♯ semiquavers.			

Cue: 0:05:53	Shot: 60	POV: Bass end of keyboard lid to hammers	Bar: 397
Description: MS J losing balance on hammers.			
Commentary: J losing balance staggers and slides down hammer shank. Two pans to right indicate camera is trying to keep up with J. J falls over. Music is gradually getting slower and left hand moving up octaves so whole section sounds like cartoon adaptation of twittering birds.			

Cue: 0:05:57	Shot:	POV:	Bar: 402
Description: J recovering			
Commentary: J shakes his head in recovery, makes his plans and moves determinedly. Camera pans L/R/L with J's movements, giving sense of action. Music is closure of previous section with the slowing high ostinato now taking on an anticipatory feel. J snaps off two hammers.			

Cue: 0:06:03	Shot: 61	POV: Bass strings towards hammers	Bar: 408
Description: XCU strings, hammers			
Commentary: J comes into shot, jumps and lands, sitting on hammers poised to play. Music dies to silence, followed by 2 seconds of silence creating a tension link before revenge section. J looks over left shoulder at T before jumping up to feet.			

Cue: 0:06:06	Shot:	POV:	Bar: 421
Description: FS J playing using broken hammers			
Commentary: Music cut 409–420 inclusive. Martellato played as straight quavers instead of broken semiquavers. J is playing the music using the broken hammers. Full orchestral accompaniment.			

Cue: 0:06:08	Shot: 62	POV: Downstage right of piano	Bar: 425
Description: MS J & keyboard			
Commentary: T is surprised that keyboard is playing itself. Hands in air to indicate was ready to play but not doing so. T watches for 4 bars.			

Cue: 0:06:10	Shot:	POV:	Bar: 429
Description: T covers self-playing keyboard			
Commentary: Tom tries to cover up the keyboard playing itself by joining in. T looks a little ragged. Violins move up an octave twice to give feeling of mania. Second piano part playing straight chords on downbeats. The tempo seems to get too fast for the orchestra, with the violins in particular having a difficult time. This is entirely in keeping with the diegetic nature of the orchestra. They are working with T, who is being driven by J's pace.			

Cue: 0:06:18	Shot:	POV:	Bar: 445
Description: False ending 1			
Commentary: T gets near to end of piece, breathing heavily.			

Cue: 0:06:22	Shot:	POV:	Bar: 429
Description: Continuation of previous shot			
Commentary: About to play final 2 bars but piece restarts at 429 (8 bars after previous start at 0:06:06). T appears horrified since keyboard is playing itself again. Watches for 4 bars (as before) and joins in at 433.			

Cue: 0:06:25	Shot: 63	POV: Soundboard through strings	Bar: 435
Description: Low angle through strings LS J			
Commentary: J playing. Jumps to spread legs on downbeat of 437 and drags right leg in 438. All movements tightly choreographed.			

Cue: 0:06:27	Shot: 64	POV: Downstage right of piano	Bar: 441
Description: MS T			
Commentary: T looks very ragged (fur, whiskers, coat looking rumpled, eyes drooping). Just managing to keep up with music. Cuffs fall off in 443.			

Cue: 0:06:30	Shot:	POV:	Bar: 445
Description: False ending 2			
Commentary: Repeat of false ending gag at 0:06:18. T is panting.			

Cue: 0:06:34	Shot:	POV:	Bar: 433
Description: Continuation of previous shot			

Cue: 0:06:34	Shot:	POV:	Bar: 433
Commentary: Again about to play final two bars but piece restarts at 433 (4 bars after previous restart, compressing the gag line. T watches for 4 bars and joins in at 437.			

Cue: 0:06:40	Shot:	POV:	Bar: 445
Description: Continuation of previous shot			
Commentary: T totally exhausted. On the three chords in 445 and 446, the arm of T's tails falls off, his collar springs open and his shirtfront comes up. Unlike at 0:01:31, T is not in control and self-assurance has disappeared.			

Cue: 0:06:47	Shot:	POV:	Bar: 447
Description: Continuation of previous shot			
Commentary: Final chords are played almost by slaps as T falls over and plays the last chord with his torso. Applause from audience.			

Cue: 0:06:49	Shot:	POV:	Bar:
Description: Continuation of previous shot			
Commentary: Pan R then zoom in to FS J. J is pulling on tails over his dress shirt and white tie.			

Cue: 0:06:55	Shot:	POV:	Bar:
Description: Continuation of previous shot			
Commentary: Spotlight while J takes bows.			

Cue: 0:07:00	Shot: 65	POV:	Bar:
Description: Close iris to black			
Commentary:			

Cue: 0:07:02	Shot: 66	POV:	Bar:
Description: End titles			
Commentary: Closing orchestral fanfare.			

Cue: 0:07:03	Shot: 67	POV:	Bar:
Description: Dissolve to MGM/T&J Cartoon title card			
Commentary:			

Cue: 0:07:07	Shot: 68	POV:	Bar:
Description: FTB			
Commentary:			

The *Rhapsody* as a vehicle

The suitability of a pre-existing score for programme music depends on the extent to which it contains or can be made to contain topic-rich references. However, for tone poems and ballet, the speed of musical inflection tends to be at narrative speed or slower. This simply would not work for cartoons, where the rate of change is faster even than for live action movies, themselves already an order of magnitude faster than concert programme music.

It is of particular interest, therefore, why Liszt's *2nd Hungarian Rhapsody* should be a favourite with animators. The answer lies in the origin of the format of the *Rhapsody*, which may be "passionate, nostalgic or improvisatory" (Arnold, 1983: 1561). The legendary animator and producer Friz Freling said of the Hungarian Rhapsody: "[it is] one of my favourite numbers. I know it and I can manipulate it. I can make it stop, like a conductor. Or I can slow it down. That's one thing about the number: You can use a phrase, you can repeat it, and it still works!" (cited in Goldmark, 2005: 129). The *Hungarian Rhapsody* is based on the *verbunkos*, a "Hungarian soldiers' dance used around 1780 to attract recruits into the army. ... It was danced to the music of gypsy bands by hussars in uniform" (*ibid*). Like its near relative, the czardas, it has two parts, *lassu* (slow) and *friss* (fast). Liszt's markings are *LASSAN* in bar 9 and *FRISKA* in bar 118, close enough to betray the link.

The music of the *verbunkos* was often highly florid and marked by variety in tempo, both inter-sectional and intra-melodic. In addition, it was a form based on folk melodies, making it harmonically accessible and rhythmically regular. Most significantly, for *The Cat Concerto*, its highly romantic form allows the animators to set up the satire that forms the major contrast between the stuffy Tom and the upstart Jerry. The huge rubatos are played not for the heart but to parody the concert hall. Although Jerry may, at the end, conform when taking his bows by donning the uniform of the concert artist, he is the subversive element against which the formal performance is parodied.

Jerry's little home (seen at 0:02:01) is in the piano, the symbolic home of music. His shorts are on display and he has pinned a washing line across the music stand. He is asleep, oblivious to the high art around him. It is Jerry who introduces a boogie-woogie at 0:04:34 (thereby using a jazz form as a satirical leveller) and who is prepared to mutilate the piano, changing keys for a mousetrap or breaking off hammers. However, these and other plot lines are enabled because of the flexible, partitioned nature of the score.

The opening eight bars are marked *Lento ed a capriccio*, a potential conflict in directions. *Cappriccio* is an ambiguous term, potentially meaning joking or whimsical but also having connotations of virtuosity (cf. Paganini's Caprices) whilst having seventeenth-century associations with improvisation. Likewise, the markings at the *Lassan* (bar 9) are open to conflict with the music. *Andante mesto* (*mesto* means mournfully) would imply funeral march in style and rigidity, supported by the bell-like pedal note. However, the Hungarian style would be to treat bar 12 with extreme rubato, delaying the final semiquaver as long as possible, directly in conflict with the original meaning of *Andante* (from *andare* = to walk), implying regularity. Generally, upbeats (and other intermediate weak beats) may be extended substantially with the final note in the bar forming a gestural anacrusis to the following bar.

In the University Society Edition, the first 11 bars have 8 instructions (excluding accents, dynamics, pedalling and phrasing). More significant than the editorial or composer's instructions, however, are the general stylistic methods of playing such music. Physical gestures, extremes of timing and variety in touch are commonplace. The tonality regularly moves between minor and relative major, often in answering phrases, offering tonal class associations with the frequency of cadenzas or smaller flourishes creating a faceted piece, capable of interpretation in many ways.

Overall structure

As indicated above, there are too many fragmented sections within the score to be able to produce a coherent summary of the internal structure. However, there are three major musical segments (given here by bar numbers):

1–8	Introduction	(0:00:58–0:01:33)
9–117	Lassan	(0:01:33–0:03:33)
118–448	Friska	(0:03:33–0:06:49)

Within the cartoon, these can be mapped onto the structure of the action thus:

Introduction	Establishing the concert and Tom as a concert pianist
Lassan	Jerry being mischievous and Tom's attempts to control the situation
Friska	All out war between the two, with Tom losing control

The introduction and the preceding shots without music are essential to establishing the character of Tom. He is an arrogant, self-confident performer, totally in control of his environment. His eyes are closed for most of the time (even when walking on, bowing and sitting down), partly from musical reflection but also to state that he needs neither sight of the stage nor the keyboard to be able to perform. The opening chords in the orchestra confirm, through heroic topic, Tom's strength and ability.

The Lassan starts by allowing Tom to restate his musical credentials, but after only a dozen bars, Jerry is introduced. The rest of the *Lassan*, on the whole, represents Tom's superiority. He controls Jerry via a flick (0:02:34) or a gentle hit on the head with a tuning lever (0:3:13) but saves malice for the *Friska* (e.g. 0:05:16). Jerry is a nuisance but one that does not deflect Tom from his purpose of playing the piece.

The Friska is initiated by Jerry slamming the piano lid on Tom's hands (0:3:33), the first time that violence is introduced and it sets off the start of the action of the cartoon. The directors also play their part in the structure by designing the lengths of the shots to correspond with the relative levels of action. This is a graph of the shot lengths:

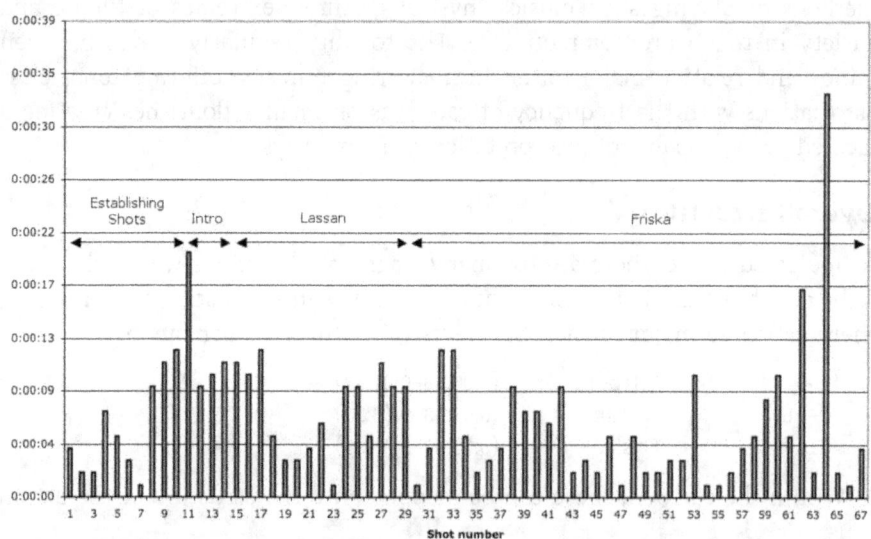

Figure 1 THE CAT CONCERTO

> Shots 1 to 7 (0:00:00–0:00:24)
> Titles and establishing shots.
>
> Shots 8 to 17 (0:00:24–0:02:24)
> Slow part of the *Lassan* before Tom and Jerry see each other.
> Average shot length of 12 seconds.

Shots 18 to 29 (0:02:24–0:03:33)
From bar 35 (*capriccioso*). A livelier section of the *Lassan* in which Tom and Jerry first interact.
Average shot length is 6 seconds – half the length of the previous section.

Shots 30 to 42 (0:03:33–0:04:54)
First part of *Friska*. From start of warfare to the piano stool scene.
Average shot length of 6 seconds.

Shots 43 to 59 (0:04:54–0:05:53)
Up to point of Jerry's recovery from being battered and his taking control.
Average shot length 3 seconds – half the length of the previous section.

Shots 60 to 64 (0:05:53–0:07:00)
Primarily, Tom's distress.

The variance is too large to determine a sensible average. However, shots 62 and 64 are both on Tom and last 50 seconds between them.

With the average shot length reducing from 12 second to 6 seconds to 3 seconds, the apparent action receives energy in the same way as rapid editing in a live action movie. It can now be seen that the macro timing of the cartoon, as determined by shot length, musical section and action, work together to provide an impetus to the point of Tom's downfall. A decreasing average shot time, accelerating music and a move from control to mania lead towards to the repeated false endings.

The false ending

In the finale of Haydn's String Quartet Op. 33 No. 2 ('The Joke', one of the 1782 Russian Quartets), Haydn tricks the listener by fragmenting his theme and leaving pauses between the statements. Apocryphally, this was to catch out the chattering women who attended his concerts by having them believe the piece to be over, only to restart amid their conversation.

The structure of Haydn's final 38 bars is:

- 133 – Establishing dominant via appoggiaturas
- 136 – One bar rest
- 137 – Establishing dominant 7th via appoggiaturas and rhythmic diminution
- 141 – Statement of 8-bar *rondo* theme, ending on dominant-tonic
- 148 – Pause (fermata of unspecified length)
- 149 – *Adagio*, subject and harmony based on *rondo* theme, ending on dominant-tonic
- 152 – Pause (fermata of unspecified length)
- 153 – First 2 bars of *rondo* theme

155 – 2 bars rest
157 – 3rd and 4th bars of *rondo* theme
159 – 2 bars rest
161 – 5th and 6th bars of *rondo* theme
163 – 2 bars rest
165 – 7th and 8th bars of *rondo* theme
167 – 4 bars rest
171 – First 2 bars of *rondo* theme

Haydn's technique seeks to delay the closure, restating the dominant at 133 to 140 and the bars rest between each part of the *rondo* theme 153 to 165. Even if the listeners had not thought the *Adagio* to be closure, they may have picked up the pattern of bars rest and assumed that 166 was the end, especially given the extended number of bars rest at 167. Having been caught out by 167, 171 states only the first two bars of the *rondo* again and the listener may have expected more but the piece ends there, on a dominant-tonic pattern. However, the cadence is not correspondingly rhythmically perfect; it ends on the 2nd bar of a phrase and with the 1st violin playing after the other three instruments.

Haydn's joke here is on the audience. Closure is delayed and even cancelled. The joke is eventually played out using a combination of Morreall's (1983) Incongruity and Relief theories: normal classical methods of closure are stretched, causing humour within the ending, and the recognition that the piece has finally ended will allow the tension to be released.

In *The Cat Concerto*, Bradley uses a different technique. He wants to delay closure but not to trick the audience; instead it is to trick and ridicule Tom. The structure is:

421 – Jerry starts playing, Tom joins in 4 bars later
445 – Strong statement of IV-V^7
429 – No resolution of V^7, music restarts at 429 (8 bars after previous start)
445 – Strong statement of IV-V^7, as before
433 – No resolution of V^7, music restarts at 433 (4 bars after previous restart)
445 – As per score to end

Unlike Haydn, Bradley delays closure but does it by interrupting the IV-V^7-I pattern twice and by restarting later within the piece each time. The two replayed sections are therefore progressively shorter, creating a sense of acceleration (aided by the accelerando in the soundtrack) which, in turn, adds greater stress to Tom's playing. The method and technique of closure adds to the ridicule that is played on Tom and, in relation to Morreall's (1983) tripartite theory, corresponds to the superiority realm.

Conclusion

As the above analysis shows, music in *The Cat Concerto* has played a pivotal role in both the foundation of the film and the realization of comedic intent. Through analysing the structural elements of the music we have seen how music plays a shaping element, providing coherence and form to the macro structure of the animation. Music has also provided the foundation for satire, drawing on long-standing perceptions of 'high' art versus 'low'. It might be argued that cinema's triumph over the concert hall, with regard to the success and viability afforded composers of the former, has proven the superiority of 'low' art over 'high' art formations. This was certainly played out in the later careers of Hanna and Barbera, who reduced both the animation and sonic content of their work to its bare basics, with phenomenal success. There may be more than a hint of this subversion in the structure of *The Cat Concerto*. Finally, what is seen in the analysis above is that the episodic and flexible nature of the score provides opportunities for farce in the form of physical comedy and sight gags. This was essential to animation comedy then, and continues to be an important feature of the genre (see Coyle, 2010).

Notes

1. The rules for which year an award is given are to do with initial showings, which may include limited screenings. Tom and Jerry cartoons were to receive 13 nominations and win seven times.
2. The score for *The Missing Mouse* (1953) was written not by Scott Bradley but by another cartoon specialist composer, Ed Plumb.
3. Most notably Goldmark (2005).
4. *Rhapsody Rabbit* was released on 9 November 1946 and *The Cat Concerto* on 26 April 1947. In the former, Bugs Bunny is playing the Rhapsody on a piano with a resident mouse. The storyline is so similar to *The Cat Concerto* that there were heated arguments between Warner Bros and MGM about who got there first.
5. Milt Franklyn was Stalling's assistant and arranger from 1947 until the latter retired in 1958. Franklyn was a natural successor to Stalling, although, constrained by studio budget cuts, was never given the opportunity to fulfil the promise shown in the handful of cartoons that Franklyn scored by himself prior to Stalling's retirement.
6. The cartoon includes part of the overture from *The Flying Dutchman*, *The Ride of the Valkyries*, Siegfried's Horn Call, part of the overture and Bacchanal from *Tannhäuser* and fragments of *Rienze*.
7. The song 'On the Atchison, Topeka and the Santa Fe' (music by Harry Warren, lyrics by Johnny Mercer) would have been well known to cinema goers in 1947, having won the Academy Award in the Best Song category for 1946. It came from the MGM film, *The Harvey Girls* (1946) and is an example of reusing the

MGM catalogue, partly to avoid copyright problems and partly to promote the song.
8. The music credits come from MGM's *Daily Music Report*, dated 25 March 1946, held in the library of the University of Southern California.
9. When chase scenes were required in 1960s cartoons, for which the production budget had been substantially reduced, it was common for loops to be created, meaning the same items would be seen flashing past the chase characters. This is typically true for Hanna-Barbera shows. Such mechanisms are completely absent from this, the golden age of animation.
10. Pachman had been dead for 34 years by the time of the cartoon's release and, although footage may have been available of his playing style, I have been unable to substantiate Strauss's claim.
11. Bathos is a form of anti-climax by which the self-important can be made to appear ludicrous.
12. The animators also stripped the mechanism of the piano internally so that gags could be more explicit. There are no dampers and the hammers are above the strings, instead of below. Likewise, Tom's fingerings, movements and positioning on the keyboard are sometimes accurate but often simply representational.
13. Jerry would never have been allowed to permanently cut off one of Tom's digits. Whilst it might occasionally be allowed for cartoon characters to have their head come off, both body and head would continue to be animated and alive prior to rejoining. Disney's own animation code (Klein, 1993: 48–49) and the unwritten code of the other studios would not cause in injury that might cause blood to be seen.
14. MGM was, of course, the main studio of the Hollywood musical and the 1940s produced many hits. Two years before *The Cat Concerto*, Gene Kelly had starred in *Anchors Aweigh* (1945) and performed a dance number with Jerry Mouse (Disney had turned down MGM's request to have Mickey Mouse dance with Kelly). This scene in *The Cat Concerto* seems to return the favour by having Jerry dance in a Gene Kelly style.
15. The first is one of genuine surprise, the second is a deliberately silly face, the third is blowing a raspberry at Tom and the fourth is a pose as if from a Wilson, Keppel and Betty Sand Dance.

References

Arnold, D. (1983). *The New Oxford Companion to Music*. Oxford: Oxford University Press.

Coyle, R. (2010). *Drawn to Sound: Animation Film Music and Sonicity*. London: Equinox Publishing.

Goldmark, D. (2005). *Tunes for 'Toons: Music and the Hollywood Cartoon*. Berkeley & Los Angeles, CA, London: University of California Press.

Jones, C. (2002) Music and the Animated Cartoon. In D. Goldmark & Y. Taylor (Eds.), *The Cartoon Music Book* (pp. 93–102). Chicago, IL: A Cappella Books.

Klein, N. (1993). *7 Minutes: The Life and Death of the American Animated Cartoon*. London: Verso.

Morreall, J. (1983). *Taking Laughter Seriously*. New York: State University of New York Press.
Strauss, N. (2002). Tunes for Toons: A Cartoon Music Primer. In D. Goldmark & Y. Taylor (Eds.), *The Cartoon Music Book* (pp. 5–13). Chicago, IL: A Cappella Books.

Originally trained as a concert pianist at the Royal Academy of Music, **Peter Morris** moved into research in areas such as artificial intelligence, mathematical modelling, human interface design, systems usability and mapping the usage of the Internet across Europe. Realizing the folly of all of this, he returned to music and has spent 10 years researching music for animated cartoons and especially the compositions of Scott Bradley. This resulted in Peter being commissioned to create a suite of Bradley's Tom and Jerry music that was performed at the BBC Proms in 2013. Other research interests include computer-mediated composition, especially using SuperCollider, and the work of Stephen Sondheim. Peter is currently a Senior Teaching Fellow at the University of Surrey in the UK.

Index

Academy Awards 3–4
Ackroyd, Dan 93–109
Animal House (Landis, 1986) 52, 71, 94
Annie Hall (Allen, 1977) 3–5
Apter, Michael 16–17, 20
Aristotle 2, 15
Austin Powers films 9, 74–91
Austin Powers in Goldmember (Roach, 2002) 78, 84–7
Austin Powers: International Man of Mystery (Roach, 1997) 78, 80–2
Austin Powers: The Spy who Shagged Me (Roach, 1999) 78, 83–6
Awaara (Kapoor, 1951) 215
'Awaara Hoon' ('I'm a Tramp') 215

Barbera, Joe 224–56
'Be a Clown' (Porter) 122, 124–39, 144–5
Beetlejuice (Burton, 1988) 113–14
Belushi, John 93–109
Bernstein, Elmer 9, 29–50, 51–73, 92–109, 114
bhava-rasa 211
Bizet's *Carmen* 11, 198, 225
Blazing Saddles (Brooks, 1974) 24–5, 27, 66–7
'Blue Shadows' (Newman) 64, 68–9
'Blue Shadows' (Rogers) 69
Bradley, Scott 224, 227

clowns 129–39

Conti, Bill 94
Copland, Aaron 51
Coyle, Rebecca 7, 11, 118, 253

Devi, Sri 217–18
dissolves 68–9
'Do Not Forsake Me' (Tiomkin/Washington) 52, 65–7, 71, 72

El Camino de Babel (Mihura, 1944) 10, 172–8
El Destino se Disculpa (de Heredia, 1945) 10, 172, 178–85

Fear 93
Freud, Sigmund 4, 149

Garland, Judy 129–45
Ghostbusters (Reitman, 1984) 9, 52, 92–109, 113–14
Go, Takamine 190
Gordon-Levitt, Joseph 122
Gosho, Heinosuke 192, 193
Govinda 219
Greenaway, Peter 18, 194

Hammer Horror 10, 110, 114–15, 120
Hanna, William 224–56
Haydn's *String Quartet Op. 33 No. 2* 250–1
High Anxiety (Brooks, 1977) 24–5
High Noon (Zinnerman, 1952) 52, 65–7, 71

Hindi cinema 11, 205–22
Houlihan, John 75
Hum Aapke Hai Kaun (Bharjatiya, 1994) 211

incongruity 8, 11, 14–28, 205–8, 213–14, 218, 220, 252

James Bond films 74–5, 105
Jour de Fête (Tati, 1949) 20–2
Jūku no Haru 192, 196–202

Kaasua, komisario Palmu (Kassila, 1961) 10, 148–70
Kadekaru, Rinshō 191, 195–7
Kaneshima, Reiko 198
Kassila, Matti 10, 148–70
Kelly, Gene 129–45
Kishore, Kumar 216
Koestler, Arthur 15–16, 20

Landis, John 9, 29–49, 51–73, 93, 94, 103
laughter 4–7
lesbian spectacle 111–12
Lesbian Vampire Killers (Claydon, 2009) 10, 110–21
Liszt's *2nd Hungarian Rhapsody* 248

'Make 'Em Laugh' (Freed/Brown) 122–8, 139–45
Martin, R.A. 15, 17, 26
McIsaac, Ashley 191, 197–8, 199–200
Mozart's *Marriage of Figaro* 9, 30–49
Mr India (Kapoor, 1987) 217
musicalized drama 11, 194
Myers, Mike 74–91

Nabbie's Love (*Nabi no koi*) (Nakae, 1999) 10, 190–203
Nakae, Yuji 190–202
Neighbours (Avildsen, 1981) 93–4
Newman, Randy 52, 64–71

Noborikawa, Seijin 194–5
Nut Busters (Markman, 2003) 105–7

O'Connor, Donald 10, 139–47
Okinawa 10, 189–203
ondes Martenot 95, 97–8
opera buffa 30–1, 46–8
Oring, Elliot 17
Ōshiro Misako 191, 195–7

Parada, Manuel 10, 172–88
Parker, Ray Junior 100–1, 104–5
parody 52–73, 74–91, 110, 113, 120, 174, 211, 225, 248
porn parody 106–7

Reitman, Ivan 92–109
Ritter, Tex 65–6

sanshin 189–203
Saturday Night Live 4, 39, 77, 93, 104, 122, 145
Scott, Tom 93
self-parody 52–73
shima uta 189–203
Singin' in the Rain (Donen, 1952) 122, 123, 149–50
Sitaaron Se Aage (Bose, 1958) 206
spectatorial misdirection 59

'The Ballad of the Three Amigos' (Newman) 64–5
The Blues Brothers (Landis, 1980) 93
The Cat Concerto (Hanna and Barbera, 1947) 11, 224–56
The Comic Strip 110
The Magnificent Seven (Sturgis, 1960) 51–72
The Pirate (Minnelli, 1948) 123
The Silhouettes' 'Get a Job' (1957) 44–5
The Stooges 18–20
They're a Weird Mob (Powell, 1966) 22–4

¡Three Amigos! (Landis, 1986) 9, 51–73
Thriller (Landis, 1983) 103–4
Tom and Jerry 224–56
Trading Places (Landis, 1983) 9, 29–49

vampire porn 112
vampires 110–21

'Wah Wah Ramji' ('Lord Ram, You've Done Well'), 211–12

Walker, Johnny (Badr'uddin Jamal'uddin Qazi) 206–10, 214
What's Opera Doc? (Franklin, 1957) 225–6
Wiseman, Debbie 114–19

Yukichi, Yamazato 197, 203

'Zara Rukh Ja' ('Stop For a Minute') 206–9
Ziv, Avner 16

www.ingramcontent.com/pod-product-compliance
Lightning Source LLC
Chambersburg PA
CBHW071834230426
43671CB00012B/1960